Sounds of the River

Sounds of the River

A MEMOIR

Da Chen

HarperCollins*Publishers*

HarperCollins books may be purchased for educational, business, or sales promotional
use. For information, please write: Special Markets Department, HarperCollins
Publishers Inc., 10 East 53rd Street, New York, NY 10022.

FIRST EDITION

Designed by The Book Design Group / Nicholle Morgan

Printed on acid-free paper

Library of Congress Cataloging-in-Publication Data
Chen, Da.
    Sounds of the river : a memoir / Da Chen
        p.   cm.
    ISBN 0-06-019925-3
    1. Chen, Da. 2. China—Biography. 3. China—History—Cultural Revolution,
1966–1976—Personal narratives. I. Title.
CT1828.C5214 A3 2002
951.05—dc21   2001039215

02 03 04 05 06 ❖/RRD 10 9 8 7 6 5 4 3 2 1

to Sunni

On the wooden door of the old Chen mansion, my grandpa had painted, with powerful strokes, a nostalgic couplet:

Colors of the mountain will never leave our door
Sounds of the river will linger forever in our ears

Throughout Grandpa's life, Ching Mountain, with its ever-changing colors, was his hope, and the Dong Jing River, with its whispers, thunderous shouts, or—sometimes—just its silence, was his inspiration.

Acknowledgments

I thank the following people for their contribution to the making of this book:

Sunni, my beautiful wife, loving partner in life, and brilliant in-house editor: each book born is a testimony of our labor, hope, and love.

Victoria and Michael, for the purity of your innocence and love.

My dear mother: your smiles are the best encouragement and inspiration.

My father, who is the reason I write always.

My uncle Chen: your love for us all in Yellow Stone will always be a part of me.

My sisters and brother: with you, I become part of a lush canvas.

William and Alice Liu, for unfailing love, faith, and support in more ways than I can count.

Elaine Koster, a super agent and dear friend, who not only discovered me but also continues to help me grow as a writer with your guidance and faith.

Robert and Myrna Walters, for your love, laughter, and the gift of an American dream. Bob: you were a great man, true artist, and a beautiful soul.

Leona and Robert Murray, for helping me every inch of the way when I landed in the prairie of Nebraska.

Cathy Hemming, president and publisher of HarperCollins, for your leadership, wisdom, and for making this sequel possible.

Susan Weinberg, senior vice president of HarperCollins, Perennial, and Quill, for your sensitivity, infectious enthusiasm, and publishing savvy.

And my editor, the late Robert Jones, editor in chief and vice president of HarperCollins: You were a man of wisdom, art, and letters. Thank you for making my book shine.

Author's Note

Most of the names in the book have been changed to protect the privacy of individuals. Also, the name of Beijing Languages Institute has since been changed to Beijing Languages and Culture University.

Chapter One

The Beijing-Fujian Express! I had dreamed about the train, not once but dozens of times, in color. Each time it was different. Once, it had wings. Another time, it had the formidable head of a golden bear, the curling tail of a lion, and flew off to an outlandish place where strange headless animals danced and welcomed me with slimy arms. I had awoken in a sweat. But this was reality. The express loomed large before me as I stood on the platform with my brother, shaking hands.

"Don't forget where you come from, little brother," my quiet brother Jin said, sucking in a large mouthful of smoke. His hands were a little shaky. "And watch your luggage closely. There are bad guys out there. Even when you're asleep, try to wake up once in a while to check on your things."

I nodded, all choked up, looking at my toes. From now on, it was just me against the world—an exciting but dangerous place. The three-day journey on this monster would take me to the capital of China. Soon Yellow Stone, the small village that had nurtured me for the last sixteen years, my family, and my grandparents' tombs would be far away. The blue Pacific would be but a memory.

I hugged Jin. With tears in his eyes, he held me in his sweaty arms. The train whistled long and sharp, echoing against the mountains. Jin pushed me away and bit his lip. "Go, brother. Write us as soon as you get there, and then one letter a month like we promised Mom and Dad, okay? Don't let us worry."

I nodded and jumped onto the train. The mixed odor of sweat and some unnameable smell attacked me as I studied the route to my seat. The overhead luggage racks reminded me of a butcher's store. Bags big and small were packed right up to the ceiling. Lots of other objects hung from the rack, swinging overhead. Old farmers were squatting, lying, and sitting against their large sacks of farm produce, jammed in the aisle. They smoked pipes and chattered away. I wished I had wings to carry me through this throng to my seat in the middle of the compartment. It looked like I might even have to step on the old men's heads and shoulders to get to my destination. I bent down, found a tiny space on the floor to set my feet, and moved slowly along, murmuring to the old farmers, "Grandpa, please let me through."

I was six feet deep into the crowd when one funny-looking old man smiled at me with his yellow teeth. "First time on the train, young man?" he asked in heavily accented Mandarin.

I confessed with a nod.

"You might wanna go back and empty your pot before coming through again."

It made a hell of a lot of sense, so I shoved my way back to the beginning of the compartment again, visited the windy loo, and slowly made my way back with an empty bladder as the old man suggested. I picked my way to my seat, stepped on a couple of toes, and received a few slaps on my leg for punishment. I sighed as I stood before what I believed to be my seat. An old lady was sitting in the spot matching my ticket number, looking out the window with a smirk on her face.

What should I do? If I followed the tradition of Yellow Stone, I should bow to her since she was my elder, and beg with politeness for her to let me use my seat. As I weighed my opening line, six pairs of eyes stared at me. The old lady winked, held her head high, and looked out the window again. She was playing it cool.

"Grandma, if I am not mistaken, you are actually sitting in my seat," I said, forcing a small smile. My other seatmates looked on with jaded curiosity.

There was no response from the lady, not even the slightest movement of her proud head.

"Excuse me, you are sitting in my seat, old comrade!" I said in a firmer voice.

"Me, in your seat?" She turned and sneered at me, wrinkling her already wrinkled nose. The whole crowd turned their heads.

"Yes, here is my ticket."

"It don't do you no good. I was here first." She shook her head and crossed her chubby arms over her big chest.

"No, no, you are wrong again. I was here first, way before you were. See the luggage up there?" I pointed at my pathetic two pieces, now buried under the heavy pressure of some huge sacks of dried goods. "And these people saw me here also." I looked to the four men and one woman around me, begging for support. Their expressions remained blank. *What a lame crowd.*

"No, I'm not moving. You, young man, can stand till we reach my stop. Then you can sit."

Finally a bespectacled seatmate spoke up in a weak but precise voice. "This young man was here first, and he has the ticket. You ought to move."

A few of the other people nodded their agreement. *High time!*

"See? Please move. I have a very long journey."

"How long?" she asked.

"To the last stop, Beijing."

"Then there's no hurry for you to sit. You will have plenty of time to sit. My stop is only the first from now."

"Where is that?"

"Hangzhou."

I wasn't too sure, but it sounded very far away. I hesitated.

"Young man," the bespectacled man said, "you don't need to think about it. It's twenty-four hours away from here."

Another man joined in. "Old lady, you ought to get out of here."

She sat there stubbornly.

"I'm going to call the conductor," I said firmly, deciding to leave the sticky old lady to the hands of authority.

"Don't call the conductor, please. I'm moving right now." The old lady suddenly stood up and quickly collected her things. She ducked her head under the hanging luggage rack and stared angrily at all of us.

"What's this world coming to? No one gives seats to older folks anymore," she murmured and sniffed as she disappeared into another compartment.

I sat down, and the man with the glasses said, "She looks like a train bum, someone without a ticket. You know, if you sit in a seat, the conductor doesn't even check your ticket. He only checks the ones in the aisle."

"I see. Thank you for your help." It was not exactly a smooth start, but I forgot about it as soon as I sat down and waited for the train to pull out. I had been waiting for this moment for a long, long time. The train, the crowd, the cheering, the good-byes—I had rehearsed it in my mind many times and had even practiced wiping my tears of excitement as I waved good-bye to my loving family on the platform. I had imagined waves of emotions choking my heart, lungs, then throat until tears poured out. As the train departed, I would reach my arms out the window as my family chased the train along the platform until the train left them behind. Then it would be just me and the world ahead of me. But, as I came to realize, things often didn't turn out the way I imagined. The only similarity was the last part. I was a village boy, heading for the biggest city in this country, thousands of miles away, all alone, with fifteen yuan pinned to the inside pocket of my newly tailored trousers.

The train whistled for the last time and gave three short coughs and an enormous puff of dark smoke. I strained my neck, looking for my brother, knowing very well that he had had to run back to catch his bus home to Putien. From there he would have to ride on the backseat of a bicycle from Putien to Yellow Stone. He wouldn't be home till midnight. If he missed the bus, he would have to wander the large city of Fuzhou looking for a cheap place to stay for the night and go home tomorrow. I worried about him not having enough money.

The train jerked twice and we were on our way. I sat by the window and closely watched every inch of land flying by. The trees raced like long-distance runners. The Ming River changed colors, and the mountains that flanked us changed shades in the setting sun. I let the breeze wash my face as my feelings welled up. I kept seeing Mom wiping her tears with her apron as she waved good-bye, my dad stopping the bus in the middle of the road as he passed pears to me, and my grandpa's coffin burning up in flames. Then I thought about buffalo and the endless green fields of Yellow Stone. I wished I could see them one last time, but it was too late. The train was running at full throttle and slowly curving around the mountain. Suddenly the ending had ended and the beginning had begun.

As the sun set on the rugged mountain ridges, we began to cross the border of Fujian into Jiangsi Province. Lush mountains, layers and layers of them, piled up on both sides, guarding the edge of Fujian like solemn soldiers, never tiring. The Ming River, meandering along the bottom of the valley, gleamed thoughtfully with the last glow of the day. My Dong Jing River was miles and miles away now, and my Ching Mountain would have looked small compared with his brethren here. No wonder geography textbooks called the province of Fujian an isolated territory, where the emperor was so far away that sometimes people didn't even know what dynasty they lived in.

On the southeastern side, Fujian bordered the Pacific Ocean. On the northwestern front we had mountains and mountains. We could have started a kingdom or a republic, sought independence from the emperor, and no one would have minded. I sat there at the window feeling proud of coming from such an odd, geographically dangerous, and challenging land. Who wanted plain fields with no mountains to guard you and no sea to front you?

For the last four hours, we had passed through tunnel after tunnel inside dark mountains. There were six more hours of mountains to cross before we saw flat fields once more. Small wonder that for thousands of years the pampered emperors preferred cuddling under the quilt with their concubines rather than making the effort to visit their subjects in this outlandish territory. I couldn't blame them for just sending their footmen to collect the taxes. If the men didn't die from starvation, the horses did. And the treacherous Ming River had sunk many a boat venturing into its shallow rapid currents as they came down angrily from the mountains.

I was an obvious novice at the train-riding game, being the only passenger still glued to the window. Eighty percent of the riders had fallen asleep in various positions—against the seats, in the aisles, back to back—all nodding with the rhythm of the train. They were tired after the long journey from their dusty counties and the fight to get on board this machine, the only express out of our mountainous province into the mainland of China. There was a certain peace and quiet among the snoring. The train driver could have dozed off and the vehicle could have flown off the flimsy rail, jumped off the cliff, hit the Ming River, and no one would have known.

We came to an unannounced stop near a small mountain town. The station looked shabby with its tiled roof half blown off, and a stationmaster who wore shorts and waved a small, yellowish flag. The little houses clinging to the mountainside gleamed with sad little lights in the twilight. I wondered what the people lived on.

The light in the car suddenly went on. All the passengers awoke with blinking eyes.

"Dinnertime. Every passenger please get your money ready for your share," the loudspeaker blared. I could feel the mass movement of people reaching into pockets and the counting of little bills.

"Aren't you buying?" my seatmate with the glasses asked me. He had been asleep since the train started moving.

"Oh, I don't know," I mumbled.

"What do you mean you don't know?" the man asked with a curious smile.

"I mean, I don't know what they're selling," I said, while in fact, I was so hungry I really didn't care *what* they were serving.

"Well, regular train food, which is soupy meat with vegetables over half a pound of steamed rice. It's the same three meals a day all the way to Beijing, young man. You might like it in the beginning, if you're really hungry, but I guarantee you'll be sick of it by day two, and want to throw it up by day three."

"How much is it?" How bad could meat taste over steamed white rice? Give me a break. I could eat that every day, 365 days a year, every year of my life, and still love it. The guy hadn't had any moldy yams lately, it seemed.

"Cheap," he said casually.

"How much?" I was my own provider now. The fifteen yuan in my pocket was supposed to last me a couple of months. I had divided it up evenly and figured on five fen per meal. I had brought my own pencils, some paper, and a couple of jars of pickled vegetables for a rainy day. Every fen counted in my financial condition.

"Thirty fen per share," he said, putting a one-yuan bill on the counter.

"Thirty fen?" I repeated incredulously, frowning and sucking in air. A little steep for a dinner for one. Now I wished I hadn't eaten the pears Dad had given me. I had shared them with Jin and we had both savored the treat, but if I hadn't eaten them, they would have been a delicious dinner.

The aisle was piled with farmers, some still dozing, some talking. The dinners were on a wheeled cart that had to be pushed along the platform outside the window. Passengers stuck their heads out of the windows, waving money in their hands. The salesman in a once-white uniform shouted and cursed among the thrusting hands, grabbing money angrily from the hungry mob.

"Exact change only or no dinner!" He threw dinner boxes at the passengers, who received them gratefully.

"Gee, that's worse than begging," I said.

"What are you going to do? People have to eat," my seatmate said, fishing out change.

"Can't we buy something else?"

"Sure, look at those kids." He pointed at a flock of boys and girls, aged eight to twelve. Some had their infant brothers and sisters strapped on their backs. They all carried baskets of food for sale and rushed to each window, pushing up their baskets and shouting, "Rice cakes, sugarcane, salted bean curd, roasted chicken."

"Well, that's quite a variety," I said.

"You've got to be careful."

"Why?"

"Sometimes the food isn't good. Other times they take your money, waste their time poking in their basket waiting for the train to move, and then run off. What are you going to do? Jump off the train and chase them?"

"Little thieves."

"Yeah, hustlers, even that tiny thing with a bunch of flowers in her hands." He pointed at a girl no older than six or seven, waving a few long-stemmed red flowers, smiling at us with her big eyes. She saw us pointing at her and stopped, clinging to our windowsill, smiling and begging in accented mountain dialect. We shook our heads. She lingered and I felt terrible for her, such a pretty little child, so young and vulnerable. She must be selling things to help support her family.

She looked away and moved on to another window. An old man reached out with a small bill. The flower girl smiled with her white teeth, took the money, and stuffed it into her pocket. Then she busied herself trying to choose a stem from her basket. In the meantime, she moved backward with small steps, farther and farther away from the unsuspecting old man. Then in a blink she was gone, running off into the woods.

"Hey, what are you doing? Give me back my money," we heard the old man shout angrily.

"What did I tell you?"

"I can't believe my eyes," I replied.

The dinner cart was under our window now. I counted my money, chewed my lower lip, and made my first expenditure as an independent man with the borrowed money from my family. The man threw me a box of hot food with grease stains left on the box by his fingers. This was the most expensive dinner I had ever bought. I opened the box. The strong aroma of meat with soy sauce teased my nose—it was divine. Two long strips of lean pork lay on top of white rice. Next to that, cabbage glistened with pearls of oil. It weighed heavily, confirming my belief that it was, after all, a rich meal.

My seatmate poked the food with his chopsticks and frowned. I sensed we didn't come from the same background. I played a guessing game in my head about the identity of the man while shoving in my meal down to the last grain of rice. I left the meat for the very end. It was so good that had I been alone, I would have licked the bottom clean. As I put away my dinnerware, I still had come to no conclusion about my seatmate.

"I see that you enjoyed your meal," he said, putting away his half-eaten box and fishing out a rare, expensive brand of China's first generation of filtered cigarettes, Phoenix.

"It was all right." I stifled a burp and toned down my high praise for the treat.

"I'm glad you liked it." He weighed his lighter in his right hand and asked, "Would you happen to be on your way to college?"

"Why, yes. How did you guess?"

"You look too young to be a state worker, too old to be a high schooler, and too dark-skinned to be a city kid. Why else would a country boy be sitting on a train at this time of the year besides going to college?"

"You made quite an observation there."

"What college are you going to?"

"Beijing Language Institute."

"A very fine liberal arts college. What major?"

"English."

"Fabulous major."

"You think so?"

"I know so."

"Thank you."

"My congratulations to you. Have a smoke?"

"I better not."

"Why not? Have a blast, college man. To freedom with a bright future. You should celebrate." He pushed a filtered one into my hand and lit it for me.

"So what line of business are you in?" I asked, savoring the good taste of an expensive cigarette.

"An interpreter."

"An interpreter? What language?"

"English."

"Well." My mouth must have dropped open two inches.

"I work for the Sports Ministry and got called back to Beijing for an important meeting. You know, getting ready for Bangkok."

"Bangkok?"

"Yeah, the Asian Games."

"Wow, the Asian Games!" I was actually sitting opposite a real live interpreter who made a high living speaking that fine language, English, interpreting for the top athletes of our country. I sucked in a large mouthful of smoke just to get a buzz going so I could enjoy this man's fairy tale in a dazed condition.

"I've been there five times."

"You mean Bangkok?"

"Yeah." He nodded. He looked out at the fading daylight. Darkness was falling slowly. He was in the mood for a chat. "The city never sleeps: nightclubs, restaurants, cafés, and the girls." His eyes gleamed with colorful memories. "You know, those pretty prostitutes."

"Oh. Oh, I see what you mean." Girls equaled prostitutes.

"In our system we don't have that, so you wouldn't know. It's a social curse." His eyes were still dazed, probably with past images of those girls dancing in his mind, which he called social evils only with his mouth. "But you will see when you graduate and get picked up by a top government ministry to travel to foreign countries. The outside world is amazing. Young man, you are heading for a bright future. English majors are so hot you could actually pick your job: international business, journalism, diplomacy, the embassy, anything. Girls love guys who speak English, even the rich Japanese girls."

"Japanese girls?"

"Yeah, porcelain-skinned beauties. I was served on both sides by two cuties when I was attending a meeting in Tokyo." The guy was too much. He had been everywhere. "They respect the language of English, not because it was the language of Shakespeare but because it is the language of wealth, tradition, history, and pop culture. Naturally, whoever speaks it becomes idolized in their mind."

"Well." Very enlightening information, both on the subject of Japanese kimonoed cuties and on the fine language of Shakespeare. The interpreter had found himself a totally captivated victim on whom to unload his wisdom. Here I was, a country boy by any measurement, heading for a college to study English. Who better to impress than a naive fellow like myself? But I liked it. It was exactly what I wanted to know on the eve of my college life. I had lived for such stories in my dreams—high living, far away from Yellow Stone, full of the tango, champagne, and fine-skinned women. *Give me more of that stuff, pal.*

He went on to describe his trip to Paris, especially the women. He sighed with admiration. They had an attitude. *I was sure they did.* And Africa, the landscape and the women were a little dark, but they shone in the glaring sun. He said he could see why they were considered beautiful also. The only place he had not been was America. "New York," he whispered with a kind of worship. Next time, if he was lucky, he might accompany the minister himself to visit the UN. But he knew all about New York, the long-legged Broadway showgirls, the movie stars, and the girls again. He talked about women as if that was the only reason he liked or disliked a place. Each nation was ranked by its women's beauty. It was a different way of judging a place. I sat there thinking about it, long after he dozed off into his girl-stuffed dreams. I saw him smile in his sleep. *Good luck, pal, and thank you for your beautiful fairy tales.* I wished to live every detail of it when I was done with my studies. The future was so near I could almost touch it, like the stars shining outside my window. Somewhere between Fujian and Jiangsi, I slumped over in my seat and fell asleep.

I spent the next two days of my train ride watching the rich plains of Subei, seeing farmers wearing bamboo hats pop up and down in the green fields like puppets. Buffalo bent their heads, dug their hooves deep into the mud, and stared at the sun with a sneer in their eyes. They surely worked hard everywhere. My seatmate slept most of the way. But when he woke up, it was to talk about girls again. He said that by comparison, girls from Singapore would rate the highest as wives, and he added that he wasn't talking beauty contest. Inside, he said, pointing at his heart. He chain-smoked, boasted, and slept. I was getting a little sick of his limited range of subjects by the second night.

On day three, the train was running on the deserted red soil of northern China. You could feel the dryness in the air. Sad little huts with tiny windows dotted the horizon. Skinny mules, dragging huge loads of hay, stood by the rail with dripping noses, counting the cars of the passing train with their wooden eyes. Their masters whipped them hard as soon as we passed by. Their thin legs looked as if they would crack under their burdens at any time, and their tummies were so thin that their walls seemed to be rubbing against each other. I knew they hadn't eaten for hours.

I got into the routine of climbing over each seat to get to the now smelly toilet. The farmers slapped my legs and demanded that I drink less water. They laughed and pinched my flesh. I began to notice that my feet were swollen when my shoes began to feel extremely tight. I tried squatting on the seat, but that only made them numb. So I slid off my shoes and hid my feet deep down under my seat so that my seatmates wouldn't find the smell intolerable. The pork and vegetables over rice began to taste like wax. I wished they had loaded it with more sauce or pepper to spice it up. I lived on two meals a day to save money and to boot up my appetite. It didn't work. The lack of sleep made my mouth feel like rubber, and my tongue weighed heavily like a thick tail. I'd need a gallon of soup for an overhaul when I finally got to my impossibly far away, seemingly unreachable destination.

"Hey, young man, within two hours we will be there." My friend looked as if he had aged a few years.

"Two hours?" My mind came to attention as if I'd been kicked in the back.

"That's right. You are here."

Despite the weariness, my heart still managed to dance the steps of excitement. I stuck my nose against the windowpane, watching the suburbs of Beijing fly by. The houses grew thicker as the trees grew thinner. The fields had a green but dry look to them. Lush southern China, the Dong Jing River, and Yellow Stone seemed only like a distant memory. Beijing was suddenly a reality.

Buildings began to pile up before us on both sides. Roads, crossing and overlapping, became a complicated chess game. I saw more cars and trucks and fewer people. Suddenly the speakers on the train began to play our national anthem with a sweet dramatic narration by a Beijing-accented girl, announcing our arrival at the capital city. Patriotism surged in me and I wanted to stand up to salute the great city, but my feet were as heavy as lead sticks and my body felt as if it would break into pieces with but a single touch. My fellow passengers were too busy unloading and looking for their luggage to think patriotic thoughts.

The interpreter pulled out a business card and gave me a snappy handshake before he disappeared into the throng. In four years I would have my own cards and be able to drop names like he did. I collected my things and lay them under my feet, patiently waiting for the train to stop. It was the last station. It wasn't going any farther. The admission letter had said that there would be people from the college to meet me. My heart was in my throat as I saw the crowd at the station; there must have been tens of thousands of people. I grabbed my things and followed the crowd through an underground tunnel. As I passed through a gate, the city of Beijing jumped out at me with the familiar structures I had seen so many times in postcards and calendar pictures. There were people and bikes everywhere. I dropped my things at my feet and looked up. To the left of the entrance flew a big red flag. The afternoon sun was in my eyes. I squinted and looked again. I saw it now. It read proudly, *Beijing Language Institute,* and there was a minibus waiting with a few people beside it waving smaller flags in their hands to welcome newcomers. My heart jumped with joy, and I dragged my things toward the flag. I felt like a man who had just hiked across the Sahara Desert, finally reaching a beautiful oasis with the promise of water—a lot of spring water—spouting from the earth.

I am safely here. Thank you, Buddha!

I am finally here. Thank you, Mom and Dad!

Chapter Two

With my luggage in hand, I inched toward the flag. I regretted not scrubbing my face before getting off the train. I regretted a lot of things. Those
guys might turn me away, mistaking me for the fuel boy who shoveled
chunks of coal into the burning mouth of the furnace. They would think
I had jumped the train. I wiped my face with my hand a couple of times
and took a deep breath with a wide open mouth. Three days of debris were
hidden in the cracks of my big and ugly teeth. With a light puff of breath
I could easily pollute a five-yard radius of air space. It would be safer to
keep my mouth shut until I got to my dorm and could overhaul myself
with loads of soup and scrubbing. Nervously I went under the shadow of
the red flag and looked up at its symbol. No mistake. The right college, the
right bus. It was an oasis.

   "Hey, the guy is here," I heard the old driver shout from his driver's seat.

"You?" Three young men turned and glared at me. "Are you the country boy from Fujian?" one of them asked. Typical city slickers, they wore long-sleeved white shirts even in this steaming summer heat.

"Yes, I am," I said.

"Is there a need to ask, stupid? He's as dark as charcoal," another guy said. "Where is the Shanghai girl?"

I put down my trunks, ready to whip out my letter of admission, my only proof of identity.

"Get out of here, you're a skinny high schooler." A tall fellow slapped my shoulder, which sent me rocking like a wobbly three-legged chair. "What did you do before coming here, fish by the sea?" he joked with a big smile.

"Just about right," I said.

"You really did? You mean deep-sea fishing?"

"You bet! Deep sea, shallow sea, everything. Where do you think I got this shining tan?" I stretched my neck to show them that even the most hidden creases were a solid bronze color. It was a real tan. I wanted them to know that I came from a land of sea and sun.

"Well, very impressive but no more details, please. I thought you guys from the countryside were born dark-skinned." The guy slapped my back again, sending me halfway up the bus.

"Maybe and maybe not," I said with good nature.

"Gee, since when did our college begin picking up fishermen from the deep south," the third student said, not as a question. He picked up my trunks and threw them to the floor carelessly. What an attitude. But I had no intention of starting my new life with a skirmish here.

"Let's go," the fat driver shouted.

I reached over to shake hands with the three students. Only one accepted my hand, and very briefly. The other two pretended to look away and headed for the bus. I stood on the ground, puzzled, refusing to think that there was any element of rudeness involved. It might be that city folks, who hadn't seen enough of open nature, remained uptight at heart. But handshaking, as far as I knew, hadn't been replaced by any other type of formality in China.

The driver, a jolly guy with a ruddy face, gave me his sweaty hand and I shook it firmly. I was a man now, and I should learn from this moment on to deal with the outside world by myself, to be an astute judge of character. Most important, I should act confident and be eloquent. People loved a good talker. Dad's words rang in my ears. I wished he had told me more.

The bus cranked along through the unruly crowd. I was its only pickup. I was flattered by this special arrangement. It would be the first item in my letter home. The whole town of Yellow Stone would know about my VIP treatment soon, and they would talk about it in the fields and on the street for a while. I searched for the right words about the right subject to converse with my new friends, but nothing good came to mind. I looked in their direction with a smile on my face, hoping eagerly at heart that one of them would volunteer to give me an introduction to the city or just say a word or two about the tall, impressive buildings that we were passing by. The three students had left me alone in the corner and were chatting with such a strong Beijing accent, mixed with a heavy load of local slang, that I could hardly understand what they were talking about. Each occupied a row of seats on the empty bus, one lying in the shape of a pair of closed scissors, the other an A, another draping his feet on the row in front. They had put on their sunglasses and were laughing and whistling. In their conversation, I heard the short guy mention something about the girl from Shanghai they were supposed to pick up. She hadn't shown up yet. He was upset and blaming the tall leader for the mishap. The two stood up and threatened to throw the tall guy off the bus. They fought for a little bit, then calmed down. I sat in the corner, keeping my ears wide open, pretending to be looking out the window. I laughed silently at the three horny animals hidden under those fair skins, sleek looks, and fashionable clothes. They were out there to pick on innocent prey at the mouth of the pipeline. What better opportunity than at the train station? After a long exhausting trip, any girl would lean limply on their shoulders and let their oily tongues give her a tour of the strange city.

It seemed impolite to stay by myself on my side of the van. I made my move and walked toward the tall guy. I hoped to join them, to begin socializing with my new college classmates. As if my footsteps disturbed him, the tall guy looked at me from the corner of his eyes and moved a few inches away. I wasn't sure whether he was being rude or simply joking with me. But the clouds of doubt were soon cleared when he gestured for his friend to shut up and said to me, "To be frank with you, you're a little smelly. For the time being, there won't be any handshaking or anything like that. I don't mean to be rude. I hope you understand. Thank you." He delivered the line with a sly smile. But the rudeness was more than the thin smile could conceal. The other two chuckled and then casually took up talking where they had left off, ignoring me as if I didn't exist.

I was so caught off guard by the insult, I was rendered speechless. I turned and grabbed my things and moved a few more rows away from them. Anger choked my throat and made my heart pound like drums. Welcome to Beijing, you skinny country boy. I couldn't understand why good-looking humans behaved like that. In the tradition of Yellow Stone, I would have given my last bowl of precious rice to a visiting guest from afar, for it was the honorable and decent thing to do. Why were they treating me like this? Was I worth less to them because I wasn't from a big city and didn't have the right clothes and right accent? I pondered these questions as the bus pushed along the crowded avenues of Beijing. I bit my lip to make me forget about the city rats chatting like a bunch of birds, but it didn't work. My fists clenched tight. I wanted to take the tall guy and punch him right in his fine mouth where all those foul words had come from. I wanted to see those white teeth fall out, piece by piece, dripping with blood.

The sun was slanting westward, hovering over the treetops. I figured it couldn't be more than half past three. As we drove along famed Forever Peace Avenue, the fatigue faded away from me. We were at the heart of the biggest city in China, rubbing shoulders with hundreds of cars and trucks. Tiananmen Square looked empty, with little people moving around like ants. The sun was setting over the golden roofs of the Forbidden City. The sky was quietly blue, but no one among the busy crowd seemed to notice. I guessed that the days when I spent hours staring at the setting sun dipping into the western hills were over. The water here no longer told fairy tales, and the moon masked the howling of the mountain foxes. I wondered if the sun told the same story here as it did in Yellow Stone, or if the wind whispered the same forecast about the weather. I looked up at the sky and saw clouds circling the edge of the sky in the west. The clear weather would stay for two more days, a Yellow Stone farmer would say. But the sea was hundreds of miles away from here. The inland climate might be a different guessing game altogether.

I leaned against the glass, watching bicyclists pedal by in the hundreds like a school of young fish swimming against waves in the shallow parts of the Dong Jing River. Their clothing was so formal and different. They were sweating in the humid afternoon heat and still wore socks almost to their knees. City people! I shook my head. Folks back home would laugh their rotten teeth off at the absurdity. We called that "dressing to death" in the summertime. The sweat couldn't get out, and fresh air couldn't get in. There was no ventilation, simple as that. Flowers withered that way, and trees perished if wrapped up. There was a reason why Yellow Stone men had been wearing nothing but the briefest briefs in the warm months inside or outside of their houses for thousands of years.

The city thickened, then thinned, and soon we were running along its western tip, on the well-known road where twenty of the best colleges were scattered. The driver, seeing me so totally ignored by the three young men, turned to tell me briefly that farther west was the empress's Summer Palace and the Fragrant Hills where royalty spent the summers and autumns seeking forbidden pleasures outside the tall walls of the Forbidden City. I was living a forbidden dream of my own. I must be the luckiest Yellow Stone man alive.

My heart jumped with joy as we slowed down and the grand entrance of our school came into view. The plaque bearing the name of the college had been handwritten by Chairman Mao, and its gold characters shone in the setting sun. There were three guards walking the beat. They waved to us and opened the huge iron grille gate. Inside, everything was landscaped as if it were New Year's Day and everybody had gotten a haircut. The grass grew evenly like a sheet of carpet. The trees grew out of small holes in the cement. One was left to wonder whether they had first planted the trees or cemented the yard. Their tops had been rounded as if cut by a huge pair of scissors, like all of their brethren lining the elegant and neatly designed yard. The main office building soared to the sky with two long wings sprawling farther into the campus. The entrance must have been ten or even fifteen stories high—so large that people looked tiny entering it. There was an air of aloofness and absoluteness about the place, every bit the appearance that I wanted it to have. On this flat plain of northern China, this would be my Ching Mountain, a landmark to look to when I drifted afar, an anchor to chain my rope to when the currents of life threatened to sweep me off my feet. I was not in Yellow Stone anymore.

I sat back, slowly savoring the first impression of my college, a mysterious, elegant, and quiet enclave carved out of the land of Beijing. I felt loaded with pride. Without a doubt I had ascended to a higher plateau, and

I wanted the rest of the world to know that the younger son of Chen had arrived, finally.

The trio, chatting all the way among themselves, dropped me off at a small brick building among the peach trees without so much as a good-bye. I waved to them, thanking them. They didn't respond with the same enthusiasm. The tall fellow, whose name I did not know and had no intention of knowing, nodded slightly and looked away as the bus swiveled around the narrow road and disappeared into the woods. I wished never to see those faces again. And I wished even more that my roommates would not be as snobbish, that they would be people with whom I could be friends and have some fun.

I picked up my luggage, lying on the road, and dragged my feet to my new home. My name would appear on one of the doors on the second floor, the driver had said. Finally this was the end of my long journey. My heart beat with the rhythm of joy. I looked around, searching for soil, the body of the Earth God and the source of all the earth's blessings. I found it right at the foot of the peach trees. I knelt down and grabbed a handful and felt the grain of the soil. It was drier and lighter in color than the soil in Yellow Stone. There the soil was dark and soft, rich with rotting leaves. Grandpa had said that one could tell a place by the smell of the soil. A prosperous locality had thick soil and a poor one had thin and light soil. This was the land of many emperors, and the soil should taste sweet. I had almost licked the dirt in my hand when I realized that there might be people watching me. Soil tasting might not be something to be associated with, on top of my fisherman's image. I spread the dry soil evenly on the ground and felt comforted by the thought that I had touched the earth and was again connected to the land.

My home for the next four years would be a two-storied red brick building surrounded by tall trees. I lugged my way up to the second floor. The hallway was dim, with a little light at the end. The floor was smooth cement showing the wear of its age. The air was suddenly cool. I read the names on each door and silently prayed that mine would not be next to the stinking toilet or drafty stairway. And please let it face the road, not the woods, for I feared dark nights alone, and the thought of many strange ghosts was never far from me when night fell.

On the door of 216, I found my name printed below two others, Bo and Hong. I wondered who they were. My mind raced, searching through all the Bos and Hongs I had encountered, hoping to find a matching image to help me deal with them. None surfaced. From my scanty knowledge of surnames, Bo and Hong were rare in my native province of Fujian. They were definitely of northern descent. Grandpa, in his life, had had his share of encounters with the northerners. He had admired their stature, distinct long faces, and fair skin, which he suspected came from the bread they ate all their lives. Most of all, he had pointed out that they were honest and sincere people who kept their promises.

I straightened my shirt and wiped off my face the sweat and black stains of charcoal soot spat out by the train. If it had been the doorsteps of my home, I would have dumped my things outside and run for my parents. But it was different now. The outside world was one of formality, politeness, not public displays of indulgence. I sighed as I knocked on the door.

A tall young man opened the door, and behind him stood a shorter guy. The tall guy had a worn sweatshirt on, looking casual yet stylish. The short one wore an old army uniform buttoned to his neck.

"Looking for someone?" The tall guy spoke so fast I missed what he said. Judging by the intonation, I knew it was some sort of question.

"I am the new student from Fujian. I saw my name on this plate here." I pointed at my name, pulling all the tired muscles of my face to form a small smile.

He studied me slowly, inch by inch from head to toe and back again. Then he looked at the short guy and said, "Please come in. I am Bo and this is Hong, your second roommate." He used his hand to spin the short guy around by the head.

"Ni hau, jien dao nimen hen gaoxing." I bowed deeply and told them I was very happy to see them.

They both responded somewhat unexpectedly, ducking their heads like a pair of cranes.

"What kind of ceremony is this? Don't tell me you're from Japan?" Bo said.

"No, we do that at home, and I would not know any better." Remembering the lesson from the bus and how those Beijing boys had recoiled on seeing my paw extended to them, I was unsure whether to shake my new roommates' hands or not.

Hong stood there smiling, a little shy. Bo tilted his head to his right and narrowed his eyes in concentration, trying to understand my opening speech. "Did you say something about your hands?" he asked after a long pause.

"*Duibuqi, duibuqi. Wode Fujian coyin tai zhong.*" I apologized for my heavy Fujian accent.

"You do have a strong, I mean, very strange accent, and you're here to study English like us?" His eyes studied me again, up and down. A trace of uncertainty flavored his voice, lingering like good liquor.

"*Duibuqi, duibuqi.*" Sorry, sorry. I could not understand why I had to apologize to my new roommates, but I did it because I thought I must sound ridiculous to them.

"Do you want me to help you move your luggage?" Hong finally opened his mouth, still smiling.

"Pardon me? I did not understand your question," I said slowly to Hong.

"I said I could help you with your things," he said slowly back with the help of his hands.

"Sorry, sorry, there is no need for that. I have been carrying them since Fujian a few days ago. See, it is light." I lifted them up and walked in the door with the stride of a giant. I wanted to show them there was nothing wrong with me except for my stupid southern accent.

"That is your bed up there." Bo pointed to the top level of a bunk frame. "The one under you is Hong's, and mine is over there by the window. I don't like bunk beds, never did. Sorry, guys, but I was here first."

I said, "No problem, I like climbing trees. It is fun."

"Country boy. I am glad to hear that. As you can see, there is only one desk in here but three chairs. Yours is by the door," Bo told me, "and you are welcome to use the table." He gestured to the table next to his bed. There were all kinds of books lined up on one side. At the other end was an electronic device, fancy stuff that my cousin Tan said the rich city boys always had. I couldn't see how I would be able to share the desk with him, but I appreciated the courtesy extended.

"Is that a radio?" I ventured.

"Radio, yes, but it's more than that."

"You mean it's a recorder?"

"A stereo recorder. Do you know what it is?"

I shook my head.

"From this ear to that ear. It's from the great country of America," he said slowly to let me digest the significance of his announcement.

"America. Well! How much does it cost?"

"It is not the money. You cannot buy it in this country."

"Well! A stereo recorder." I was excited about someone owning a piece of modern wonder that I had only dreamed of in my little town of Yellow Stone. I actually roomed with a rich kid. I wanted to write my friends about it. It would be a news item short of nothing.

"Here, let's listen to some Western music."

"Western music? Is it allowed?" I was told that Western stuff corrupted your mind and softened your heart. The ban on it had never been lifted as far as I knew.

Bo smiled wickedly. "Yes and no. Don't worry, the last time I checked, the central government was softening on the issue."

"He's the insider," Hong said, pulling out a chair for me to sit down. "For undisclosed news, Bo is our guy."

"I don't want to get into trouble listening to the stuff. Where I am from, they could put you in jail for listening to the love songs broadcast from Hong Kong."

"That's the outlandish Fujian mountain and border policy or whatever you call it. You're in Beijing now, the center of everything. You can't live like an ancient man under feudalism anymore. You've got to liberate yourself from those shackling ideas, college man, be independent and free. Here is something to start you out, Johann Strauss, 'The Blue Danube.'" Bo gently touched a top button. Music flowed out like a trickle of water from the very beginning of its source. Soon it richened, thickened, surrounded, and overwhelmed me like water flooding the small room. With the first note, my corruption was complete. My weariness was gone and my mind was somewhere in a dreamland full of beautiful girls in long Western gowns, dancing in circles in the arms of tuxedo-tailed men with blond hair and blue eyes. My heart tingled with softness and gentleness. The music ended before I knew it.

"What do you think, Fujian man? You just heard your first waltz. I bet they don't listen to that sort of stuff on a fishing boat or wood-chopping expedition."

I shook my head. It was true. The background music in Yellow Stone was the buffalo mooing to a clouded sun, the mountain foxes howling at the full moon, and the gentle wash of the Dong Jing against the grassy banks on a windy night without stars.

"You're corrupting the country boy already. His parents aren't going to like it. Let him make his bed and settle in, Bo." Hong helped me put my sheets on the bed. They laughed when I pulled out a bamboo woven mat and a mosquito net from my hometown.

"What is this? There are no mosquitoes here," Bo said.

"How come? Without the net, they could bite you to death."

"It's the city here. There are no manholes open. We have sewage systems here. There are no mosquitoes, not one."

I tilted my head and listened carefully. The familiar humming of those nasty insects could not be heard. There was only the quietness of the evening now. A land of no mosquitoes! Sleeping in a bed without a net would be like walking around the street without clothes. I climbed onto my bed. The final touch was the pillow, handmade by Mom. My thick mattress felt soft and bouncy. Under it was wire woven with spring coils. At home, I slept on a hard wooden board, on bundled dry hay topped by my bamboo mat. What started out fluffy at the beginning of winter had become flattened when spring came around. And because I had no meat on me, it always felt hard. This was many steps up the ladder. What was common here in the big city became my treat. Everything was wonderful. The only thing missing was the night pot that I was used to grabbing right under my bed when my water was full. I was afraid that in my sleep I might mistakenly grab Hong's head in the middle of the night. I smiled as I tested the softness of my bed. I had made mental notes for my first letter home, but my draft kept changing and enlarging. In my mind, I promised my mom, dad, sisters, brother, and my dear friends at home that it would be full of treats and surprises.

I slept dreamlessly for the next sixteen hours. When I woke up the next day, hunger was stabbing me like a knife. As I blinked at the glaring midday sun outside the window, my heart sank like heavy lead. I was terribly homesick. The excitement of arriving in a new place was over. I had begun a life alone in a world among strangers. I sniffed the air; it smelled different. The sun was cooler, and the little patch of sky I could see from my bed seemed bluer. Even the whispering of the tree leaves in the gentle breeze seemed like a foreign tongue. What did I do now? At home, I would call my mom for food, and she would scurry around the kitchen and reappear with a bowl of something steaming and tasty. Dad was always around sucking on his darkened pipe, watching my every move with fondness and love.

Even when I upset him with a bad deed, he would control his temper, give me a pointed criticism, and leave it to me to cure my own evil. I loved the way he guided me through tough times with real stories of long ago. I missed all those summer nights when we would talk over freshly brewed tea, sitting in our back garden, watching the moon dangle over tree limbs. My three very affectionate sisters no longer bustled over me. If my four best friends were here, we would take to the woods, break out a new pack of cigarettes, smoke, chat, and maybe wrestle a little. Then we would sit back to daydream about the pretty girls who came to our minds and the witty ones who stirred our hearts. And the sun would set and night would fall and the sea would bring a gentle wind as if to cleanse the day's foot-prints away. We would go to sleep and the tiny power station would quiet down and all lights would be dimmed. Only the moon would rise to shine on the dark earth. That was the inevitable cycle of Yellow Stone. I already missed everything it was and the things that it was not.

Hong suddenly burst into the room and broke into my thoughts. "Finally up. Did I wake you?" he asked in an accent that brought reality crashing back.

"I was up already and wondering what to do about food," I said, stretching my back and jumping down.

"Here, I picked up all your food coupons at the office for you." He passed me a bundle of tickets printed with the name of the college and the quantity of food represented.

"What do I do with them?" I asked as I weighed them in my hand.

"The government gives each of us coupons for thirty-six jin [about thirty-three pounds] of food each month, twenty jin in flour, ten in rice, and six in corn. You use it any way you like. I know southerners like you like rice, but we like to eat steamed round bread, our famous *mantou*."

"That's great." I thought of the days when thirty jin of moldy yams had to last our whole family for the long and chilly month of March. This was the good life. Thirty-six jin of food for a sixteen-and-a-half-year-old boy. Mom and Dad would be so proud of me if they knew. My first government food ration. I had food now, plenty of it.

"I see you're happy about it," Hong said.

"Very happy, believe me. You city people could not understand. I could feed my whole family with this."

"Really? I thought everyone got this much every month."

I shook my head. "Not where I come from." I refrained from saying more. I didn't want to give away too much about my past yet. Like Dad said, look around first, make no fast friends, and only say 30 percent of what you really want to say.

"Let's go to the cafeteria now," I said with a smile.

Chapter Three

In the center of this leafy campus, two smokestacks stood against the blue sky. They were the heart and soul for all who called it home here, like the spear of a chapel in a small village, like a beacon tower by the sea. Food ruled, north or south. A layer of grayish smoke lingered among the discolored white poplar leaves, gradually dissolving into the blue background; the higher it rose, the lighter its color.

A chimney with smoke reminded me of Yellow Stone's setting sun, my mom's kitchen, and food—good-smelling food that I waited all day to devour. A smokeless chimney brought chilly feelings down my spine and cutting pains in my stomach, for it usually meant something was amiss. Mom must not be home or might be sick. Food in many ways equaled Mom and Mom, home. Here, I counted on food to distract me from of this homesickness that kept poking at the very depth of my hollow heart. Hope was high.

"This is our cafeteria."

My antennae shot up, my nostrils flared, and my dry throat pulled my adam's apple up a notch while my stomach churned like an empty washing machine with a lonely coin clinking in its swiveling walls. My strong sense of smell had long gone ahead of me in search of a good sniff, and my eyes searched meaningfully for a culinary ambush. The smoke I inhaled awoke my dormant hunger. My knowledgeable nose did not fail me— pork shoulders roasted, calf livers soaked in strong liquor and weak spice, loaves of fried dough dripping with drops of fat hello, and rack of tender lamb grilled rather than smoked. My mind could have gone on for a while, but the threshold to the congested dining hall had caught my toes.

"We keep our bowls here, iron preferably, on these shelves," Hong said as we entered a large hall. "But you've got to be careful. Last time the epidemic hit, half of the school was sick."

"What epidemic?"

"Hepatitis B."

"Why?"

"Because all the bowls are together."

"I'm healthy as a cow. Nothing is going to hit me."

"I wouldn't be so sure. See that guy?" He pointed to a tall, lanky Chinese fellow with a gaunt look and dimmed eyes. "He's a French senior, varsity volleyball star. Got knocked out by hepatitis B. Now he's a skeleton and nobody wants to be near him."

"Well. I better carry the bowls with me in my bag."

"They will make fun of you."

"Who?"

"People."

There was a crowd here. All sorts of people swam in this unruly dining bazaar, a garden of colorful hair—red, white, black, yellow—and a rainbow of skin colors—white, black, bronze, yellow, and pale. More perplexing and confusing were the variety of hairstyles—braided, shaven, crew cut, shoulder length, hip long, lion loose, and dog tousled. I was shocked to the core.

Seeing my fallen mouth, Hong said, "You know you are in the most international college in the world, don't you?"

"But I did not expect this!"

"The color of their skins?"

"Yeah, and the hair. Did you see that girl, with *blue* hair?"

"Da, calm down. You're walking with your lower chin."

That didn't stop my jaw from dropping even lower. "And did you see that one with the ring piercing his nose?"

"They pierce everything, try belly button."

"Ouch! In Yellow Stone we only pierce the nose of our buffalo to put the rein through."

"Keep your buffalo thoughts suppressed, okay? Let's get to the food stand before they run out."

"Who are these people, and where did they come from?"

"They are here to study Chinese, history, philosophy, and some are here to do herbal medicine. Those loudmouths, yeah-yeahing, are Americans." He pointed at a table of youngsters sitting on their table, resting their feet on their chairs.

"The pasty white men with squinting eyes are Brits, and those are Frenchmen, drinking, and their women, skinny and beautiful. You won't miss our Japanese friends; they bow more than they should. And the Africans are the friendliest bunch; they gather under the trees smoking, drinking, and just hanging out. The rest of them come from fifty other countries in this world that I can't even begin to name, like the island of Madagascar."

"Well," I exclaimed, resting my hand on my hip. "I am just as foreign as they are here."

"If not more."

"I'll do all right then," I said proudly. The virginity of my homogeneous Yellow Stone existence died a sudden death. I felt pleasantly pricked by the assault of this palette of human faces: some too white as if molding in the damp crease of spring; others too black, grilled under the baking sun; still others mixed with borderline colors, more bronzed than dark, more gooey cream than healthy white. I must appear too yellow, like a banana, to all the above. But they all looked beautiful.

What a boiling world. So big yet so small. So different yet so similar. Around me all the languages of the world were being spoken, tossed and looped around so freely and carelessly that I wondered why I needed to study English, why I had to grow another tongue from its very root while the language was already so very beautifully spoken and musically whipped together around me. The closest thing to this was English spoken from the mouth of Professor Wei, who always chose her words so carefully and gingerly, as if each word were a pearl not to be dented by the accidental click-ing of her teeth. But here English, a butterfly that I tried to catch with my blind ears, was being used not with care but with joy, with shouts, with free will and stomping feet, like song, like poetry, like a dream.

"Where are they going?" I asked, seeing all the colorful foreigners branching into another hall.

"The foreigners' canteen."

"We're not allowed there?"

"Very good, Da. You're not provincial at all. We, the Chinese, eat on this side, and they, their side. We can't cross the line, but they can come on our side. You got that?"

"I see. No dogs or Chinese allowed over there." I referred to an old colonial door sign.

"Exactly, we're second-rate citizens here in our own country."

"Why?"

"This is our foreign policy. The open door policy is not quite open yet. All foreigners are being treated like royalty because they bring in hard cur-rency."

"What is hard currency?"

"Dollars, francs, and Japanese yen versus our *renmingbi,* the rubbish."

I gripped my pathetic stipend coupons tightly and said, "But aren't you happy that we are in such a privileged environment to learn English from genuinely native speakers?"

"Yeah, but you'll see to your frustration that this is a fucked-up place."

"I don't mind being second-rated as long as I can learn something good and leave."

"You will, soon."

I shrugged at his prediction and looked around me. The foreigners' side had a clean look: white tables with linen, forks and spoons shining, fine china, and cute little flowers in the middle of their tables. The food smelled alien to my nostrils. And there were no lines. They all sat down and ate as in a restaurant, with cloth stuffed down their collars, waiting to be served by uniformed waiters. I flared my nostrils and sniffed blindly. "What is that smell coming from their side?"

"Creamed coffee."

"Creamed coffee?"

"Another invention of capitalism and residue of colonialism. They want coffee bitter but not too bitter, so they milk the cows to make cream so that they can dilute it. And of course, it has to be sweetened by the sugars husked from the sugarcanes by the skinny sugarcane farmers in the mountains so that the bitter coffee now tastes like sugar water with pasty lining."

"You sound as if you have tasted it before."

"Hate it. The cream gives me diarrhea."

"You seem pretty angry with those foreigners," I said.

"It's not the foreigners I'm mad at. It's our spineless government that allows this policy of segregation to exist."

"I don't want to eat there anyway," I said thinking of my monthly ration.

"Precisely. That's why they don't need to segregate the red-hairs from us. Only the insane would walk over there and spend a month's wages for a dead turkey meal."

"They eat turkey?"

"A big deal somehow."

"I have never seen a real turkey before."

"Would you stop saying you've never seen this and you've never seen that before."

"But it's true. I haven't seen lot of things before. This world is brand-new to me."

"It's brand-new to me also. Just pretend that you've seen it and done it."

"You're a city slicker."

"Born one and will die a smiling one as well. Now let's get in line."

"I still can't believe that those foreigners wear bibs like babies."

"Not bibs, napkins, you silly!" He whacked my head.

Our side contrasted starkly with theirs. The floors were sticky, pulling my rubber soles with each step I took. The hungry crowds were loud. The lines were thick and undefined, sort of like a hive of bees buzzing in front of two pathetically small windows where food came out.

"Why are only two windows open for hundreds of us and a whole dozen over there?"

"Because you're fucking Chinese. And remember that all your career here."

"For a happy thought, Hong, what's the dish of the day?"

"Cabbage with sliced pork, cucumber with sliced pork, pork spare ribs, rice, *mantou*, and corn porridge," he read.

"Well, I'm impressed. There is so much meat." I was thinking of cousin Tan's story, meat for everything.

"Bad meat, Da."

"Meat is never bad." I played the defender of the flesh. "Believe me, I know."

"No, you don't know. There is not a slaughterhouse within a hundred miles of here. All this pork came from western China, and the lamb and beef from Mongolia."

"How do they stay fresh?"

"Freezer. Slabs of dirt-stiffened meat trucked in and stored in the freezers here like corpses in a morgue."

"Do they stay fresh that way?"

"Never. In fact, one year a third of Beijing children got sick with vomiting, diarrhea, and nauseating stomach pain after eating yellowish goat fat gone bad from Mongolia. I, for one, will never ever touch that shit again."

"Well, thank you for your appetizing introduction. Everything just doesn't seem as appealing after your mouth has blessed it with your comments."

"Hey, what can I say? I'm only a city slicker. The cucumber dish looks good." He eyed another guy's bowl steaming with the oily dish.

"How much is that?"

"Thirty fen."

"Thirty fen? That's expensive."

"Expensive?"

"Yeah. That's a little above my budget."

"What budget?"

"The stipend."

"That's never going to be enough. Didn't your parents give you more money to spend? You're going to need it."

"I think I'll just get the cabbage." Five fen. "And the corn porridge." I only needed one stipend ticket for that.

"That's good too, but you're going to be hungry. All that cabbage and corn do is gnaw at your tummy as you go into the fourth and fifth class of the day."

"Well, I grew up eating mainly vegetables. I will do just fine."

Hong shook his head, not understanding. "No wonder you're a skinny little monkey."

Counting the money I had with a permanently alarmed mental abacus, I screamed to have my independence retracted. I didn't want independence if it meant responsibilities. I was not used to having to account for myself. I spent what I had and never worried about tomorrow, much less the day after tomorrow. There was always my worrying mother, who would wipe her hands on her apron, and my all-useful father, who would straighten out any wrinkles. And if he could not, his friends or his friends' friends could. But now it was just me and me. The stipend was dead money that could not breed more of its own.

Gingerly I passed my coupon through the oily window where all I saw was the beady eyes of a tired chef, smoking a thick roll and chatting with his fellow chef. He scooped with a big ladle and dropped a third of my five-fen cabbage outside the rim of my bowl.

"Could you add some more, chef?" I asked.

"Why?"

"You spilled some of my portion."

"That is your portion. For five fen what do you expect?" He stuffed two *mantous*, white steamed bread, into my hands and threw me my two bowls, accidentally dipping his dirty thumb into my soupy cabbage. I picked up my food and followed my friend.

"What's the matter with the chef?" I asked Hong as we sat down.

"You see, you have to understand something. They think that you look down on them because you're a young hotshot, the prince of modern society, and they are on the waning road heading for nowhere being chefs, having to cook for you, the great college brats. So they treat us like that out of spite and jealousy. I have seen hair in the food, dirty nails and stuff, but what are you going to do? You just close your eyes and swallow it."

"He stuck his thumb in my bowl!"

"Well, then your cabbage should taste great. That's the tradition in China's glorious culinary history; chefs' farts, sneezes, sticky armpits, and phlegm all add to the mystique of its great flavor."

"The health department should be here to check on them."

"They can't check on them every day. Why do you think we all cherish the dish called Stinking Tofu?" Tofu marinated in rotten fish sauce.

"True, I love it myself, but my favorite is the chicken wrapped in banana leaves and baked with dried cow manure," I added to prove his theory.

"Come on, I'm about to eat, Da. No more cow shit, all right?"

I squeezed the *mantou* with my hand, and Hong commented between his teeth, "Feels good?"

"Soft."

"Like a girl's breast."

"I'll take your word for it."

"You miss your rice?"

"Yeah." I nodded. Any rice would be better than this, but I knew that eventually I would have to like it. This was China's policy: Eat what you grow. The dry climate in the north grew only wheat; the humid and damp south grew rice. It would have cost too much to transport it throughout the nation. I chewed the soft chunks of the ubiquitous *mantou*. It wasn't bad at all. It was kneaded without a touch of salt or sugar, but the chewiness brought out a grainy sweetness. The doughy consistency would even be better for my purpose. It was durable, like a pair of good tires that would run a long way. I needed durable food. I loved durable food. "You eat this every day?"

"Every meal. And everywhere you go in Beijing there is *mantou*. All thirty million citizens here are always in some stage of tackling the *mantou*: chewing, swallowing, digesting, kneading, farting them out, and crapping them into manholes. It's one big *mantou* city and capital of hot steamed buns. Get used to it."

"How do you feel now that you've chowed down both of them?" Hong asked curiously.

"Stuffed."

"Good. Now it's time for the corn porridge. It fills up the gaps and holes left unfulfilled by the chunky bread." Now there's one thing you have to watch out for," Hong said as we left the table.

"What's that?"

"The fart."

"The fart?"

"It will come to you unexpectedly, my friend. *Mantou* does that to everyone equally. The finer your digestive system, the louder it works, like a woodwind instrument. And I, as your roommate, beg to know in advance if you decide to blast the music. I mean whenever."

"Don't worry, my friend. You'll always be the first to know, for you happen to be sleeping right under me."

He slapped my back. "Now the trick is to make a big one small and a small one vaporize totally."

"Easy for you to say. How do you propose to do that?"

"Clap your ass tight. The opposite of pushing out your shit."

"Opposite of that? Won't it back up the leaking gas and form a burp?"

"Theoretically, yes, but don't you be cute with me. It never works that way. The trickiest one is the mute one, and for that, I advise you leave the room whenever you sense one coming. They are A-bombs. A big no-no in this civilized Beijing."

"Isn't it a no-no just to talk about it in this civilized Beijing?"

"No. Firstly, it's a precaution. Secondly, it falls under the category of humor. Fart humor is a preoccupation here. We've got a whole lot of it."

I had to laugh at Hong's sly wit and pinched his right ear until it turned purple. He reminded me of a Beijing opera clown or a comedic cross-talker who made a living making fun of things important or petty. We left the dining hall happy, satisfied, and with a slower gait than we had come in with. In the quiet of a garden, I burped into the autumn breeze, and Hong farted a *mantou* fart—a squeaky little squirrel of a leak. The wind made both vanish, leaving no impact on the atmosphere, no damaging ripple, no resulting flood, no catastrophe of any sort, just the victorious smile of getting away with both, unharmed. I rubbed my expanded tummy. My first meal on the campus, and only a small ration and a tiny stipend had been spent. I loved it. That thought by itself tripled my delight as we sauntered onto the campus.

When the day was ebbing, I picked my way across the campus looking for a spot to spread the small bag of soil that I had brought from Yellow Stone. I still remembered the very feeling when I had pinched those rich dark grains from the riverbank. This soil bore witness to my childhood and those of my father and his father's father. In these grains were contained all the particles of my past: recorded sounds of the silent river, captured colors of the rampant land. It carried the stains of Yellow Stone farmers' stinking feet and their yellow spit. I was happy holding it close to my cheek, listening to the silent dream of all the naughty many-legged insects, deciphering the clucking of green frogs sitting on floating lotus leaves in the thinking water, dreaming, just dreaming and reflecting on a land so tiny yet loving.

Beyond the beaten soccer fields, the grass kicked randomly and replanted carelessly, lay a forest of willows, dancing but not singing because the breeze here was more stagnating than liberating. The sea was far and the mountains away to the west. I jumped over some red berries, crawled over a short wall, swiped away the gossipy willow twigs, and in the recesses I found my little leafy paradise on the edge of the universe. The ground was crawling with my little friends: nut-stealing rodents; earth-digging rats; meaningless millions of insects with legs over heads and heads under bellies; Mafias of robins and *wu-ya*s; and quick-mouthed sparrows creating a noisy aerial disarray, flying out of their nests and into their nests, interrupting a late afternoon mating. I ventured in and looked around this world within a world. Instantly I felt peace. If I closed my eyes, I could listen to the muteness. I untied the silk bag and slowly dusted the soil onto the land. The dark, rich, damp soil of the south kissed the dry, sandy soil of the north; they merged and settled; they became married and buried. Old thoughts forgotten, new dreams begun.

From now on I would be protected because my soil had spoken to the local Earth God and the token of soil was an embrace, a handshake, a bow, a marriage proposal imposed, and acceptance extracted. A done deal. I had a right to be here now. I would not offend the motherland with my stinking feet anymore. I am welcomed. When I am sick, the earth will cure me. When I am sad, it will comfort me. When I jump, it will make itself soft for my landing, and when I fall, it will glove my face and cushion my neck. I am part of the land and the land part of me.

Chapter Four

There were twenty-six freshmen majoring in English at Beijing Language Institute in the Class of 1983. I was assigned to Group Two with another eleven boys and girls who had come from big cities in China. I was told that language study required smallness so that we would each get more attention from the skillful teachers. The better the school, the smaller the class.

"We have the smallest class in this land," said our class president, a long-chinned fellow, an older guy from Beijing who had already been chosen to that position even before school had officially begun. It was only later made clear to us that he was the only Communist Party member in our class.

I realized that my classmates were already all talking in English, simple sentences tossed out to each other in their red-faced introductions and carefree chatting. Their intonations were curving and dramatic and their pronunciation refined and accurate. But as I stretched to catch the drips and drops of their humming dialogue, I couldn't understand it all, only that it was English. Those words now flying before me sounded a little familiar. I had read them and tried to speak them, but I had never heard them spoken back to me in such a speedy, fluent manner. My big plan of beating the city folks was thawing before my eyes. They were *joking* in English, and even their laughter sounded different. I wondered what people talked about when they socialized here. In my hometown, I would have asked, "Have you eaten?" and the other guy would say, "I am stuffed." Next, a Yellow Stoner would ask how tall your wheat was or how far along your pregnant mother swine was, and what you planned to do with the litter. What did the city folks chat about?

I was still buried deep in my thoughts when my busy city neighbor disengaged himself from the girl next to and said, "Yun, here from Beijing." He extended his hand.

"Hi, I'm Chen Da. Nice to meet you." I shook his hand.

"Move your toes off my bag."

"Oh, sorry."

"Where are you from?" Yun asked. He was a white-skinned, tall fellow.

"Fujian."

"Toes don't lie."

"What did you say?" I looked down at my toes. "Arhh! The dirt under my toenails. I don't like socks."

"You don't wear them."

"I'm planning on wearing them when the cold winter is here."

"I suggest you do not wear them at all. They stink." He laughed, and two other boys joined in. It wasn't funny, just demeaning.

"Don't be bothered by that, it's just a city joke," Yun said. As I was warming up to talk to him, he turned and resumed chatting with the girl next to him. I was left holding my unspoken words in my mouth.

I didn't know whether to be rude or polite, friendly or cold. What an awful place to start, with so much to learn. I straightened myself. I was used to a classroom filled up to its brim. At Yellow Stone High School there had been sixty per classroom. Cousin Tan had told me in his knowledgeable manner that he sat with another ninety in his college finance class. But here, with our desks lined up in a U shape, it was small and intimate, the perfect stage for ultimate embarrassment as soon as I opened my mouth. A bigger class I could have swum through without having to be called on or even noticed. I could have studied on my own, waiting until I caught up with the others. But here it was not to be. The moment of truth was coming soon, and soon enough in coming.

Our first class was in phonetics. I sat waiting with poise and deference for my first college teacher. The door opened, and in came a stout, middle-aged woman, dumping a sack of books on the podium. I had already heard of her reputation. She was the Beethoven of phonetics, the doctor of your tongue, but seeing her was a totally different matter. I had to swallow my gagging when I saw that she was sadly, grotesquely cross-eyed to the point where there was no focus of her vision at all. My Professor Lulu saw double. Twelve students became twenty-four. What a roomful of shifting twins. What a name and what a face—long and big, about a third of her stature. And what a big mouth—a third of her face. No wonder she made a living on it. She was born to be good with that mouth. If Dad were here, he would have told me instantly that it was no good for a woman to own such a mouthpiece. A woman's big mouth ate her husband, while a man's big mouth only ate big meals. I pinched myself for having these terrible thoughts about my teacher, whom I yearned to be taught and coached by.

Then she opened her mouth and something beautiful and magical happened. A finely, delicately tuned English melody flowed out. She stretched every facial muscle to get the nuance of each sound, setting an impossible, spotless example of a pure, blue-blooded linguist who rode the wild horse of another language and tamed it under her muscled thighs. She dazzled us all with her accurate, crystal-clear sound and fluency. She kept going, obviously saying something funny since my classmates were laughing. I kept silent. Soon my classmates were rocking with rowdy laughter. Lulu must be doing something really ingenious. Her crossed eyes shone with animated light. Unfortunately, I wasn't getting it at all. But I chuckled nonchalantly to the rhythm of my classmates' laughter, hoping not to be caught with a blank face. The class laughed some more and I chuckled some more, making sure that I was the only one who could hear my throaty vibrations. A famous folktale came to mind of a rotten flutist who pretended to play absorbingly among a lively band in an ancient court. He was getting by fine, making a nice living, until one day each musician was requested by the emperor to perform a solo. When his turn came, he was quickly beheaded, which might shortly happen to me. My solo performance was to come soon enough.

Lulu pointed her sausage finger at a tall Shanghai girl, Ling, asking her something. Ling, of course, dispatched her singsong talk in English, and the teacher nodded with pride. I nudged my neighbor, Hong, and hissed, "What's going on?"

"Introducing ourselves."

"Ah." I had done this little speech about myself so many times that I could do it in my dreams. Dia, my old friend, used to be a victim of my drill and would shout to be told what I was yakking about in that foreign tongue. Now I knew how he felt.

The teacher nodded and applauded as she went along through the class. The closer she got to me, the more jittery I felt—fat stage fright, threatening more than just shaky legs, threatening possible heart failure with my mind completely gone from my body.

"Comrade Chen." Lulu penciled my name on her list, one eye looking at me, the other at my neighbor, the defocusing of an eye-crosser. I stuttered, which I rarely did, and took a breath to start again. Out came the Yellow Stone version of an English speech. "My name is Comrade Chen Da. I'm from Yellow Stone, Putien, Fujian Province. It is a beautiful village surrounded by rice fields." Her eyes rolled clockwise. "My score on the college exam is three hundred eighty, and I am sixteen and a half. I come from a farmer's family, and no one in my high school has gone to college to study English before." Her eyes rolled this time to the roof of her forehead and stayed there until I formally announced, "The End."

Lulu was quiet. So was everyone else. There was a sense of gloom and depression, discomfort and held-in laughter. Then Lulu repeated, "The End?"

"Yes, The End," I said proudly.

She burst into a rippling chuckle, then leaned on her elbows and laughed with her big long face all wrinkled up until her tummy ached. She finally rested her head on the podium. The class was doing the same thing. Girls huddled together; boys shook their heads and wiped their tears. It was perfect. What was better than an opening number by farmer Comrade Chen, doing his plowing with his thick tongue? They laughed while I rotted in ignorance, not knowing why I was so honored. I shrugged a nervous shrug and chuckled, my new way of dealing with things. I chuckled a little more when I saw that the class had not yet ended its joyride. I started to laugh with them, as if we were laughing about something that was happening outside the window to a total stranger that no one cared about, and by doing so, hoped that I was less of a target, that they might even forget whom they were laughing at.

Lulu's saliva was spluttering out. She had to wipe herself with a white handkerchief. Finally she drummed her podium for the class to stop. They did stop, but one girl whose curls got in the way of her red lips let out another giggle and the class let loose again. An untamed dam burst, threatening to drown the running bull, me, in their spittle of laughter.

This time Lulu's eyes were red with tears. I thought that if she laughed any harder, her eyes might uncross.

I shook my head and let my chuckles shake my shoulders, keeping a cool surface, but underneath I was boiling with anger at their cruel humor and cheap treatment. How dare a teacher of her status, in this seat of higher learning, lead it? The class slowly quieted down like an engine that had run out of steam.

"It was a perfect speech," Lulu said, patting her heaving chest. "I'm sorry."

So why the hell were you laughing then?

"Perfect because you said, 'The End.' But it was supposed to be an informal speech. You made it formal, that was why it sounded so funny," Lulu explained, and Hong was right there to translate for me.

Too little too late. I stretched my neck as if to uncoil a tangle of nerves and found nothing to say back.

"But your pronunciation is really terrible, you know," Lulu continued. "And I am here to help you."

"Thank you," I replied with my eyes downcast.

"Who taught you spoken English?"

"Professor Wei," I said proudly.

"Who?"

"A dear friend from Yellow Stone."

"No wonder."

"She is a wonderful teacher," I defended.

"I am sure she is. But the more she taught you, the more trouble we will have here."

"Why is that?"

"It will take longer to unlearn what you have learned."

I thought of the privilege that Professor Wei had bestowed on me. She had gotten me out of that dark hole, and the insult this hotshot was aiming at my idol was intolerable. Did she have any idea about anything beyond the pampered walls of this school? Did anyone have any idea? Try plowing the cold field. Try carrying manure. My mind rattled on as if those chores were my only glory. What was amazing was that I used to despise everything that Yellow Stone stood for and couldn't wait to get out of that stinking hole. But now I was proud of it because a bunch of city folks had laughed at me. It turned me into an instant defender of everything I had left behind.

The rest of the class was a blur. In pain I extracted myself from my chair, feeling the deadly craving for some cigarettes. Others flew by me, girls in pretty skirts flirting with boys in nice slacks and silky shirts. I bet none felt the same urge I did. They all came from wonderful families, were pampered, and could only read about lives lived like mine. They did not understand me. They ran out and celebrated the blissful beginning of their glorious college life with other classmates in the hallway. Bo jumped on my desk and invited me to go pee with him. I shook my head, begging to be left alone.

"What's the matter?"

"Nothing."

"It is hard at the beginning. Don't be fooled by others' appearances. They might be just as bad as you are."

"I am bad, very bad."

"Time will cure it all."

"Thank you. By the way, what is UN?" I had caught the phrase from Yun's introduction.

"United Nations."

"That guy used to work there?"

"Yeah. So?"

"He has been to the UN?"

"So, maybe you will too. And stop acting naive. You're in a city now. Act like you know shit."

"But I don't know shit."

"Nobody knows shit." He flew off my desk and was gone.

The last to leave was Lulu, the teacher. I collected my books and was ready to go when Lulu grabbed me and pushed me back down in the seat. In Chinese, she said, "You have one advantage that I did not have when I was starting out like you."

I had planned to boycott the conversation with silence, but tact and respect for teachers in general held me back. Besides, I noted sincerity in her voice. "What is that?" I asked.

"Thick skin."

"In my village, saying one has thick skin is an insult."

"But not here. Thick skin is good in the city. You'll go a long way with thick skin. Do you know I also came from a dirt-poor farmer's family?"

"You did?"

"Yes, that's why it was very endearing to hear you give that speech. You were brave, very proud of yourself. I saw myself and wished that I had been brave like you instead of a shy, miserable kid from the country."

"But you sound like you've been abroad and all."

"Never. But many believe so. In fact, an Oxford professor once thought so too. But I learned all this from tapes and reading mountains of books."

"What is the trick then?"

"No easy trick. It's a long journey ahead of you. Let others laugh at you. It doesn't matter."

"Easy for you to say."

She smiled. "Just work extra hard and you will figure it out."

"Your pronunciation is so very excellent."

"Marbles. I used to put marbles in my mouth while doing pronunciation drills."

"Marbles? Why?"

"Marbles are like leg weights to a marathoner in training. Once they're dropped, you'll fly."

"Where do I get them?"

"No need for that now. Go spend a couple of hours in the language lab; they have a lot of good tapes and recorders. I don't know why you could not be on top again if you apply yourself."

"What do you mean?"

"You have the highest score coming here."

"I do?"

"You did not hear it? Everyone was telling their scores."

"I couldn't understand eighty percent of your speech." I reduced the percentage a bit.

"Your ears will be trained soon enough. Feel better?"

"Can I have some private lessons with you?"

She drew in a long breath, thinking. "I'm very busy. I act as an inter-preter for a ministry in the afternoons, and evenings I translate foreign news items for a news agency. Sorry." Hurriedly, she left, just another city slicker.

As my classmates raced off noisily to the congested dining hall for their well-deserved lunch, I found myself wandering off aimlessly into the deserted woods, scared and deeply troubled. It had been five hours since I had last eaten, but hunger was the last thing on my mind. Fear had replaced hunger, and now it lay heavily on my chest, giving my empty stomach tides of mild jabs, a sensation that I had never felt before. In the quietness, where I found it safe to express myself, I felt the desperate urge to just let go and cry. I had never felt so alone and helpless before. There was no one near me to talk to. Sitting on a tree stump, I held my knees and sobbed like a baby for a good five minutes till my sleeves were all wet and my head was numbed. How I wished my family was right by me, and dammit, how I wished I wasn't so homesick on top of being so scared.

But five minutes was all I needed. The torrents of tears had cured me, and the gut-wrenching crying had cleansed my fear. I lugged my school-bag up and headed back determined more than ever to fight the fight of my life. Fuck lunch, fuck nap, fuck political meetings! I wasn't born to be stepped on like this, not before, and never again.

In this emotional moment, I remembered Dad's advice about the wis-dom of water. He had once shown me a large piece of rock in the moun-tain that had been penetrated through its heart by a dripping spring of water. Diligence, he had said, would defeat the biggest foe, and I thanked him for that. I was the water and everything else that stubborn rock. Drip by drip I would negotiate, and bit by bit I would conquer.

I rushed to the sound lab, a tiny place hidden in a deserted corner of the campus. I grabbed all the tapes I could borrow in English and buried myself in a corner booth, practicing the tricky phonetics of this alien but beautiful language, intending to make everything that wasn't mine, mine. The recorder was an old model, a big coffee table thing that ground along like a squeaky gramophone. Slowly and carefully I stretched my lips, twisted my jaw, and clucked my tongue, trying to mold the precious English words into flawless marbles. As my mouth went dry, I tried swal-lowing some saliva and went on. When my head slumped down, dozing off, I pinched my earlobes until I woke up.

The sun was forgotten and political meetings missed, but I didn't give a damn. It was my secret defiance of a system long gone and rotten; my first act of intellectual freedom in this land of ideals.

All seemed fine until one day our dean appeared in our classroom, demanding to see me in his office. This man held the key to my future. I wasn't ready to make matters worse. Nervously I followed him downstairs to his office, where he sat down without inviting me to sit in the empty chair. I waited for whatever he had to say. He looked at me with narrowed eyes. Nothing except coldness was emitted by this northern bearlike fellow. His Mao jacket was neatly buttoned to the last button, announcing his rigidity in following the dead man's fashion. It was a state of mind doggedly set on safeguarding Mao's tomb till his own death and beyond. "You have been skipping the political studies class in the afternoon." His voice was low and very serious.

"To study. I was in the lab," I explained.

"Study?" He ground his teeth, making his neat sideburns ripple and cheekbones rise.

"Yes, I have a lot to catch up with. Extra diligence is required on my part," I said, trying to convince this venerable dean of my conviction.

"Wrong attitude."

"How could I be wrong? Aren't I supposed to be devoting all my time to my studies so that our country doesn't waste a penny on me?"

"Wrong, wrong, wrong. And I am surprised how wrong you are in assessing your current task, especially considering your background."

"My background?"

"Yes." He opened a file in front of him. "I see that you are from a landlord's family in the south."

He knew the impact of that casually dropped line. He knew that anyone who had a connection with that damned word *landlord* would shrink at the tip of that cutting sword. It was a dirty secret, a skeleton, a disgrace, an incurable handicap, an ugly birthmark. I was quite shocked to hear him drop the bomb. The Cultural Revolution was long over but obviously not yet dead. And this was the office of the dean of the preeminent Foreign Language Department. Who was this monster? Did he hope that the specter of the Cultural Revolution would return? Did he keep a tracking diary of bad deeds others did to the dead revolution so that he could shout *revenge, revenge* as innocent people were hanged and shot in the head?

"But"—he flipped the file closed—"the times have changed. We are not talking landlord or no landlord anymore."

Times obviously haven't changed enough for you, you fossil, you intestinal buildup, you filthy philistine. I almost shouted the thought. Instead I said, "I did not choose to be the son of a landlord. I am my own body and mind. President Deng has wisely changed any discrimination against us. Why did you have to mention my background?"

"I mention it only when I find the usage of such information appropriate in assessing a situation. It wouldn't make a difference on your way up, but it does on your way down." He leaned back. "Where you are, there are many temptations. We have on our campus all the capitalistic, bourgeois-minded liberals with their corrupted lifestyles and very, very dangerous behavior. And the worst of them are the Americans. That's why we have three guards in the front entrance and another three at the back gate around the clock. No outsiders are allowed in here. Socialization between foreigners and Chinese is forbidden, and you bet we work hard on containing their contaminating influence, but still we find cheap girls smuggled in taxis into the foreign students' dorm to do their dirty thing. They call it love. I call it prostitution. We even caught a few girls climbing the walls to meet white and black students alike. They have the money, the hard currency, the cigarettes, perfume, and everything else. And here you are in the midst of everything, the most corrupted spot in China, coming in from the countryside. I, as dean, worry about your political growth here. But political meetings aren't the only things we have to keep control over you. We also have our model students, openly or secretly reporting to us directly about your daily conduct around here. Do you understand what I am saying here?"

"Yes, sir." Very well.

"I am warning you and the other students not to get involved with them at all. If you have a visitor, limit the visiting time to minimal. And do not let your visitor contact foreign students."

"But aren't we supposed to be friends with them? Show them our culture and language and learn theirs in return?"

"That is only an empty policy. In the past, we did not allow any Chinese students here on campus. You students are experiments, so to speak."

"Experiments?"

"Yes, to see if and how you react to poisoning Western influence, being together with them every day and eating in the same cafeteria. The results of these experiments are simple. Good students get good jobs. Bad ones, which you are in danger of becoming, will get rotten jobs or no job. And keep in mind that we have the power to pluck you out of your class and return you to the country to make sure we're not wasting our money on some destined loser. That can happen if you further offend our policy here. From now on, I want you to attend political meetings every afternoon. Do you hear me?"

"Yes, dean. I will be there."

"You had better be. It's not a choice."

Angry and frightened, I left the meeting with a shockingly changed perception about this place that I now called home. I imagined eyes, hooked and sharp, watching my every move. Those spies, who were they? My roommates? It could be any one of us. Your dream talk tonight could end up on his desk tomorrow. What a lovely place to grow pure friendship. To get ahead, all you needed to do was report on someone, step over his dead body, and promotion from that bearish man would be guaranteed. This campus was just an old drama with a new cast, and politics was still the deadliest toxin threatening our existence. I had innocently thought that the old shackles of political mumbo jumbo had been thrown away and dumped into the South China Sea, that I was liberated, and this was a new beginning. But I was wrong. I was still trapped in this sinkhole of Communist crap, only this time it was in the disguise of freewheeling intellectual pursuit.

The meeting delayed my class in beginner conversation with Ms. K. Lynch, an Australian linguist and a former kindergarten teacher with a wheedling way of speaking. She was whiter than paper and paler than the sickliest patient. She had a mop of shining hair the color of yellow corn and blue eyes that one could swim in. She came from the muggy coasts of Australia; big-boned, freckled Aussy feminism with all the goodies going for her, including a set of visibly proud breasts, which always preceded her arrival by a few inches like headlights. She had somehow found her cocoon of life temporarily suspended in the no-man's-land of China, teaching eager young minds to speak like native speakers.

Rumor had it that she was divorced, thrice! To top our curiosity totem pole, she was dating a shining black African revolutionary leader in exile from his native country, who had come at the invitation of the great but dead Chairman Mao. Each morning the couple could be seen kissing and canoodling, one black, one white in a sharp contrast of beautiful skins, saying their reluctant good-byes for the short daytime separation, the intolerable not-togetherness. One could only imagine what happened behind the door of their residence.

Her love life, a life so illustrative of one's beliefs, aspirations, and wonders, set her up in our minds as a revolutionary herself, not in less glory than her boyfriend/guerrilla war hero. She dated openly, happily, unafraid, with shouts of lust and songs of love in her eyes, with no intention of marrying the man she was sleeping with, as she loudly told anyone who asked. "Heck, no, not after three whopping failed marriages," she said. Had she been a Chinese woman, she would have been condemned. They would have called her "a broken shoe." But somehow, because she was white and blond, it was okay. And not only okay but laudable, for she had told the previous class that it was she who had fired her former hubbies. They were all losers or beaters when drunk, and she did not take crap from them. And that made her a living example of a modern Western woman, her fame sealed as she openly, lovingly leaned on the shoulders of a pitch-black African, kissing him as they parted.

When I tiptoed into her class twenty minutes late, all the students were already paired up and engaged in busy dialogue. With me stranded, she volunteered to be my speaking partner. And what a traumatic experience that was.

"Are you deaf or something?" she asked.

"I don't understand you." I shook my head helplessly. I dreaded doing this to every teacher who came through the door. My ability to comprehend the spoken word was so poor that all I could do was smile this silly smile, nod when I was to shake my head, and shake it when I should have been very, very quiet.

"You . . . should . . . choose . . . another . . . major, . . . Comrade Chen," Lynch said painstakingly with both ends of her full mouth sagging in disappointment.

I should choose another major. I got it only after she replayed her judgment three times in the noisy class.

"No. You should teach me English," I said back slowly.

"Di . . . ffi . . . cult."

"Ea . . . sy. I can be good with time."

"No." She shook her head. "They are good," she said, pointing at others in the class.

"I can be better."

She just shook her head and walked away to others not needing help.

Disappointment was hardly the word. How could she judge my potential just because I could not, for the time being, comprehend those strings of words so quickly spoken? Did she have any idea that I had never seen a recorder before, much less had any opportunity to speak? *Give me some time and I will catch up.* But she did not care. I was left alone in the noisy nest of my talking classmates for the rest of the hour.

Lynch came by after class with an interpreter in tow—Hong—and asked me to make an appointment to see her. "What appointment?" I asked Lynch directly. But she batted her long, blackened eyelashes at me and turned to talk with Hong. Her attitude could not have been more insulting. I wished she knew that. Helplessly now, I asked through Hong in Chinese what was the need for an appointment? We in China just popped in for a visit.

Hong shook his head and told Lynch, and Lynch laughed good-naturedly, in obvious sympathetic kindness. "Westerners make appointments, do you understand?"

"No, I don't. Why can't I see you now?"

She had to go freshen up.

"What is that?"

"Powder my face and smoke my cigarette."

"I could follow you."

She rolled her big blue eyes and laughed with a rocking rhythm that shook her headlights wildly. She flipped over her thick day book, frowned, flipped some more, frowned again, and finally penciled something in but then stopped and asked, "Is this a good time for you, Comrade Hong?"

I said I didn't need Hong there to translate for me all the time because I understood. She used her wheedling tone again, and we finally agreed on an appointment a month from then. That was after she had readjusted the date because of the urgency of the matter. Had I been a house fire and she the firefighter, I would have burned to the last dangling shingle.

I might be temporarily deaf, but I wasn't mute. I decided to take Lulu's advice about having thick skin and speak as much English as possible. In class I took my time and spoke my long sentences to the nodding disapproval of impatient teachers. All eyes would be on me as I gurgled on like a rooster choking. I could feel their sneering eyes that said, *"Come on, get on with it,"* but I went about my business as rhythmically and calmly as the long sentences required. Heads would shake, eyes would roll, and little chuckles escape, but I had my learning to do. No one was going to hurry me, not one syllable. I had the duty and the right to do so. Worse yet, I simply adored those lovely big words and interlocking phrases. I collected such words as *however, therefore, whereas, in the meantime, wherewithal,* and *whereabouts* like gold ingots. My classmates frowned with disgust, and Lynch narrowed her blue eyes, examining me like a doctor. "Use simple words," she shouted. But if big words were not used and spoken, I protested, I would never get to learn and understand them. Like a Nazi officer, she drilled the tip of her pointy chalk on my forehead. "You're a terrible English speaker," she would say. The class laughed while the teacher walked away, dismissing me with her patented bodily trio of shoulder shrugging, eye rolling, and head shaking. Someday she would understand me better.

Not all my performances went unnoticed or unpraised. In my English literature class, Ms. Tang—nicknamed Black Rose for dressing from head to toe in black, normally worn only by widows—was surprised when I answered her fetching question of what constitutes simple pleasure.

"A dip in our Dong Jing River," I said.

She dipped her head, letting her black-rimmed glasses slip a notch down her elegant nose, and studied me as if I were a rare species. "Very good, Comrade Chen. But no one knows what your Dong Jing River is. Here, I have an even better example of the phrase." She produced a pack of Kleenex tissues from her black jacket pocket. Carefully, with her thumb and index finger, she pulled a soft white tissue out and waved it before everyone. Then with her eyes closed and head tossed back, she dabbed her nose with it. One could sense the pleasure of the simple tissue rippling from her head to her wriggling toes.

"She is having an orgasm, Da," Hong whispered into my ear.

"I've never seen anyone having more fun with a piece of paper," I whispered back.

"You know why?"

"No."

"Her husband is permanently stationed in another country."

"A cold bed with a cold heart. No wonder she is in black."

"Never a cold heart. Look at her. Her sex appeal is bursting through her tight seams. No man should leave his wife alone like that. It's a shame." Hong gave a wicked wink. I elbowed him back.

When Black Rose finally overcame her emotional attachment to the tissue, she folded the used paper and dropped it into a small plastic bag, sighing with satisfaction. "This little bundle of luxury is from my dear husband in San Francisco. You know that he is an attaché there. It only costs a dollar, but I could never live without it."

"Pathetic," Hong chided softly.

I raised my hand. "If it costs a dollar, then it can't be a simple pleasure."

"Money is not the issue here," she said.

"But it is. A dollar equals ten yuan, which is one-third of a worker's monthly wage, Ms. Tang."

She sighed helplessly, shook her head, and shrugged, her black earrings dangling. "We are not in the mathematics class, Comrade Chen. Leave your abacus somewhere else. Literature has nothing to do with money." She shot me a scornful look.

My true mentor was one Mr. Tu, who was an abnormality among the pale, blinking intellectuals. The Big Tu, as he was called, looked like a corn-husking farmer on a pee break. Vertically he was a tank; horizontally, a bigger tank. His blunted hands dangled clumsily by his sides and often groped his cropped hair in puzzlement. His cheeks, pitted landmines of black-heads, had visible holes left behind from his having squeezed one too many youthful pimples. His face, another horizontally generous display of meat, was dragged wider and made more emperorlike by his thick lips, which gave one a sense of the scarcity of words and weighty thoughts. He paced rhythmically back and forth on his wide feet, which had distorted a pair of extra-wide shoes so that the uppers became the soles and what did not become sole became holes through which the suffocated fat toes could peek and breathe. And breathe they did. The whole classroom breathed of his toes and the mileage they had locked in. However, he was one tank of a vocabulary teacher. The first thing he taught us not to say was one particular word that he emphatically called "a very strong word."

"Don't ever use it if you can help it," he warned us.

The culprit was none other than *fuck,* which he introduced without knowing that it did more harm than good to our spongy young minds because of its emphasized vulgarity. In one sample sentence, he let loose a can of worms. "My fucking foot fucking got caught by the fucking chair in the fucking kitchen."

At the end of the class, everyone knew that word, and worse, how to use it figuratively and literally.

His speech in English was peppered with big words, which impressed me a great deal. Red-faced, he struggled with long sentences. Sometimes the sentence got so long he lost the tail of it, or rather the tail lost him, and he would stand at a loss, blinking like a kid in overalls. "What I'm trying to say is—which—that—whose—whom—whereby—therefore—thus—hereto—therein—" The more he tried, the more entangled he got in grammatical knots and syntactic confusion.

But he was an endearing man. His gappy smile revealed the innocence of a farmer with dirt-crusted fingernails and muddy toes. Each long sentence—the result of his scientific and mechanical compilation of alien words, crammed but not digested—was a breathless effort. Some longer ones deserved the standing ovation given to a tenor whose breath has run out but whose vocal cords still vibrate as he climbs to an impossible high note. It was that aspect of him that led me to the conclusion that I had found my role model. He did not have to say he was a farm boy whose father was still plowing those blasted northern lands of China. I knew it. I also knew his glee at being here with his toes sticking out of his windowy shoes, because I was he. Big Tu also seemed to have seen the farmer in me in leaky disguise. He picked me—also sporting a crew cut—out of the whole class of pretty boys to answer the very simple question "What is another word for *interested*?"

"Intrigued."

"Very good, Comrade Chen." He was intrigued. "Are you the student who came from Fujian, which is a farming and fishing province that faces Taiwan, which is our enemy?" Only Big Tu would ask a suicidal question like that.

Readily, I took the challenge to offer a Yangtze River reply. "Yes, sir. I'm that student who came from the faraway, proud province of Fujian, which boasts not only abundance of grains, fruits, and fish but is also well known for its scholars in history who have made great contributions to our culture."

I became his favorite student.

Chapter Five

Though a city man now, I still lived like a Yellow Stone farmer. Every morning at sunrise I woke with the birds that sang and scratched for food among the fallen leaves outside my window. My nap was a five-minute doze at noon with my head planted on the petals of an open book. I learned to nap quickly and eat fast like a soldier on a battlefield. I tried taking a short nap once in the dorm, but my quickie didn't sit well with my roommates, who preferred napping for two or three hours, depending on the day and the mood. In Bo's case, if no one woke him up he could snooze till four o'clock, and then it would be exercise time. My short nap ruined their perfect afternoon slumber, so I lugged everything I needed for the day in my bag and stayed out studying till midnight, when I would sneak back like a mouse into our dorm room while my two roommates snored away. I wished I were weightless because even my tiptoes caused them to turn in bed in subtle protest. I was but a shadow to them. Our encounters were simple hellos and good-byes. Hong asked me to watch my health, but Bo only looked at me with a distant, troubled expression on his face.

Finally one day Bo stopped me and asked, "What is the point of life if you live like this every day, Da?"

"Like what?"

"Like what? All you do is study alone every day," he declared.

"If I don't study like this I feel awfully empty at heart."

"But studying is no cure for your homesickness," he said like a doctor.

"Since when were you a psychologist?"

"Since I was five and left in my grandpa's care by my loving parents who flew to France for our great country."

I turned and looked at him.

"Da, I am your friend if you want it. All you need to do is spend some time with us. Missing your family and shutting yourself out is going to kill you."

"Who says anything about me missing my family? I'm enjoying myself," I denied.

"Enjoying yourself? I've seen you falling asleep with your family photos in your hand."

I was silent and choked.

Now he grabbed me and said, "Come here, Da. Let's smoke." He tossed me a filtered one.

I took it. "I thought you didn't smoke."

"I did as a kid to cure my depression. You wouldn't understand what it feels like to be left alone thousands of miles from your parents. I had a hollow hole this big." He used his hands to form a big circle.

"I do understand, believe me. But it seems strange that you city folks also have pain and suffering."

"Of course we do, Da. At times I lie in bed imagining what kind of idyllic life you must have lived back home with a loving family and simple friends who would not betray you."

"You'd never want to live my life there, I can vouch for that, Bo."

"And you'd never want mine either, an empty life surrounded by luxury."

"I'll take luxury anytime."

"Not if you have no one to share it with. My mom used to ship me large containers of food, toys, clothes, bicycles, books, and foreign things that others would die for. I used to wait with my grandpa at the port, watching the ocean liner come in and waiting in the car from the ministry to pick up the goods. The happy feelings only lasted while the toys were still new. I used to think that Mommy would jump out of the container as well, but she never did." Bo was misty-eyed too.

"I can't believe we suddenly turned into girls." I rocked my friend's shoulders. "Why did you stop smoking?"

A dark cloud covered his face as he sniffed and wiped his nose with his ever-present handkerchief. "Since I stopped breathing through my nose and cigarettes lost their flavor."

"What is the problem with your nose?"

"Plugged all the time."

"You should see a doctor."

"Forget my nose. Let's cure your homesickness first. Now listen to me. Stop being a stranger and spend more time with Uncle Bo. Talk to me when you have problems. I care, unlike those other jerks. And if you're alone here on weekends, feel free to use my tape recorder. I know you like my Russian folk songs." He smiled.

I was quite touched by his caring and thoughtfulness. It was, after all, the first time anyone here had reached out to me and offered his kindness. I thanked him profusely and promised to do just as he advised.

But as time went by, I came to realize that Bo was not always there for me when I needed him. In fact, he wasn't even there for himself most of the time. His moods seemed moored to his nose. When his nose began to bother him, he would turn into an edgy, thorny cactus. His bushy eyebrows would knit together, his long nose grow longer, and his eyes become colorless. He would look at you with a deadly stare, not talking or smiling. At times like this, I would try to sit and chat with him. He would shove me off his bed, saying, "Can I be alone, please?"

I would reply, "No, I'm your friend and your classmate. You have no right to drive me out."

He would grit his teeth and shout, "Get lost!" and I would say, "Didn't you tell me to open up to you when I needed to? Now that you're all moody, you should open up to me and let me help you."

"It doesn't work the other way around! Get the fuck out of here!"

Taking the cue, I would lug Hong with me to leave him alone.

One day I came back to find his bed cleared and things moved. Hong, lying in his bed like a curled banana, passed me a note from Bo. It simply said: *Come see me in room 201.*

I rushed to the dark end of our dorm building where an empty room sat among spiderwebs. Bo's familiar Western music foretold his presence and his mood. I knocked on the door. Bo jumped out to grab me excitedly and demanded, "How do you like it?"

"I love it."

"See that?" He pointed his thumb backward at a white machine.

"What is it?"

"A refrigerator. Let's have a beer and some ham or, if you like, some orange juice instead or maybe a Coke?"

"You have a refrigerator?"

"This is a small one Dad bought for me." He threw me a local beer and I thirstily drank it.

"How did you get this room?" I asked.

"I pried open the lock and changed it. No one except you and Hong knows where I live now."

"Your secret is safe with me, but sooner or later people will know and you'll be in trouble."

"Trouble is my name. I will tackle it as I go along."

"Why did you move?"

"I didn't think our marriage was working, Da," he said, smirking.

"Funny, Bo. Seriously."

"I thought dorm life would be more fun, but it wasn't. I told our dean that I wasn't used to living with others. I'd always had my own room since I was born. I can't stand sharing anymore."

"It's my fault. I kept waking you up."

"No, the fault is within me. The rest of the billion people can share a room with others but not me. I am sick, Da. But now this is my paradise."

"Well, I am glad it's working out for you."

"Everything is perfect except for one little imperfection." Bo looked around and sighed.

"What is that?"

"You haven't noticed?"

I shook my head.

"You dummy, we have no hot water. Only the foreigners' buildings get

hot water eight hours a day. Don't tell me you haven't taken the weekly
shower in the public bath yet?"

"I haven't. I missed the Wednesday schedule. Couldn't find the place."

"Good thing I can't smell. You must be full of odors."

"That and many other things. I haven't done any laundry yet."

"No wonder I see you wearing the same thing every day," Bo exclaimed.

"You got it. It's my third round of wearing this same shirt."

"Get out of here before you fill my beautiful home with your smells."

"I'm leaving."

"But do drop by often, for I am going to be so blissfully alone without
you guys."

"I bet you are."

One Wednesday afternoon, I took myself out of my routine to confront the
pile of dirty clothes and my own bodily smells. Mom was an expert on
clothes washing. In her life she had broken two thick, clunky washboards.
No small feat for a small lady with delicate fingers. I repeated the five-step
washing technique that she had taught me as I lugged my fat bag of dirty
clothes to the mossy public washroom. Soak, soap, knead, rinse, and dry.

She warned me not just to soak and dry; the clothes would not wash
themselves. "Never let people see that you have rings on the collars. It's
shameful," she would say. I was to soap them heavily and rub them till the
rings went away; otherwise the rings would become permanent and no girl
would marry me. I had laughed and said that if I could win the college
seat, I would have no problem washing my own clothes. She said dirty
clothes would attract rats and used the example of my grandaunt who had
lost one of her wrinkled nipples to munching mice because she had delicious stains on her chest that she never washed off. The mice had a mouthful and Aunt Susie lost one dim headlight.

I dumped all my clothes into a large sink and filled it up with soapy
water. I had to thank the Communist Party, which had had the wisdom to
build a ribbed cement washboard into the sink. I used my two fingers to
pinch up my clothes, piece by piece, and soap them thick and slippery.
Mom's words popped up again. Check your pockets now for debris, and
pull the inside out to wash. My pockets were filled with treasures: *mantou*

crumbs getting soggy, pencil bits, crumpled paper, half an apple, wet matches, and some cigarettes. *Thank you, Mommy. I wish you had told me more.*

I started kneading them hard, first the sleeves, then the front and the back. I used a hard brush made of palm leaves to work on the greasy collar ring. Mom had warned me specifically not to use the brush for the collar. It was cheating, she said, because the harsh brush would ruin the collar, and soon the shirt would be collarless. The best way to do the ring was to patiently rub it between your hands, but patience wasn't something I had aplenty. By the time I was down to the last three pairs of stiffened and slippery trousers, I did exactly what Mom had warned me not to do—I soaked them and rinsed them, skipping all the other steps in between. With water splashing all over the floor and myself, I wrung the pants into twisted loaves, shook them out wrinkleless, and hung them along one of the ropes in the breezy yard. Proudly I looked at the flying flags dripping and drying. I wondered then why Yellow Stone women always sang while washing their babies' diapers in the Dong Jing River. Were they out of their crazy minds?

Next I walked the whistling walk lightheartedly to the public bath, which looked, sounded, and smelled like a slaughterhouse. People stood in two long lines—men in one, women in the other—before a miserably small door, waiting for open showerheads. The whole campus of a few thousand intellects had to shower at the same time in the same place, one day a week when hot water was available. The flat-roofed bungalow hotly breathed out the odor of dirty humans getting scrubbed through its small windows and chimneys. The bathers' wet feet dampened the front yard in a fan shape, fading into the dirt road and beyond. The comers looked dirty and their hair greasy, but the bathed were red-faced from the hot steam with hair loose and carefree.

An old lady with bound feet, the cashier, asked for five fen for the bath. I paid for it hurriedly, grateful for my turn. The steam had fogged up the glass in the doors, and I almost went into the women's side. The old lady caught my tail and threw me forcefully back to where I belonged—the men's side.

"Honest mistake," I said.

"Heard that one before, you horny pervert. Those women would have beaten you to a pulp."

"Sorry, it's my first time here."

"Make sure it's not your last. Go on, the line is long out here."

Others behind me shoved me inside. Nervously I undressed, hiding my private parts with the casual draping of my towel. A Yellow Stoner, I had rarely stood naked before others. A dip in Dong Jing River entailed taking off your pants quickly behind the bushes and jumping in nimbly. To come out of the river, I would tear a tree branch to cover my grassy gears. But here the city folks, pasty with loose hanging flesh, stood in the caressing steam chatting casually about things not suitable as subjects between two naked men. One professor was telling another about his wife's kidney stone surgery, demonstrating on his big belly while others looked on carefully. Two young students were chasing each other and wrestling, their dicks lip-synching, knocking violently between their thighs. Others were shaking hands, not caring where the hands had been. I hurriedly bowed to Professor Tu and tried to disappear to a corner where no one would see me. But Tu, being a generous man, waved to me to share his showerhead and scooted over, making room on the bench. Nervously I nudged next to him.

In a slaughterhouse, he would be a beefy slab carried by four men to be served as a dinner for a hundred, while I, a skinny rack of lamb, lunch for a thin old couple with dwindled appetites. The hot water glided smoothly from my head to my toes but not in Tu's case. His belly button was a deep puddle holding gleaming water, while the breasts, a set of loom-ing terraces, made the water detour and plunge from two chunky nipples. I scrubbed myself quickly and was ready to hop out when Tu made a pro-fessorial request for me to scrub his sizable back. I used to do that for my dad, and I had no problem doing it for my mentor. Besides, he certainly needed some help there. So I soaped and scrubbed him like a good boy. But his back had an oily quality. No matter how hard I tried to wash the grease off, it spread right back. So I scrubbed hard and he moaned delight-edly. I scrubbed even harder, intending to give my favorite professor max-imum pleasure.

The water was hot, the heat clawing, and the steam sticky. I felt a little dizzy. It was totally relaxing. I forgot about everyone being naked here. It was one big body-rubbing vertical wrestling game. But something alarmed me. Tu's head began to dip to one side, resting on his shoulder. I asked him if he was all right. He did not answer me. His eyes were closed and he was leaning against me, slipping farther and farther off the bench.

"Are you all right?" I asked urgently.

He shook his head.

"Are you feeling dizzy?" My dad, who had high blood pressure, would sometimes sit down suddenly and lean on anything around him.

He nodded.

"Do you want to get out of here?"

He nodded again, slipping farther.

The weight was too much for me. My heart tightened up. This man could have a stroke on me if he wasn't taken out right away. I shouted and begged another fellow to help me. We dragged him to the less steamy locker room. There we laid out a large blanket for him to lie down on. His nakedness lay in total display while he recovered slowly.

"Thank you," he muttered.

"No problem."

"High blood pressure is bad."

"You want me to get a doctor for you?"

"No, I will be all right."

"I'll stick around until you are fine."

"Go get dressed, you skinny rat."

I smiled and he smiled back. The funny thing was that no one seemed to notice this pile of heaving flesh on the blanket. It was considered normal to do that in the public bath. In fact, in the old days people brought pipes and teapots and finger foods to enjoy while lying on a simple bamboo bed naked.

I stumbled out of this nutcrackers' Garden of Eden feeling less sure of my manhood, but the cleanliness I hadn't felt for days was heavenly.

Chapter Six

Funny thing about Bo was that when he had been with us, he detested our presence, but now that he was living alone, he would come by every day after midnight to chat with me. I was usually exhausted by then, while he was just getting going after a long afternoon of undisturbed napping. Our room became his midnight social spot, and his own, a sanctuary for him to retire to. Soon he extended his leisurely lifestyle from afternoons into evenings by inviting girls to his private den and dazzling them with his electrical gadgets—his refrigerator and stereo—and many sensuous tapes and fashion magazines. In the darkness from afar, one could see the silhouette in the window of him reading a magazine with a girl, head to head.

I asked him, "What are you doing with these girls?"

He said, "I like to sniff their hair."

"I hope this is all you do because everyone passing by can see your every move."

"They can?"

"Bo, you know they can." I thought for a moment, then suddenly exclaimed, "I got it! You're one of those sick guys who makes trouble in order to get caught."

"I'm bored."

"You've got your whole college career before you and you are bored?"

"I can't help it. I'm not spending a lot of time with the other classmates anymore. You know, Yun and Goo and all their cronies."

"What's the matter with them?"

"I tried to be their friend. I gave them film and stuff, but they're treating me coolly. I don't know why, but I resent that. Now I don't even speak to them."

"How could it be? I remember at the beginning you were like this with them." I snapped my fingers.

"But I am like that with you now." He snapped his back.

"Good for you. I'm a loyal person you can trust. You know I have four sworn brothers at home who would probably die for me."

"You do?" Bo's eyes lit up. "Did you do the cutting the vein thing for the swearing?"

"Not quite but something very similar."

"I knew it! You are cool. There's something about you. What else did you do as a kid? Tell me, tell me."

"I was in a gang that did a lot of bad things."

"Man, I always wanted to be in one of those, but my grandpa locked me in every day after school."

"I did not become one of them to have fun, you know."

"For revenge then?"

"Yeah, something like that."

"Well, how would you like to organize a gang right here?"

"Bo, are you out of your mind? I'm a college student now. Our society needs me to do well so that I can make a contribution to its future."

"You don't believe in that shit, do you?"

"I do. Bo, I can't believe I'm hearing this. You're from a revolutionary family!"

"Third generation and a lost generation already. I often wish my mom and dad would just defect to a nice country like America. I would join them in no time."

"You are dangerous."

"I'm forward thinking, Comrade Chen. Hey, I heard they're considering moving us into the foreigners' building."

"They are? Why?"

"So we could be spies on each floor, like the classes ahead of us."

"Spies?"

"Sure, that's what it's all about. They want you to watch things for them and report as you go along. But you could choose not to."

"How?"

"Three D's—don't see, don't hear, so don't tell."

"Like I said, you're a dangerous man."

"I know. One of these days I might be a danger to myself."

Two things happened as anticipated. Bo was caught living in room 201 without permission. He actually ran to my room to announce the news.

"Guess what, they caught me last night."

"Congratulations! What are they going to do with you?"

"Jail me in another single room, I hope."

"Seriously, Bo, aren't you worried at all?"

"No."

"No?"

"The dean said that he wouldn't even publicly criticize me. What a disappointment!"

"You son of a gun, you are powerful."

"Thank you, but I feel cheated. I don't get to be as well known. I wanted the whole school to know."

"You're a sick bastard."

"Notoriety is air to me."

"The way the authorities are treating you with such soft gloves, you might have to kill yourself to be famous."

He smiled darkly. "You know what the dean told me?"

"What?"

"That he was going to write to my father in Paris."

"That's an itch."

"Less than an itch. It's a tickle."

"So are they asking you to move out?"

"Nope."

"That's strange. They don't want you there, and yet they don't want you to move either."

"Then I guess I'm staying and winning."

"This is your country, Bo. You picked the right one, living off the glories of your dad, Buddha bless him. I wish he were my uncle."

Bo laughed all the way back to his room. But that laughter was short-circuited when we heard that the rest of our class was moving into Building 8—the cushiest of all—with hot water, twenty-four-hour security and housekeeping, and heat that started a month earlier than in the rest of Beijing. Everybody was happy and busy moving except Bo. He was not invited, and that stunned and upset him terribly. He jumped up and down in the corridor, shouting and screaming, then went to ask our dean why he was being left out. The dean told him to check with the housing personnel, so he went there. The housing cadres told him to go to the president's office, from which he was kicked back to the dean, who again kicked him back to the housing cadres. By then the offices were all closed, and Bo was left alone in the old building, rotting in his usual depression under his thick quilt.

I begged Hong to take Bo back.

"Would he want to live with us again?" Hong asked.

"Let's go ask him."

We walked over to find Bo sitting dazed in his bed with disheveled hair and still wearing yesterday's wrinkled clothes.

Bo was quite touched when we invited him back. "Do you mean it?" he asked.

"Of course we do."

"Why are you putting yourselves out so much for me?"

"Because we like you," Hong said.

Actually, Hong and I had rehearsed the dialogue. We didn't want him to lose face among our classmates. He had such a huge ego that he would be crushed and thrown into an even deeper depression if no one offered to help. Besides, we had been given a much more spacious corner room with a view on two sides. The three of us could each have a little island of space to ourselves.

Bo was almost on his knees thanking us, but he wanted to know something else. "Who thought of the idea of inviting me first. Who?"

"He did," Hong and I both said, pointing at each other at the same time.

Bo smiled. "Flawless rehearsal. Thanks."

"Not so quickly," Hong said. "Promise me that you won't bitch about Da's lifestyle."

"Done." Bo pounded his desk.

"Promise me that you won't dominate everything in here."

"Done," Bo said again. "Oh, but could I have the desk and the bed facing the south?"

"Here you go again," I said.

"Alright, alright. I'll take the northern bed," Bo corrected himself. "In fact, I'll volunteer to cut down on my music playing. How do you like that?"

"Good, so Da and I can study a little at home."

"By all means."

We celebrated our ascent in life by taking a splashing hot shower. Butt naked, with only towels around our waists, we ran noisily down the polished stairs to the total annoyance of the Chinese housekeeper on the floor. He stared at first with a look that said: *Don't enjoy it too much, you don't deserve it.* Then his smoky mouth shouted, "Slow down or you'll bump into foreigners."

"Big deal," Bo whispered loudly. "So now we have a speed limit here."

"I heard that. For your information, we do have a limit to what you can do here, you punks." The housekeeper was tough.

"Shut up, Bo," I said.

"Yeah, or I'll shut you up," Hong said.

"I'm not going to shut up because of him. In fact, I'll show him something that he'll never forget." Bo quickly yanked the towels from around our waists. Instantly we were stark naked. I didn't know whether to pick up the towel or cover my ass. Hong was even more embarrassed, squatting down like a girl peeing. We both cursed Bo as he laughed. Of course, the housekeeper was fuming and chased us with a mop, calling us hooligans! We ran till we reached the shower room where we nailed Bo down and opened the showerhead on him with splashing cold water.

"Now Bo, you will never forget this shower for the rest of your life," I said.

He was choking and gagging under the freezing water and began to shake. As it turned out, it was all a fake. Soon Bo was singing a rousing song, which sounded so loud in this poorly ventilated bathroom that we had to cover our ears.

"You know, guys," he declared, "I have to thank you for the most refreshing shower I've ever had. And for your information, you guys have lovely asses, which in both of your cases are much better looking than your faces."

I shook my head, glad that the old Bo was back, fun and carefree.

For Bo, a promise was meant to be broken. He took the best bed, facing the southeast, saying that the sun would nurse his nose and make it less noisy, which was good for us. He also said that his vision was failing and that he needed to have his bed face the brighter window where the greenness of the trees would arrest the worsening of his eyes.

"But you hardly read," I exclaimed.

"I'm trying to read more."

"And you play even more music now than before," Hong complained, reminding him of his other promise.

"Yeah, but who could resist the view, the clean air, and the warmth of this lovely place? And you have to admit that the music adds a nice touch to it. Oh, by the way, I've ordered some wallpaper to be delivered to us in a few days at *my* expense for everyone's benefit." He smiled.

"Wallpaper! We don't need any paper on the wall. This is fine," I declared.

"The white walls remind me of a hospital. You just wait for the miracle that will happen here. The girls are going to love our room."

"Girls?"

"Yeah, don't you want to have girls come here and party with us?" He winked and pointed at us. "One for you and one for you."

We smiled.

"How do you propose to bring them here?" Hong asked.

"I've already been approached by a few girls who want badly to come and visit me."

"You have? In your dreams."

"You will see tonight."

That evening we got a page from the guard downstairs, calling Bo's name. He went running down and returned with three girls with their hair all loose, wearing scanty clothes and sandals. They giggled as Bo led them into our room, showing them his view and collection of music. In the end, he said, "This is Da and Hong, my *dear* roommates, who are on their way out to do some serious studying, aren't you?" Bo herded us out into the corridor and whispered, "Listen, the chicks are here to take a shower, okay? I promised you girls, and here they are, with their hair loose, sexy and all."

"But they are here to take advantage of you, the hot shower," I said.

"Da, a man has to start somewhere," he replied.

"And a horny man would start anywhere," Hong declared.

"Well, soon these cuties will be coming every evening, and wait till you see them after their showers, all red-faced and relaxed. I've got a blow dryer. They'll have to spend hours here using it to dry their thick long hair. Did you see that one with hair hanging to her hips? I can't wait."

"Well, neither can I," I said.

"No, you guys let me work the night first. You rush off to wherever you need to go, and I'll get them hooked on this hot shower lifestyle. Soon you guys will be living in paradise with cuties coming to see you every night. Who knows? Maybe romance will flow from here. Go on now and get lost before I make you." Bo sounded convincing and conniving. The temptation of seeing those girls in a relaxed mood did something to me and Hong as we went back to our room and apologized to the girls about having to leave and all. They giggled and laughed some more. Just that made my heart fly like a butterfly. Hong wanted to linger but was quickly kicked out by Bo.

Bo soon became a victim of his own device. The naked girls were caught in the men's shower room, even though Bo had designed a schedule to sneak them in extra early before the crowd swamped in. The foreigners did not mind seeing the girls in there. In fact, they loved it and began to chat with them, which led Bo to feel resentful. He was even more inflamed when the girls accepted the invitations to come and visit those half-naked foreign acquaintances. And the doormen were inflamed too, about the whole setup. They chased those girls back to our dorm room. So now the girls had to stop coming for a while. Everything went back to normal, and Bo quickly returned to his mood swings again. One moment he was happy about all the new discoveries and goodies the new building had to offer, and the next, depressed about the routine of school and our loss of freedom, being watched all the time by the doormen.

A week later the girls were back. The long wait for the public hot shower had them itching to return to Uncle Bo. The color returned to his life with their return. This time they did not ask to be taken to the hot showers downstairs. Instead they washed their hair in the washroom on our floor, then fetched hot water from the tap in basins and washed their asses in our room, making our floor all wet. Each night Bo had to wait outside our room while those asses soaked in the basins and got washed. They would giggle a great deal while washing their private parts slowly. Bo would cling to the door, listening. That was real torture for a man as virile as he was. The girls were local high school graduates assigned to petty jobs around the campus. Their main goal in life was to find a husband with a college degree. But they could not have been more wrong hanging out with Bo, who was definitely not a marrying man. All the man wanted was to taste things, as he put it. Those girls were smart and seemed to have seen through the hollow man. The three always came together; that way Bo could not lay a finger on them. He ended up shut outside a great deal. Finally, he gave up his big plan of making our room into a romantic nest and canceled the order for that much-talked-about wallpaper.

The daily hot shower made me a new man. I looked nicer and smelled better. I took a steamy one right after dinner each night. With the day's dust and sweat cleansed, I would march alone in the setting sun to our class-room, which as time went by had become a deserted cemetery the moment classes were over. In the first few weeks, zealous freshmen would hang out there in the evening to study. Then the crowd thinned as they figured out better ways of spending the evening hours, mostly entertaining in the dormitory. Soon even those who came late and left early began to chat and laugh or just gossip. It was obviously uncool to continue coming.

"You still going there?" Bo asked one day.

"Sure."

"What is the fun there anymore?"

"The fun of having the whole place to myself. I can read out loud. It's my own stage, with silence being my sole audience."

"You must have been a real lonely farm boy who grew up screwing sheep on the deserted farm."

"And you must have been a sick city boy who jerked off on crowded buses, rubbing against unknowing females."

"You've acquired the mouth of a city man now. I think it's time you acquired some city manners as well."

"And you are going to teach me?"

"Uncle Bo at your service. Since you've been washing every day, your tan is lighter and skin a little smoother. Now you need to pay attention to the fashion style here." He bent down to pull out a pair of new shoes with a two-inch heel. "Do you know what these are?"

"Shoes," I said. "Women's shoes."

"Wrong. Let me tell you something, this is the fashion now. The taller the heels, the better. Do you know where I got them from?"

I shook my head.

"Of course you don't. Canton." He kicked off his old shoes and pants, leaving only his underwear on, and slipped into his new heels. Instantly Bo grew taller. He strutted from my bed to his, hips zigzagging and chest pushed out. He looked astonishingly good except for his thick, hairy legs, which seemed to crush the poor, slim leather shoes. He kicked his legs high like a gymnast and jumped up and down like a ballet dancer, shooting into the air, scissoring his feet. I wished he hadn't taken off his shirt. He was all hairy on his chest too, an unusual feature for a pure Chinese fellow. It looked disturbing. No one grew hair from the crotch up to the belly button either.

"Please cover yourself or I'll throw up."

"You're turned on. I can see that." He paraded on, lighting a cigarette. With one hand holding the elbow of the other arm, he smoked and rolled his eyes. "Do you know who I'm imitating?"

"Your mother?"

"Shut up. Mom's a straitlaced, model Communist. This pose belongs to one person and one person only. Marilyn Monroe."

"Monroe? Who is that?"

"Oh, you thickheaded country lad. Hello and wake up. This is the late seventies. She is only the sexiest woman alive or dead." He gave off another high kick, his dark balls peeking out from his underwear.

"You'd make a great entertainer without those *taros* lolling around."

He kicked again just to annoy me. This time he slipped on the spikes and fell on the cement floor with a dusty thump. He wrinkled his face up in dull pain and begged me to pick him up. I took my time and commented, "You deserve the punishment for wearing girls' shoes."

"You idiot! Get me up."

I did.

"If you call them girls' shoes one more time, I'll cut your balls off. Soon this will be the hottest thing in Beijing. I'm so ahead of my time, it's scary." He adjusted his underwear and tugged his twin *taros* back in.

Bo's experimental heels made him a laughingstock to all. Since they were sharp and clunky, he now could be heard before he was seen. And since he was usually late for classes, everyone would clap to the rhythm of his heels as his clicks neared the quiet classroom. At the beginning, he took it as an exciting reception, which he craved. He only laughed when the girl Ling said, "You have taken over our territory."

"So go cry your eyes out, Ling. In fact, men will be even more feminized soon," Bo theorized. That was a mistake because another girl right behind him said, "When will you start wearing your bra?"

"Yeah, and maybe Bo will be the first man to have periods," said another girl.

"Or babies."

Bo took it with a smile, liking the attention a great deal. "Does anyone want to marry me? Da, maybe you." He pointed at me.

I smiled and said, "Not until you shave off your crawling belly hair."

Bo deliberately lifted his T-shirt, revealing his area rug, causing another round of laughter.

But soon the newness wore off, and classmates began to sneer at him. The tall Yun boy one day grabbed Bo's ass, which was sticking out more because of the heels. Another time, someone put a peach pit on the floor, which he tripped over and had a hard time dislodging from the crevice of the sole. Lynch would sigh and say as she saw him come in belatedly, "Even China isn't safe from Western corruption." In the old days Bo would have taken it as a compliment, but somehow the clothes changed the man. The stranger his clothes were, the more distant and guarded his attitude toward others became.

"I love your colorful shirt," I commented one day, seeing him in a new outfit.

"You don't have to say nice things just because you're my roommate," Bo said without looking at me. Hong's eyebrows went up hearing that.

"I do like it, Bo. I admire your audacity every day, making a statement across campus."

"That's just it! I'm not trying to make a statement with my clothes. It so happens that I have the money and resources to imitate the fantastic Western world, and I like to dress like them as much as I can. Not like you." He pointed at me. "And you." He pointed at Hong. "One in a century-old farmer's garb, the other in that stupid green army uniform of your father's.

When are you going to realize that you are probably going to be wearing that same shit for the rest of your short lives? Before you know it, you will be old and die in those rags. Don't you want to try some more adventurous clothes and be different for a change?"

"No," I said looking at myself. "I thought I looked fine in these trousers."

"You call that fine? Your pants are so wide they could fit three of your thin legs," Bo declared.

"Mom still wants me to grow," I quipped, and Hong supported me with his quiet, amused smile.

"You guys don't understand me, just like the rest of the classmates. The only one who really understands me is Black Rose. In fact, I think she's a gorgeous visionary."

"Well, well, well. Black Rose," I said. "Is that whom you are striving to match up to?"

"Not striving. We are just being thrown together by social prejudice. Do you know how much crap she is taking because of her black clothes?"

"Black eyes? Broken ankles?" I asked.

"No, Da, again you fail to understand."

"You guys are too far ahead of me."

"That's right. She receives hate notes from her neighbors. They call her a bitchy witch. That's why she chooses to be alone at all times, living more within than without."

"Is that where you intend to live, more within yourself than with us?"

"I have to."

"Well that sucks, Bo. That's strange and wrong."

"Da, there are few choices in life."

"True, but one of them is that you be yourself and not be so defensive. We are with you whatever you wear. Right, Hong?" I kicked Hong's leg.

"Right, you have our support, even though we might be behind you thousands of years in fashion."

"And I promise never to talk about your lifestyle anymore," I said.

"Okay," Bo said, calming down a bit and reaching over to clasp our hands.

"But tell us, are you in love with Black Rose?" Hong asked curiously.

"No. You degrade our relationship. We are more like soul mates."

"Soul mates! That's even worse," I said.

"Why is that?"

"Most husbands don't even get to be soul mates."

Bo nodded thoughtfully and said, "I like that."

"Tell your soul mate to give me an A next time in her lit class," I suggested.

"Me, too," Hong piped up.

Bo smiled mysteriously at me. "I actually saw your paper on her desk the other day."

"You went to her house?"

"Do tell, Bo."

"My lips are sealed," he declared.

"Well, my ears are open whenever you decide to unseal your lips," I replied.

"You're hosing us, Bo," Hong declared. "I don't think I can fall asleep tonight, thinking of you burying your head between her thighs."

"And I would hate to have her angry hubby show up here with a gun or a knife," I added.

He raised his arm to strike us, but we were already gone.

Bo was a true visionary. All over Beijing, heels got taller and thinner, as if the flatness of the Cultural Revolution had given in finally to the hills of a modern era. A pair of powerful one-inchers would have a girl walking in a constant downhill dash; precarious two-inchers, an impossible tiptoe; daring three-inchers, a tumbling suicide on the uneven surfaces of the streets. At first only girls with nice figures wore them, which made their bodily advantages more noticeable. Soon older women with crushing and overflowing weight caught the fashion, but the heels only highlighted the curse of their wrong curves. Arthritis, thickening soles, hardening corns, and even broken ankles and dislocated hips were all blamed on the invented heels-on-a-hill.

Then, as Bo had predicted, men took the plunge as well. They spiked up on heels so that they would not look too short to their synthetically grown counterparts. Richer folks sailed round on good heels that were nailed firmly to endure exertion on the rocky road. But cheap knockoffs, whose heels were glued on, left many men and women peddling around on uneven footing when one of their heels unexpectedly got caught between cracks of pavement or just detached after rain wetted the dry glue.

Bo, picture-perfect Beijing high fashion, was all torn jeans, torn T-shirt, and heeled shoes. His mustache had grown itchingly long and bothersome.

Sometimes bits of *mantou* stayed hanging there without detection, so he carried a mirror with him that he checked frequently. In class he held the mirror between his thighs, face down, to avoid the teacher's detection. But Bo loved himself too much; he ended up looking at himself long and hard, oblivious to whatever else was going on in class. The teachers did not like that. They poked fun at him, but none seemed as hurtful to him as the labeling by Black Rose, who called him a narcissist, which of course sent us all busily checking our pocket dictionaries. The entry deftly read, "A self lover," and everyone laughed long and loud. Bo took it with a smile twitching his mustache, pretending to be calm and cool.

That night, with lights out and the three of us lying in bed, I said good night to them. Hong replied nicely, as he always did, but Bo was a little agitated, sniffling and blowing his nose with hankies, turning and tossing. I always used this time of day to silently go over new words and catchy phrases before drifting off. The word *narcissist* got stuck in my head. I was having a hard time pronouncing it correctly. Too many screeching *s*s. In a whisper, I tried the pronunciation again but missed one of the *s*s. I sensed Bo tossing again to face the wall. This was the kind of stuff that kept me awake, not having mastered the nuances of a word. I tried the long string of odd syllables again. *Narcissist!*

"Would you shut up, Da?" Bo sat up suddenly, turning on the light. "So I'm a goddamned narcissist! If you dare repeat that word again, I'm going to throw you out the window!"

"What are you so angry about, Bo? I'm only trying to learn the word."

He was fuming. "Do you know that she is the biggest narcissist of them all? She couldn't pass a puddle of rainwater without checking some part of herself."

"Bo, she was just trying to teach us a new word, that's all," Hong soothed.

"And what could be a more appropriate example than you? Thanks to you, I'll never misuse the word, nor will I forget it. I think you're overly sensitive, Bo," I said.

"Sensitive?" Bo fumed. "Of course I'm sensitive. I considered her my special friend and mentor. Do you see how hard I study for her classes while I am lazy in others? And how eagerly I try to please her with my compositions that I care little about? She led me to believe in myself. You don't call a friend a narcissist in class!"

"Gee, lighten up," Hong said. "You're acting like an angry lover or something."

"No, we're not lovers!"

"Well, you certainly sound like you are," I added.

"Have you been in love before, either of you?" Bo challenged.

Hong shook his head.

"Not personally," I said. "But I've known people who have before, my friend Sen. It ain't pretty, though. He was wrecked, bitchy and moody just like you are now. I wouldn't wish that on you."

"Why not?"

"You're kidding," I replied. "You're talking about a married woman here."

"What's wrong with that?"

"She has a husband!"

"But she is lonely."

"That's good. That means she misses her hubby. If she wasn't feeling lonesome with her man away, then you'd have a real lonely lady."

"Da, shut up. You're interrupting Bo's juicy story here," Hong said. "Bo, to find out whether you're in love, all you need to do is ask yourself, are you in love?"

"I'm not," Bo insisted, but he seemed a little stirred by the word *love*.

"Just ask," Hong coaxed soothingly.

"Okay, okay. Am I in love?" Bo repeated slowly and thoughtfully.

"Go on, ask again," Hong cheered.

"Am I in love?" He closed his eyes, meditating.

"Cut the self-inquiring crap. Did you get a hard-on the last time you were with her?" I demanded, offering him an easy way out.

"Da, you ruin it all." Bo cast me a blaming look. "Love has nothing to do with a hard-on."

"It has everything to do with it, Mr. Purist. Just ask a spring running cow."

"Would you shut this guy up while I conjure up my feelings for a logical conclusion, Hong?"

Hong jumped on me and smothered me with my quilt. I threw him down, sat on him, and continued, "Did you, Bo? I'm talking those monster poking hard-ons that no handcuffs could rein in."

Bo thought for a while, scratching his head and finally admitted, "Yes,

I did. A very big one when I was in her house last time." He paused again as if suddenly bitten by truth. "Maybe I am in love with her. Gee." He straightened up and gave a smile of relief.

"That's gross, in love with your teacher?" Hong exclaimed.

"I told you to talk to your dick," I commented proudly.

Bo didn't seem to care about or hear what we said. He was all excited now. There was that truth-has-set-me-free sudden revelation glow on his face. His eyes were shining and his face all dreamy. In a singsong voice he said, "Oh, she is so elusive, philosophical, and poetic."

"Bo, I think she has trapped you," Hong warned.

"No, no, no. That's absurd," Bo said. "I just realized that I have been the one so desperately thirsty for her."

"Wrong, Bo. Wait till you hear this . . ." Hong interrupted.

"I'm right, I know I am," Bo insisted. "Boy, love is so powerful!" He touched his chest, finding it hard to contain himself and shouted, "I'm in love!"

"Slow down," Hong said. "You're falling for someone not worthy of your love."

"How dare you say that?" Bo said angrily. "She's my goddess."

"Yeah, yeah, yeah. You're not the first to be in love with her. Any seniors can tell you that," Hong said seriously.

"Rubbish. Our relationship is special, while others are purely academic."

"I wouldn't be so sure," Hong insisted.

"Shut up! That just goes to show that no one really understands us. Not you and not you." He pointed at us.

"Okay, we don't understand your mysterious world," I soothed. "But I do have two things to offer about your love affair."

"Go ahead."

"In Yellow Stone, there is a traditional award given to one sleeping with another man's wife."

"Is that right? You award those guys there?" Bo asked quite happily.

"Yes, with his own eyeballs after they're poked out with oyster shells."

"Yuck!"

"And they chop off his balls like they do to young puppies."

"You're a barbarian," Bo pronounced. "But what's the second thing you have to say?"

"The second thing is that I don't believe a single word about your special relationship with her. I think it's all imagination."

"You don't believe me?"

"No. She doesn't act in love with you or anyone else for that matter."

"That's a trick of hers, you idiot. I'll show you that she does care for me."

"You do that," I said. "In the meantime, I'm returning to our real world. Thank you for your fairy tales. Let's go to sleep."

"Come on, let's talk some more. You guys are such rats," was Bo's last, disappointed comment of the night.

Chapter Seven

On weekends the campus was one lonely monastery and I, the monk. The honeymoon of the maiden month of college life had left the city students thirsty for their families and bubbling with the motion pictures of their new life. They abandoned the campus like defeated soldiers. Only a few stayed, and they were all male. Gloomy men with sunken cheeks and hollow eyes roamed around looking for things to do, anything to do. Each soul looked scarier than the next. Their eyes emitted loneliness, hungry for warmth and companionship that was unavailable. When those eyes zoomed in on you, their loneliness became yours and the gloom got gloomier.

With this emptiness flooding my soul, I felt the pulling sadness of homesickness again. I was a leaf of a boat adrift in the midst of the ocean. No matter how strong I thought I was, I felt weak at heart, and that weakness was enlarging each moment I stayed in the shade of these emotional waves.

The laughter of long ago, loving faces rotated around me like a montage. Sweet Yellow Stone became a dreamland I visited gently at night. Many times it blurred in my teary eyes. There was no Yellow Stone anymore.

I dashed off some of the most crazed and teary letters home. The letter writing would inevitably end in spasmodic sobs and many silent kisses of good-bye on the paper. They were sealed with yet another kiss. If the postal system did not collapse, they should arrive home in a month with broken corners and opened seals as they were read by official eyes and reglued by invisible hands. The letters would gather a bit of Beijing dirt and yellow dust from the coastal cities and villages. The state of the broken envelope itself would be a testament to my dogged love for my family. When it arrived, Dad would open it with his trembling hands to the annoyance of my mother, who would be busily and blindly looking for a pair of scissors lest a word, a syllable, be cut off and left unread.

This Saturday afternoon, I decided to beat my loneliness with my own flute. I retreated to my paradise to play a few old melodies that Dad had taught me. I bopped over the grassy wall, swiping the willows' bangs, and positioned the bamboo against the wick of my lip. Out flowed the time-less "A Trip to Gu Su," my father's favorite piece. With eyes closed, my soul traveled back thousands of miles to the southern tip of Yellow Stone. Dong Jing was but a silver lining; Ching Mountain, a little *mantou* standing. The music thinned to a trickle, ending with my little finger fluttering, an ethe-real breathing, a breathless breath. I stayed in that mood, that construct of mind, for a good five seconds and would have stayed much longer had it not been for unexpected applause from an uninvited audience.

"*Hen hau. Hen hau,*" said a bearded foreigner with a semi-Mandarin tongue. Very good!

"*Nali, nali.*" Not at all, I said, turning pink.

"Do you speak English?" the man asked.

"A little."

"Very good. Your music is beautiful."

"Thank you."

"My name is Robin Ball. I'm Norwegian. I am pleased to meet you."

"My name is Chen Da. I am pleased to meet you."

What next? He did not know enough Chinese nor I, English.

"You study Chinese here?" I asked.

"Yes, I do. And you, English?"

I looked around the paradise and asked, "Do you come here often?"

"Yes, with my girlfriend. We like the outdoors." He winked.

I got it. A man and a girl in a dreamy, fluffy little spot out of sight of the world. I kicked the dirt against him and he jumped.

"Now, seriously, would you like to play for my friends tonight?"

"I would love to."

"Come to our party then."

"You are throwing a party?"

"Yes, every Saturday night. What else is there to do in this ghost town?"

"What else, indeed."

"And you will enjoy meeting some of my friends."

"I will be there."

"With your flute."

We said good-bye.

Party with foreigners! Good-bye, my loneliness. Hello, rock and roll. I kissed my slender flute for bringing this good luck. I had a feeling that wherever I went, my flute would always be more popular than I. If the flute could play itself, I might not be invited at all. But I didn't mind. I was the bellows that made the music dance. I played another song in celebration of my limpid flute diplomacy and eagerly headed home to study a few more hours before having to sacrifice the Saturday night for the party.

That night I washed myself really clean and put on my nicest shirt, a white one. My leather shoes were polished with a wet towel and shone nicely as I trotted to Robin's building.

Robin Ball was a sailor, adventurer, and Christian believer, but mostly a man. He showed his virile brilliance through his dazzling blue eyes. The blond hair only magnified his handsomeness. On his shoulder leaned a red-skirted, supple, thin serpent of a girl whom he introduced as Paula with his right arm around her narrow waist, which was accented by her big chest. His other hand cupped a wineglass, whose contents reflected back the festive prismatic lights that he had adhered to the windows. There was no doubt he was the host of the night. He fondled his girl, a red-lipped, high-cheekboned Spanish senorita, as he stood by his door, nodding and acknowledging the coming and going of a drinking crowd simmering in a music that I could not identify. The beat was urgent, with a guitar plucking like cup-sized raindrops on a tin roof. Then there were footfalls like the hooves of a thousand horses and bulls in flight, first slow, staccato, then quickening into a random mess. The crowd—all colors, all shapes, night ghosts, day ghosts—moved their butts uniformly to the rhythm; jeans broken, shirts torn. Algerians, Turks, Brits, Americans, Japanese—all danced along the cement hallway of the foreign students' building, spilling out of his gleaming dorm room.

"Da, grab a beer. This is the place to be on Saturdays."

"Thank you for inviting me. I am overwhelmed."

"Wait till you see Paula do her thing."

"What thing?"

"The Spanish dance."

The girl nodded with her pointed chin and swayed possessively, letting the redness of her dress rub against Robin's outer thigh. Paula's tongue came out to lick the rim of his Viking ear. A few strands of his blond hair got wet as a result. He chuckled at the tickle and wrinkled one side of his face in pleasurable response. "See what I have to tolerate?"

His Spanish love did not take the joke as a joke. She bit his earlobe, grabbed his butt with her paw, and walked away in annoyance with a zigzagging movement of her body, her waist a zig and her hips a zag.

"Here, take a Budweiser."

"What is a But-Why-Sir?" I asked.

"But-Why-Sir? A German beer. Universal cure for a man's impotence. Let's drink to it."

I probed one can and it tasted great. "I could get used to this," I shouted amid the din.

He grinned. "Look at these people here. What would they do without this gold liquid? They are alive and happy." He burped and refilled his wineglass. "If you want to learn good English, this is the right crowd."

"This dancing, drinking madness?"

"Yes, this is the best the world has to offer. Now, did you bring your flute?"

"Yes."

"Good, I want you to do your number right after Paula does hers. She is starting."

"What is the music that she is dancing to?"

"Spanish bullfight."

Paula's footfalls were calculated—toe, heel, knee, thigh, hip, breast, and bare shoulders, broad and bony. Her eyes stared at an invisible bull. Her feet skirted the imagined beast. Two dainty fingers pinched the silky hem of her red dress. The other hand twiddled a flower stem above her dark hair in perfect symmetry, an unbroken communication, the feet speaking to the hands, head tilting to her shoulders, breasts bouncing with her little jumps, and the tapping of her heels giving her hips a hippy jounce. Music poured and swirled like a cascade from the cliff of stereo loudspeakers. The whisper of a humid Spanish night, the lilt of Gibraltar's salty sea breeze, a bloom of Barcelona, and the little love of this Viking's heart.

Paula took off her heeled shoes, revealing skinny bare toes, and duck-walked back to Robin, spinning herself into a whirlwind of redness, dizzying not herself but the crazed crowd, drinking, drunk, and still drinking, though too drunk to be drinking.

Robin closed in on her clumsily, a big-boned man with the thin grace of a stick, rocking his butt in thrusting rhythm to meet her. They touched each other as the music trickled away. Her dark hair poured and ran free on his broad shoulders, smothering him. Buried, he shouted, "Let's drink some more."

"Paula! Paula! Paula!" the crowd roared.

"Now it's your turn."

"My turn?" I was recovering from the vibration of Paula's footfalls. My heart still lay on the floor that she had scissored, glided, and cut into pieces, and my mind napped in a mysterious land far away. My nose smelled those rumpled grasses, strangled by the stampede of bulls running, and my ears listened to echoing silence hidden in a dreamy valley. All that was doubled with the wickedness of the urging beer that rocked me like a little boat, moored, but whose knots were loosening with every swelling wave. A perfect mood for a trip to my Gu Su, wherever it might be. If there were no Gu Su, I could invent one. Everything was possible and everything eerily wonderful. Nothing mattered as much—loneliness, homesickness, cold teachers, colder classmates. Nothing mattered as much as I mattered to myself. Beer. Long live beer!

I pondered how to unknot the secret of my music for these foreign minds. They looked at me, holding this piece of bamboo with holes, without a clue to what magic it could bring. It was up to me to enlighten them about things Oriental. I stumbled with a clumsy introduction to my piece. "There was the horse riding, the willow, the lake at night, and missing a girl whom the rider loves. . . ."

"That sounds like good ingredients for some real hot sex," one party goer inserted.

"Is he looking for an ancient Chinese girl?" queried another.

"Even better with bound feet."

"Go on, play it."

"I am sorry my accent prevents me from explaining things better and more clearly."

"Stop apologizing, you did fine. Go on."

I closed my eyes and fluttered my tongue, tightened my lips, and out flowed the very melody that I had been playing since I was young. The crowd listened, drunk, and got more drunk listening. Some closed their eyes, imagining, while others leaned on their friends' shoulders, humming along. The music trailed away but the silence lingered. A reluctant but knowing applause rippled from Robin. Then the shouts of *Nice! Beautiful! Gorgeous!* erupted.

"Music needs no introduction," Robin observed. "Have a smoke."

"Here, smoke mine, a Rothmans." Paula pulled one out from the royal blue package. I took one and puffed on it hungrily. Yellow Stone could not have been further away from my mind. Putien was a shadow in the ancient past, and Fujian but a joke. I belonged here, in a strange way, among the shiningly beautiful black Africans, bearded Yemenites, bread-white Europeans, and tanned Spanish. They did not detest my accent. They liked my flute; they must like me. I was surrounded with questions of this and questions of that. Homesickness slipped away like the nightly tide.

Robin smiled from his wet bar, which he presided over. "Enjoying yourself?" he shouted in his clipped English.

I nodded back silently.

The night was beautiful. I was as drunk as the next fellow as I waddled home, singing and humming. I passed our doorman, Old Mao, at the entrance and saluted him with a big grin. He wrinkled his nose, shaking his head. I could not care less what he thought. For once in a long while, I was drunkenly happy again. Crushing my bed, I fell into a dreamless sleep.

I awoke the next day to find the noon sun shining on my hot bottom. Feeling sinful and wasteful, I grabbed my books and ran to my paradise, ready to tackle the day with readings in the sun. But when I hopped over the short fence, barely missing a little green frog, I saw Robin and a circle of his friends sitting on the grass, holding hands and singing.

"Hey, you, come here," Robin yelled at me.

"I'm sorry to disturb you. What are you doing here?" I asked.

"We're gathering here to worship God. I'm a Christian, Paula is a Catholic." He stood up, pointing to each as he went along. "Abdullah from Yemen is Muslim, and Hui Ton, my Cambodian friend, is Buddhist. Grace, Australian, is Baptist. Robert here from Cameroon has yet to decide what he is going to be, and we are having a good time."

"Didn't I meet you all last night?"

"More than likely. That's how I recruit my members."

"You throw parties to recruit them?" I was a little shocked.

"Consider it guerrilla tactics in the jungle of Communism. Besides, there is nothing wrong with baiting. Have you heard of Rice Christians?"

"No."

"In the early stages of Christianity in China, the pastors would open their doors, giving away precious rice to hungry people and then making them into believers."

"So you're a liquor Christian?"

"I'd say beer Christian," Robin amended.

"Partying on Saturday and praying on Sunday," I muttered.

"Saturday is for sin, but Sunday for spanking," Paula observed, winking at me.

Everyone laughed.

"Please go back to your activities. I have to get some studying done," I said.

"Wait a second. Sit here. This is a beautiful afternoon. A little bit of fellowship here won't hurt you, Da."

"I really have to go."

"Then you're not invited to my next party." Robin was joking because his eyes told me so, but the trick worked. Besides, I felt drawn there by the smiling faces around the circle. Pieces of sunlight danced on their faces as the trees swayed in the breeze. Paula started a new song, and they broke a gap for me to sit between skinny Hui, the Cambodian, and the Australian girl, Grace. The song was pretty, the kind I imagined Professor Wei back home singing in the Yellow Stone sunset tradition. The tune was gentle, like willow twigs sweeping. Robin, the party animal, led the flock like a shepherd. As his lambs nibbled away at their harmony, he smiled and looked at his girlfriend, whose beautiful voice soared above the others.

When she hit a high note, he acknowledged her with a nod and she beamed. Between them vibrated the sweet melody of a secret love.

They read from the Bible in English, taking turns reading verse by verse. Robin would pause and query, and one of them would answer. But it was Paula who grabbed most of the questions and answered them in lilting English. They fought over tricky points in the Bible and resolved their mis-understandings with kisses. All the rest of us quietly enjoyed their heated discussions. Robert of Cameroon, a pitch dark African, would squeeze in his weighty interpretations with his thick red lips. His responses, though brief, were welcomed with applause, which made him blush clumsily. Abdullah had a pair of big, shifty eyes. His head of hair was curly, gripping tightly like a rug to his head. He would explain in a mixture of English and Arabic. Grace was a quiet but very pretty white girl whose childish voice contradicted her height.

The meeting ended with each of us hugging and shaking hands. I chuckled when I saw Abdullah clinging to the tall Grace in a lingering hug. The little Arab sensed my smirk and winked back at me over Grace's shoulder. Hui told me that he lived in the same building on the same floor as me. I promised to visit him.

"Visit us often," Robin invited. "There is always fun and God. I am the only magician who can make them both go hand in hand." He grabbed his girl with one hand and the Bible with the other. I hugged them both good-bye, and they waved to me until I disappeared among the trees.

Robin was the second Christian believer I had met, but how different he was from my beloved Professor Wei.

Chapter Eight

I was making galloping progress in my English studies. In class, I understood almost all the instructions in that language now. It had taken two months for my deaf ears to be cured. The foreign words now glided against my eardrums with musical dings and pings. The mystery was pierced, and I no longer admired those city guys who considered themselves superior in class. They had been superior when we started out, but they had gotten lazy. All my classmates believed that this language study was a piece of cake. As long as they could yak in class, they were content. Much like Bo, most of my classmates began to take it easy. Some girls got plump, eating too much starchy *mantou* and sweet chocolates. Others began dating and going through the nightmare of torturous teenage love. Often there were inconsolable sobs and unexplainable catfights. That newly minted unity among the city folks was falling apart. They no longer ate at the same table or went to see the same movie. Some of them did not even speak to one another. Studying became the last thing on their minds. The mystery of college was over, and a more adventurous life awaited them, not books. Girls and boys began to wear fancy clothes like Bo's. Evenings were for smooching and the afternoons for baring their budding bodies and playing with the opposite sex. The classroom now was a serene place and the library an empty temple filled with lonely books.

Their happy-go-lucky attitude was encouraged by Karen Lynch, who advocated that language learning was all about socializing and that one should use language in the context of life as much as possible. That they did. And that was the only thing they did. She encouraged us to use and learn only simple words such as *get, make,* and *do.* When I once used the word *stupendous* to describe a building, she stood before me, faking anger like a kindergarten teacher to a toddler. "Yuck!" she said and stuck her tongue out before turning back to her podium.

"*Stupendous,*" she repeated. "Where did you pick up a garbage word like that?"

"In Jack London's books."

"Who?"

"He is only the greatest writer I have ever read."

"And the last one you should read any more of. Jack London, hah!"

The class laughed, an ignorant laugh. I bet none of them even knew who he was. If any of them ever read any of his masterpieces, they would forever shut up in deference to such a great man who had died too young and written too little.

But all this slacking and low morale only pleased me. Where others saw despair, I saw sunlight. Nothing beat the exhilarating feeling of gulping down buckets of knowledge while your competitors rested on bales of dry hay, chewing sweet carrots like that rabbit in the race. My turtle mentality pushed me to get up even earlier and go to bed later. My bundle of flash cards filled my schoolbag. There was not enough time in a day for me to regurgitate what I had learned. Only in the waning hours of the day, in the eerily quiet night, would I chew over the learned words of the day, relishing the real taste of pretty words and beautiful phrases such as *nostalgia, willow bay, nip and tuck, nape of a neck,* and *tiptoe.* But my favorite of all favorites was the phrase *the white silence,* London's coinage for Alaska. I often lost myself imagining that vast, snow-covered land across the mysterious Bering

Strait. And there were those images from James Michener's *Chesapeake,* the *Mayflower* fighting its way through the misty bay, autumn geese in the sky; and summer oysters in the riverbed. I basked in the beauty of a language that had taken root inside me and promised a prosperous blossoming.

For midterm, I recited a lengthy paragraph from *Martin Eden,* my favorite book, which lasted for a good fifteen minutes. Cross-eyed Professor Lulu did not blink the whole time; her mouth was left hanging. The section described Martin Eden falling in love with Ruth, how his world had turned into a whirlwind and how helpless love had made him. It was classic Jack London, dreamy, heartfelt, and eloquent. In that short while, as the class listened, I became him and Ruth became my lover. I fell in love, and love was beautiful. Lulu gave a delayed reaction of applause, which was followed with reluctant cheering by my classmates. They too were infected with that fever of love and London's feverish writing. I scored a shouting A in Lulu's class, even though her comment to me after the test was a sarcastic, "Jack London in a British accent?"

"I could have chosen Charles Dickens for the recitation, but I love London."

"I'm proud of you, Da."

"Thank you for your encouragement."

"By the way, I'm leaving for England to pursue a graduate degree in linguistics at Oxford," Lulu said proudly.

"Well, congratulations. Finally."

"Yes, finally."

She hugged me and I disappeared into her bosom. Her eyes were pearls of dew containing the sunlight from the window. "If you study hard and continue to do as well as you have shown us, you will be going abroad for further study as well."

"Thank you." Happiness made one generous, and generosity made her eyes focus a lot better. Lulu, in her floral dress, with her eyes smiling, looked ten years younger and a lot prettier as she walked off with a bouncing, cheerful gait.

Black Rose's test was a composition on anything we wanted to write about. Fiction or nonfiction made no difference to her. I stayed up till three one night, burning up half a pack of Flying Horses, feeling on the verge of great literary discovery with a pen pinched behind my ear and eyes narrowed, looking to the distant skylight. I wanted to write, but nothing came to mind. Childhood was too painful, and fiction was beyond me for the simple reason of a lack of vocabulary. I had little interest in science fiction and less imagination. So I went to Black Rose, asking for her darkly hued advice. She said, "Write what you know, never what you think you know."

It was another night and many more wee hours later when finally the round moon struck me. I set my pen flying, writing about my grandma. Each year around Moon Festival, which fell at the tail of summer harvest, Grandma would make her moon cakes, round things filled with meat and salted egg yolk in the middle. She would bake them for the duration of the burning of incense stick, then bring the delicious cakes to the backyard where the moon was full and hanging low. I would be so tempted to eat one, but she would hold me back to wait till everyone gathered. At the table there was always one empty chair reserved for my uncle, Dad's elder brother who had fled to Taiwan and wasn't allowed back. She would stroke the back of the chair and cry a little, then suddenly declare that we could eat. As we chewed those delicious cakes, she would murmur, looking up at the full moon, that Uncle was looking at the same moon in Taiwan and that the moon was a mirror that reflected all of our faces so that our loved ones, living in a distant land, could see them. It was five in the morning when I inked the last word.

The next day, when I went over the composition again, I almost tore it apart. It was tediously sentimental, unbefitting the youthful image I thought I had. But the deadline was today, and I only had time to recopy it neatly.

Two days later, Black Rose summoned me into her office. I entered timidly, expecting troubled black clouds on the horizon. She sat quietly with one hand holding her chin, as if pondering how she was going to deliver the devastating news of my mushy failure. I sat down, and she reached over to hold my hand.

"Mr. Chen, you've done some splendid writing. You've touched my soul."

"You like it?"

"*Like* is not the word. I am very surprised to see that you have this gift."

"Gift?"

"Yes, gift."

"Well, I'm very, very flattered by your compliment."

"I'm giving you an A, which you know that I rarely give, almost as rarely as I have flunked anyone. Not many people are that extreme. But this piece of writing is an exception. I did not expect writing like this from a freshman, much less from you. I meant no insult there."

"None taken." I was too busy soaking up her compliment. "Is anyone else getting an A from your class?"

"No." She smiled.

"Not even Yun, your favorite student?"

"Who says he is my favorite student?"

"We all thought he was."

"For your information, I only like hard workers, and you are one heck of a hard worker."

"I don't work hard enough, professor."

"You worked too hard for my composition, two nights till morning," she said mysteriously.

"How did you know?"

"You woke up your roommate."

"Oh." I suddenly realized that what Bo had been bragging about all along was not a total lie.

"Anyhow, I'm going to recommend publishing this piece of work in our department magazine."

I was ecstatic. "Thank you very much."

"I've also asked a French major, who is learning how to type in English, to type this up for you so that we can submit it for printing."

I bowed deeply to her and she smiled, revealing the whitest of teeth against her black clothes.

"Wait a second. Could you please return these sunglasses to Bo for me? He left them behind."

I took them and ran back to our dorm room only to find Bo lying in bed feeling gloomy. Another bad mood swing, I thought. His gloom was so big that it filled the whole room.

"What's the matter, Bo?" I asked.

"Nothing, get lost."

"I've got something for you from Madam Rose." I twiddled the glasses.

He opened his eyes and squinted. "Oh." He took the glasses and went back to sulking.

"Hey, sorry for not believing you. You do have a thing going with Rose, huh?"

"Fuck Rose."

"Hey, hey, take it easy. She happens to be my favorite teacher now."

"Since when?"

"Since she gave me an A."

"The bitch gave you an A?"

"Don't call her that."

"Well, she is. She gave me a low pass. That in her class equals a failing, do you know that?"

"What did you write?"

"Two pages of commentary about current fashion."

"Fashion commentary sounds good."

"Obviously not as good as your stuff."

"Hey, there's no reason to aim your anger at me. You go and talk it out with your lover."

"I despise her now. She called my writing rampant with no focused thoughts, like that of a drunk, she said. What the fuck did you write about?"

"My muddy town, my provincial grandma, and my huge appetite."

Bo shook his head, confused. "How could she give you an A and me a low pass? There is nothing hip about your subject and everything muddy, like you say."

"Well, sometimes she makes mistakes, I guess."

"I think she surely did in this case. Hard work doesn't necessarily justify good grades."

"Neither does laziness."

"I'm sorry if you take offense. All I'm saying is that she needn't overcompensate you for your lunatic study schedule."

"You think she's overcompensating me for my hard work only and not on the merit of my writing?"

"To some extent, yes."

"Fuck you. Wait till you see the publication of my prose in our department magazine."

"I'll be damned."

"Exactly." I turned away abruptly, feeling angry.

"Come back here. I'm sorry," Bo entreated.

"So am I. I thought you were a good friend who would be happy for me."

"I apologize, I really do. I'm just in a lousy mood because my nose is bothering me and Rose hurt me with this low grade. I couldn't face the crowd out there with this humiliation. One would think she would give me a better grade because I'm her friend, but no, she is one black bitch. So please forgive me for acting like a brat." He planted a kiss on my forehead.

"Forgiven, but don't use that tone again."

"Thank you, Da. I think you deserve it."

"You think so?"

"I know so."

Mr. Tu's test further confirmed my position as the emerging leader in class. His test was designed to torture lazybones and award those who worked hard and long like him. His specialty was lexicology—words. So he gave this long test of hundreds of words, which we had to explain the meaning of and illustrate our understanding of by using them in sentences. I couldn't stop smiling as I zapped through the whole test in two hours while others still lumbered along for the next two; some needed even more time. Even for me, there were some surprises. He deliberately made 5 percent of the test extremely difficult, using arcane words from older poems and earlier English writings. After that test, my classmates learned to fear him more than any other teacher. His smiling eyes and beefy face were but a mask. There was much more to this man than could be seen on the surface. I was very proud of being his student and, even more, his protégé.

Chapter Nine

Qiu—the Chinese word for autumn—brought to mind lotuses, floating on calm water, dreaming; bubbling crabs scaling noisy bamboo baskets, escaping; lychee trees sunk low with red fruit, burning; the bottomless sky, deepening; and silky clouds, thinning. But that was only my memory of Yellow Stone in autumn.

Qiu in Beijing was hollowing. The Mongolian wind raked the treetops of their red, dying leaves. Children's feet fell lightly on the layers of crunchy dried leaves. The city seemed bigger, the streets emptier, people smaller, and faces tinier. The campus resembled a lost battleground, with only the brave, naked trees standing. Warm summer breezes were soon replaced with the crisp cold air of early winter. Clothes got thicker and faces even smaller. People walked faster and a lot closer to the wall to shield themselves from the scathing wind. The sun became more precious and my heart bleak.

It was then that Robin decided to leave Beijing for warm Canton. His mission had been a success. Every Sunday a congregation of believers and fun-seekers gathered to sing hymns and read the Bible wherever they could find a safe place—in the woods, near parks, during boat rides on many a scenic lake. But his studies had failed miserably, which caused the school authorities to suspect his real purpose for being there. It was rumored that he had been questioned and his girl harassed by some secret police. And that was why they were moving, to seek another port of faith and fun.

He threw his last party on the lake of Kunming, on a windy boat. Some girls even cried as he offered good-bye with his long-limbed hugs. I gave him a calligraphy I had done about faith, and he gave me a little English Bible with a red cover. His parting words were an uncharacteristic, "Read this, and don't drink too much." Saturday nights would be less boisterous in his absence and the campus less colorful without the presence of his flowery Paula.

Hui, Abdullah, and I became closer buddies. The cold weather had a more vivid effect on southerners than on hardened northerners. For them it was just another page on the calendar. For us it was a step further into an unknown valley called winter.

Even the thickest clothing I had brought, a thick cotton coat, was no match for the needling cold. As my knees shook and my nose ran, my plan to make do with my knit underpants was hastily put aside. I hurriedly organized a town trip with Abdullah and Hui. One still made do with his Arab cloak, the thickest one, he said, and the other, his flimsy Cambodian skirt and sandals. When we got on the bus heading for the cheapest winter clothing store in town, the three of us were sniffling like a bunch of pathetic beggars, huddling for warmth in the corner of an almost empty bus.

Beijing bus No. 331 provided a wild ride. The windows were leaking, with wind blasting at the empty seats. The connection between the two compartments was loose and bundled together with broken cables. When the head was turning, the tail might not be following, so the sharp turns threw the tail of the bus like a wild bull, whipping and slapping a young tree here and a vegetable stand there. We hung on to one another, fearing for the next object this wild animal might sideswipe, our eyes staring at the balding head of the driver, who was either drunk or eager to go home to his waiting wife.

"Should've taken the taxi. This will kill us," Abdullah said with that blaming look of his.

"It's so cold in here, the windows are rattling," Hui spat out through chattering teeth.

"Come on, you cowards. This is fun. How else would you get to mingle with Chinese chicks?"

"Where are the chicks?" Abdullah asked sarcastically.

"They are coming," I said with a smile.

Soon my prophecy came true. This was a Saturday on the No. 331 that traveled along the crowded College Road. Carefree college girls began to board the bus noisily in twos and threes as we made our stops along the way. The bus was warming up, and my friends were smiling now. Abdullah gave an animal yelp when a group of tall and pretty girls got on board at the Beijing Art School stop. These beauties filled the bleak bus with hot possibilities. I fanned my face with my hands, Abdullah shook with joy, and Hui gripped his seat tightly, ready to pounce. The girls were also checking things out. They chatted and giggled, touching each other while they laughed. Their eyes glanced over us and were gone. Only one of them turned back to look our way again. Abdullah seized the chance to give her a friendly wink. The girl, whose sweater snuggly outlined her plump, budding chest, surprisingly gave him a sweet smile back. I pinched my hairy friend, but he needed no encouragement. Deserting us, he moved along the jerking bus to her side, where he stood a sad three inches shorter than the blossoming student artist. But that didn't lessen him as a pro in getting those girls' attention.

"Do you speak English?" he asked in that language. It was common knowledge in Beijing then that a white man speaking English could pick up any girl he wanted off the street. Abdullah couldn't change his skin color, but he could pretend to chat along in broken English, which was better than no English.

The tall girl's face went beet red and she shook her head.

"Can I offer you a cigarette?" Abdullah offered.

She shook her head again.

"Come on," he coaxed.

"Let me see what you have," the girl finally said as her other pretty friends watched the transaction.

Abdullah was in his element. His beady eyes shone with animal glee and his little taut body moved closer to the girl as he pulled out a thick wad of U.S. one-hundred-dollar bills.

"Oops," he said.

"What are you showing me money for?" the girl asked.

"My mistake, I meant to pull out my cigarettes." Out came his Marlboros.

It was a trick that worked miracles.

"You have so much money!" one girl exclaimed.

"He is showing off," said another.

"You want money?" Abdullah smiled. "Here, you can have one hundred, you can have another." He passed out a hundred-dollar bill to each girl in the group. They were jumping up and down, laughing and fighting over him. And without any invitation, he sat among them, smoking and chatting for the rest of the journey. Occasionally he looked our way, winked, and we winked back. He was a charmer, even with his smattering of Chinese. In his case, the less Chinese he knew the better. Those girls had the grandest time guessing what he was trying to say. The more they guessed and laughed, the more he faked his ignorance. By the time we got off at the Don Dan Shopping Center, the girls didn't want to let him go.

The tall girl asked for my name, which I reluctantly gave after Abdullah nudged me.

"Is he a good guy?" she queried through the window.

"A sweet and generous guy," I amended.

"Thank you. I might need you to translate for me if I go see Abdullah at your school, alright?"

Abdullah nudged me again and I nodded.

Abdullah, doggy eyed, bade them good-bye as we stood in the cold and windy street, staring at the cement building that housed the mammoth clothing store.

"Let's get in and find our coats," I suggested.

Abdullah, like a loyal dog, still had his eyes on the tail of the red bus. Hui and I had to push him inside the store and carry him up to the third floor where the whole shopping space was filled with heavy winter coats.

"Only two colors, how strange," Abdullah commented, recovered from his instant love.

"Black and blue," Hui observed.

"The most vivid colors of our Communist system," I said.

"It bores me to death," Abdullah declared.

"Well, why don't we get creative and all get a blue one," I suggested.

"Deal. Then we will look like an army." Hui had a soldier's mentality.

"A loose army at best."

"What is a loose army?" Abdullah asked.

"One that goes out and flirts with girls."

We laughed and asked an apple-cheeked salesgirl for three coats, blue. Even the smallest size dwarfed Abdullah. He danced around loosely in it. The salesgirl covered her mouth with her hands, laughing, and that was enough for Abdullah to continue his antics for another minute.

"Would you like to join us for a tea break?" he ventured, trying his luck with the girl. She reacted by suddenly snapping like a bulldog and calling him some of the dirtiest names I had ever heard in Mandarin. *Dog shit bastard! Dark-skinned hairy monkey foreign devil!* We paid for our coats and beat a speedy retreat.

"See, you shouldn't do that everywhere you go. Next time they might call the police and have you locked up in jail," I complained.

"What crime would they charge me with?"

"Scoundrelry. Open admiration is bad taste and foul style."

"Come on, Da, every girl likes to flirt, and every woman likes to fuck."

"How do you know?"

"I know because I'm married to three girls, and I'd better start educating you before you turn into another rusty Communist screw."

"Your Mandarin is pretty good when it serves your purpose. How come you were talking like you didn't know Mandarin at all with those girls?"

"Nothing works as magically as sweet ignorance. Women are born to be mothers. And they fell for it. Here are their addresses and telephone numbers. And she even asked for your name. She might come and have a threesome with both of us."

"You pervert." I pushed him. "Hey, let's hurry and have a picture taken in Tiananmen Square so you can send it to your family as a souvenir."

"But I don't have any family," said Hui. "The Vietnamese killed them all."

"I'm sorry, then do it for your children in the future." That brought a smile.

Dressed in three ten-pound cotton padded overcoats, we looked happily blue in the gray square. The review podium, where Chairman Mao used to stand and wave to the Red Guards, looked tiny and distant. His portrait had the forced smile of a constipated man. Mao and the square looked equally irrelevant as the people scurried by on bikes and in buses. The cameraman stood each of us in turn in a chalk-drawn square. Abdullah wanted to pose like a monkey with his hands curled, legs kicking, and mouth grinning. The cameraman stepped out from under his black cover cloth and looked at him puzzled.

"This is a serious portrait, you idiot," he shouted.

"But I like it this way."

"You can't do it that way. It is an insult to the background of the podium. I'm not going to do it if you pose like that."

"Come on," Abdullah coaxed. "I've got U.S. dollars."

"Nothing is going to change my company policy."

"Come on, how about a pack of Marlboros?"

The man smiled and shouted, "You crazy foreigner." He took the pack of cigarettes and said, "No more tricks."

"Okay."

The instant before the camera clicked, Abdullah tore his coat and shirt off. The man wanted to kill the half-naked monkey, but it was too late, the camera had already clicked. Abdullah was probably the only person to show his nipples at the eye level of a smiling Chairman Mao.

The following Sunday, Abdullah's girl called to say she was coming to see him later that day. The little man jumped up and down, excited and nervous. With a few cuts on his face due to a blind razor and shaking hands, he asked me for advice on how best to please a Chinese girl.

"You mean getting her to bed?"

"Da, do you have to be so blunt about things?"

"Okay. Nice food. Chinese girls love a man who cooks. They consider them good husbands."

"That's easy."

A few hours later Abdullah invited me to his room. Out came the head of a live mountain goat, which had been dropping pebbly crap all over the floor. Ten of his friends were in there with him.

"What are you doing with the goat?" I asked.

Abdullah cut his finger across his throat and I understood. It was going to be nasty.

Two hours later Abdullah marched into my room carrying a big plate with two chunks of the most delicious-looking meat. "Eat it," he insisted.

"Well . . ."

"Come on, eat it right now. I want to see you enjoy our favorite food."

Being a big fan of all flesh, I grabbed a chunk and sank my teeth into the sizzling, tender meat. The spice made my breathing jerky, and the garlic-mixed tomato sauce was a dream. Good meat was good meat, and I swallowed both of them in five big mouthfuls. Abdullah smiled with pride, and I slapped his back as a compliment.

The girl, Arlin, came in a floral dress that made her even prettier. She smiled knowingly at me and I smiled back. Abdullah was so busy pushing her into his room that I didn't have time to say good-bye.

Big laughter soon erupted from inside. I knew that goat meat might not be the most appropriate food for the first date, but the heart and spirit of the cooking apparently moved her. That afternoon the whole floor heard their love screams. Some loved it, cheering; others hated it, like Bo, who covered his ears with his music earphones and shook his head at me as if it were my fault that my friend was acting like that. I dashed off to the library and swore not to return until the last note of love was played out.

That evening I came home late to an angry reception by Abdullah. He had been waiting. Almost in tears, he begged me to smuggle his girlfriend out of the thicket of tight security. I agreed, though not without fear of retribution by our secret police. Since the whole building had heard her loud cries, I could easily be implicated, if not as principal, then at the very least as a knowing and pimping accomplice. But a friend in tears was a friend in need. Fear gave way, and silently I guided her safely out of our school's main entrance. She lingered a bit, tossed her hair, and opened her mouth for the first time. "I hope you don't think less of me?"

I just shook my head.

"He touched me, you know."

"I'm sure he did."

She chuckled. "I mean emotionally."

I nodded.

When I reentered the dorm, the old guard stuck out his head and said, "Hey, you, what do you think you are doing?"

"You talking to me?"

"Yeah." He gestured with his head for me to come into his smoke-filled

office with a glass window overlooking the entrance. "Sit down," he said.
I sat on his bed, getting very nervous about this.

"It's all right," he said, to my relief. "Abdullah came down to explain
to me."

"He did?"

"Yeah. Just don't get involved in this kind of thing again. Go."

I thanked him profusely.

As it turned out, the explaining that Abdullah had done was ten packs
of Marlboros. Abdullah came by around midnight that night and shoved
me a bag of magazines. "I won't be needing this stuff anymore," he said.

"What are they?"

"Pornography, the worst type."

That night I stayed up till morning to read through every single page.
Abdullah, Abdullah, you really shouldn't have done this to your poor old Da.

I felt a certain kinship with Hui because we both wore a tan, a deep southerner's tan. And we came from a land where the sun was our god and the
moon his goddess. Few other celestial objects soothed us like the heavenly
couple. But on one November day, our hearts were stolen and spirits lifted
when we saw the leaden, dreary sky suddenly filled with soft, dancing
snowflakes blown amok by a Mongolian wind. It was our maiden snow
and our third celestial wonder.

Hui and I chased the snow with our eyes closed and arms outstretched.
The earth seemed to be rising upward as the snowy butterflies fell gracefully. Hui stood silently still with snow dusting him and sliding down his
slender fingers. Soon he was white as a snowman. In this swirling white
silk, I held my heart in my hands, confessing my love for this northern wintry tale. In this perfect world, I also became a snowman.

"Get out of there. You're going to get sick," came Abdullah's shout.

I opened my eyes, causing snow to fall from my eyelashes, and saw
Abdullah bending down and picking up a handful of snow. I grabbed Hui
and quickly ducked from Abdullah's onslaught. A nasty snow fight followed, ending in a three-way slippery wrestle. Our wet bodies mutilated
the even carpet of snowfall. We lifted Abdullah up by his feet. His coat
flipped over and covered his face as we dumped him on the ground and
dragged him like a sled. In the end, we dropped grenades of snowballs into

his crotch, which sent him jumping and dancing up the stairs like a monkey on fire.

The snow was even more precious for bringing with it my first letter from home. I grabbed two cigarettes from Hui and ran to my little paradise with the letter clutched in my hand. Tears welled up in my eyes. It was my father's writing, the elegant, confident, and intolerant stroke of his calligraphy. I could imagine his pride when writing my name and address and adding the formal title of Comrade to the tail of my name. It was his first letter to his son far away and the first time he had addressed me as Comrade. I wanted to read in the utter silence of my own breathing, in pure tranquillity, for these were words of love, words of home, words of the many Chens, living and dead, words of Yellow Stone.

Puffing two cigarettes at the same time to calm my nervous fingers, I sat on the freshly minted snow, oblivious to its chill and dampness. In one breath I read my dear father's letter three times on end, each time with more tears and love, each time hearing more vividly my family's voices and seeing more clearly their eyes. I could almost smell Mom's scent, a memory from childhood as I snuggled next to her every morning in the crook of her arms, my fluffy nest of safety and warmth. I could almost touch my dad's shoulders, broad and manly, upon which I used to ride as a kid, grabbing his thinning hair, trotting with the rhythm of his walk along the shore of the Dong Jing River, silently guessing its tricky nooks and muddy curves.

Dad told me in his imperative tone that they had enjoyed reading my first letter and all the things I had written home. He and Mom had had a grand time reading it over and over again. Only a truly loving parent could have tolerated reading through my emotionally charged, incoherent letter again and again. They were doing well. He was thinking of setting up some sort of hairdressing business for Huang, my big-eyed sister. He himself was training Ke, my other sister, to play the *yan chin,* a stringed instrument played with two bamboo sticks and the *pipa,* a banjolike instrument, because our county was organizing another touring troupe to perform the traditional operas. He was one of the founders and would also be the playwright, the director, the conductor, and a general manager.

Dad, a jack-of-all-trades, could not stay away from the temptation of the artistic world. It had always been in his blood. He had done acting, writing, and composing in his youth. It was the tragic revolution that had hardened him into just earning bread and butter for the family. But now with two sons in college, his dream of an artistic life was blossoming again. From his tone, there seemed to be no stopping him. While Dad talked about big things in life, Mom's thoughts and concerns came in the form of antlike writings squeezed into the margins. They were my mom's famous afterthoughts. She would keep adding more and more, day after day, which at some point would come to annoy Dad because it delayed him from sending out the letter. In the meantime she would come up with something important in between her dozing and needlework. As she dozed some more, the letter kept growing and growing, but that was what I had expected of Mom. I read her tiny fine print carefully, for now I had begun paying more attention to whatever she had to say. Her nagging chatter became the cherished golden rules of life. Life was about details. I had learned it the hard way. I could tell her that the ring on the collar did happen, that it took a lot of scrubbing with the best soap I could buy and still shone with the stubborn grease from my longish hair. I already forgot to flip the pockets of my pants out when I dried them. The result would be wet pockets in dry pants.

Dad wrote that I should go home for the holiday because they wanted to see me. It was the first time I had been away, and they just had to get me in front of them and scrutinize every inch of me to make sure that northern China had not taken a toe or a nail from me. And about the forty-yuan train fare, he said he could manage. He asked me not to worry. The invitation was heartwarming, but I had already decided to stay on campus to save money and to study some more books while the rest of my classmates would be resting.

The letter left me longing for home even more. Many times I kissed my dad's signature, which he signed as Yu Fu: The Foolish and Humble Father. I cried some more in the silence of this beautiful snow, and half of my homesickness melted away like the thin flakes.

A few days after that, a letter of no less importance arrived with earthwormlike writing on the envelope. It was Sen's composition, the thinking rogue that he still was. His letter read unusually smoothly. He depicted the lousy moods of every one of my four friends with simple but not simplistic sentences that he had woven together with some sweat into a lyrical prose of artless charm. Misspellings were expected; they were necessary to make him who he was. A proud misspeller and a deft communicator notwithstanding his handicap, Sen said that Siang was pissed because I hadn't written sooner, but they liked what I had scribbled about: stories about white, black, and yellow girls with big chests and long, thin legs. He asked on behalf of the gang that I send some proof of my sightings. You boastful bastard, he commented, don't tempt us with your beautiful words. Send us something that we can see and touch.

I made a mental note of that.

Mo Gong also missed me, he reported. If, by any chance, his bee-raising venture was a success (which was quite unlikely), he might be able to travel north with his hives of bees, following the blossoming seasons, and I'd better be prepared to get him drunk and maybe laid when he came.

What was I, a pimp? I thought. Then shrugged.

Yi advised that tea was no good after all. He had recently had a little problem with his stomach and had now quit black tea altogether. But as a result, Sen added, Yi had turned into an intolerable, babbling idiot, tortured by the sudden disappearance of massive doses of caffeine that used to swim in his system.

Sen put his own thoughts last and asked me if I could find him some book about banking because he had been told he would inherit the job from his banker father upon his retirement. There was a simple reason for that. His two older brothers had married already. A landmark in their life had been achieved, but this roaming third son would never find a wife if he were not given a job with cushy pay. No one would have wanted him otherwise. Sen was freaking out, not because he wasn't a calculating kind of man who would fit into the banking world well but because of a deadly fear of returning to a civilized work environment after years of wandering and living an undisciplined life. I was overjoyed by the news and had little doubt that Sen would thrive as a banker.

The four of them had all signed at the end of the letter. Sen's signature was a thoughtful tangle; Siang's, a ballet of whimsical clouds; Mo Gong's, a messy web of emotions; and Yi's, a work of art with the precision of an architect. They made me want to laugh out loud. I could see their naughty faces among the trees and snow. Compulsively I dashed off a letter right back to them, promising to look out for Mo Gong, find a book for Sen, and maybe bring them some pictures of exotic foreign girls when I visited home. I explained that I would have sent them by mail, but our commune's mailman was the worst Peeping Tom. He would have read it first, then reported it to the cadre, and we would all have been in trouble.

Chapter Ten

Winter in Beijing was forbidding. New snow piled on old slush. Roads were treacherous and broken ankles or fractured hips were inevitable torts in a hasty trot. Trees, bare to their knuckles, stood ugly and dangerous. Supple twigs flapped, ingratiating themselves with the wind. Brittle branches cracked. A few brave and hungry birds flapped their tiny wings with extra gusto to stay within the choppy course of their windy flight. Winter lay bare their urges. They pecked on everything, hoping for a delicious discovery. Chilling winds lifted their fine feathers, reducing fluffy cuties to pathetic paupers. Smarter ones chipped away at the hardened snow on the ground, choking their little beaks with foamy colored ice. They chased the rubbish that chased the leaves, but when a blast of wind kissed the ground, the winds of war reversed. Now the leaves were chasing the rubbish that chased the birds.

Bo was miserable. He called in sick every day, while everyone else sloshed along the windy path of misery to school. He sat slanting against his warm quilt, eating the breakfast I had fetched for him, listening to his melting Spanish music. "Nothing is worth me getting up for a winter day like this," he declared.

"Go get your own breakfast next time."

He ignored me and continued. "I must have been conceived in the folds of this warm quilt with snow falling outside. You know, I was born in Moscow. My parents worked for the embassy there."

"And you can't get up to make it to school?" Hong said.

"No, there are no horses and carriages here. You see, I had to be drawn to kindergarten every morning, two blocks away from our embassy compound. Butter cookies and hot milk would be waiting for me. Shit, I'd like to have some white bread and melting butter. Da, you think you can get your foreign friends to bring me some of that stuff from their cafeteria to satisfy my old appetite?"

"Yeah, right."

"Da, Da, don't be so stubborn. And don't forget to come to the New Year's party ball."

"I have work to do. The finals are only a month and a half away."

"So? You still have to live and enjoy a bit."

"I enjoy too much. The October National Day, Christmas, and now New Year's Eve. I'm hugely distracted."

"But you must come for a glimpse of it. I have to show you something."

"What?"

"I will be waltzing with Black Rose."

"In your sick dreams."

"You just see."

New Year's was celebrated like any official government holiday, with a meal of extra-greasy spareribs and slippery onion rolls. No one really cared about it, for the real New Year, the Chinese one, was the upcoming Spring Festival, a month or so from now. But New Year's was New Year's. Colorful papers were thrown all over the bare trees, and large red posters shouted the clichéd wishes—*Make the yearly plan in spring* and *Make the daily plan in the morning.* The school was giving us a day off and throwing a big and loud dance party in our dining room. All the tables and chairs were pushed aside to the far corners. Sticky floor or no sticky floor, fabulous waltzes would be twirled and tangos twisted. Thousands of people would be flocking here to witness this newest rage called "the dance party," which had only recently been allowed by the government. There was a sense of history-making in the air. Everyone, young or old, would be there.

The dining hall was split into two sections, one for performances and games and the other for dancing. Boys and girls were in twos and threes, ogling each other. Laughter was heard above the din and love palpable in the air. A large crowd gathered for word games, but an even larger one surrounded the dusty dance floor. I waded my way there and saw among the bobbing heads our dear old doctor dancing with a young student. She was one of those mature teenagers with signs of trouble hanging all over her. Then again, where there was trouble, there was the good old doc.

I looked in the crowd for Bo and was disappointed to see him sitting all alone, smoking, with his head between his hands. I fought my way over to him, not an easy task with a thousand sweaty party goers pushing one another, threatening to burst the walls.

"What's the matter, you playboy?"

"Can't you see it yourself?" Bo grumped.

"Help me out here. Where's your girlfriend, the black number?"

"For your information, Black Rose's husband is home for the holiday and she is over there." He pointed angrily.

I spotted her among the crowd, in a flowing red dress. "Well, well, well, Black Rose is in red."

"She is out of her mind!"

"She is in love again. Her man made her bloom."

"Yeah, right."

"Bo, she looks stunning." Then more seriously, "I think you should forget about her. She is taken and has been taken."

"Shut up, Da! Can't you see I'm upset? I don't need your moral lectures right now."

"All right, all right."

"The Blue Danube" played through a jarring loudspeaker lost all its grace though not its rhythm. The speakers coughed and hiccuped a great deal, grunting with too much bass.

Bo shook his head. "Look at this. And they call it a waltz," he sneered. "It's worse than a Red Guard parade with rifles."

The scene was pathetic. Girls and boys, women and men, shoved one another as they lunged back and forth to the rhythm of the music. Their steps were coarse and unrefined as they lifted their feet high and stomped down loudly, stirring up the dust on the floor. Arms were stretched stiffly as sweaty men dragged confused women forcefully around. Male domination showed vividly here.

Red Rose was leaning in the arms of newly returned Mr. Rose, who sported the spiffiest blue blazer with gold buttons. He wore a silk tie with a matching pocket square. They were the most successful dancers on the floor, one of the few couples who were actually dancing and not dragging, pushing, or stepping on each other. She smiled as she glided past Bo.

"Don't you wish you were him?" I sighed.

"No. I wish she would not be that shameless."

I shook my head. "You're a crazy and jealous guy."

"Maybe I am, but she seems *way* too happy. She's never been this happy before."

"Because she's never had her man at home before."

Bo rubbed his nose and gritted his teeth.

Red Rose was waving to Bo now. Reluctantly he waved back.

"Come dance with me," Rose invited.

Bo wasn't given much choice. Rose matched her husband with an ugly senior student and grabbed Bo, who handsomely glided into the tango music. Instantly Bo went from being a limp, grumpy boy into a radiant young man. He guided Rose with ease, skillfully negotiating the busy traffic. Bo winked at me as they swept by, and I winked back. They did some difficult maneuver, and Red Rose became redder, her face blushing as the whole hall watched her being dipped and led elegantly by Bo. Her husband also stopped to watch them. Bo did some more fancy steps which dazzled Rose, making her shriek delightedly. Red Rose was enjoying herself, laughing and talking as Bo spun, dipped, and twirled her around. It was good for Bo, who was getting all the attention now, but really bad for Mr. Rose, who was watching the spectacle. My heart thumped as I observed the pulsing vein in Mr. Rose's neck. He angrily eyed Bo as though sighting a target. Each time their paths crossed, his eyes grew narrower.

Finally Mr. Rose pushed away the ugly senior and stepped up to Bo. Without a word, he took his wife back into his arms and spun away. Bo was left alone among the passing feet. Transfixed and humiliated, he waited.

When the Roses danced near him once more, Bo tensed up and pursed his lips, ready to do something stupid. The two men stared at each other. Bo stopped them abruptly and bowed down, asking to cut in. The wife paused but not the husband, who angrily dragged his wife away. What the heck was he doing out there? I thought. Bo chased after the couple and yanked at Mr. Rose's collar. The couple stopped, and the husband released his wife, who tried to stop her man. But the man was a man, after all. Some dancers stopped to see the drama; others continued as Mr. Rose gripped Bo's neck and pushed him out of the crowd. Bo was foaming and kicking, but he was no contest for the Rose man. A few cheering kids followed them; one of them even showed them the fire exit, which they took. I hurriedly ran after them, behind the trailing kids. Someone called for security as Mr. Rose pushed Bo out into the dark courtyard, shutting the door behind him. I tried to break through the door, but it was steel and hurt my shoulders. By the time I finally reached them through another exit, the fight was over. Bo was on the ground with a bleeding nose.

"Bo, let me help you," I cried.

"No, go away." He tried to get up but slipped.

Mr. Rose threw me a cutting look and tossed his pocket handkerchief at Bo, who picked it up angrily and used it to stop his bleeding.

"I see you near her again and this'll be your last New Year, you punk," the Rose man threatened.

"Fuck you, you animal," Bo cursed.

"For your information, I'm a military attaché." He opened his jacket on his left side, revealing a holstered pistol. He spat on Bo and returned to the dance floor.

"As if it scared me," Bo shouted back. He got to his feet and tried to limp after the man, but I pulled him back. He tried to throw me off, but I stopped him.

"He's going to kill you!" I exclaimed, clawing him tightly.

"He doesn't love his wife enough to do that."

"He's got a gun, you idiot."

"And I've got justice on my side."

"Justice? You tried to steal his wife."

"Because he screws around all over the world wherever he goes."

"It's none of your business."

"It is because I love her."

"Go love someone else, you fool."

"You don't understand. I had a good thing going with her," he said miserably.

"Let's go home and get some rest." I had to drag him all the way to our dorm. In the washroom I dumped a basin of cold water on him.

"What did you do that for?"

"So you can wake up and be smart again."

He was dripping like a drowned chick. There was water on his face. I passed him a towel with which he dried his head slowly. Only then, in the dim light of our washroom, did I see traces of tears on his cheeks. He had lost his love tonight; it did not matter whom he had lost it to. It was gone.

Back in our room we smoked in silence, waiting for the clock to strike twelve.

"Happy New Year," I said to him.

"Happy fucking New Year."

Chapter Eleven

New Year brought gloom to some but hope to me. Bo waded through this eternal thickness of cold thin air, sniffling and blowing his bad nose even harder. At times, he got so frustrated with his long dragon nose that he smashed it, rubbed it, and squeezed it till the demons inside were put to rest and bled like a broken cherry. But only a short while later the noisy elements would begin to act up again. Then he would scream and throw his handkerchief across the room to land on Hong's bed. Hong would gingerly pick it up with two fingers and return it to Bo. At night these episodes went on forever until a thick chunk of snot was finally blown out. Hong and I would sigh along with his sigh of relief.

We had just a month to really sink our teeth into the materials before the finals in February, but semesters were already over in my classmates' minds. Classes had ended, and the review sessions meant nothing to them.

I was the only one still up at the crack of dawn, beating the howling wind, battling dancing snow, and wading through dirty slush. At heart I was happy, with not a single complaint in this white world.

Successfully I swam through the lizard-infested exams like a champion. I had pretty much overprepared and had plenty of time to review all the answers. Never leave a test early, no matter how confident you are, Dad had taught me. There was always something to check on, a comma or a question mark, it all added up. And add up it did. I scored highest in the class in three subjects and second highest in the rest. The results were pasted on a wall. It was not hard to see that there was a general indigestion about my grades in the intestines of my classmates. They groaned, moaned, sighed, and said things like, "It don't mean nothing," with a shrug. They despised me and looked down on me as a thick-toed, dark-skinned fisherman not fit for the academic setting. But before the grades, all were equal, and I loved that democracy that rewarded cows with hardened shoulders and punished lazy cats that purred in their warm beds.

I whistled down the hallway only to be congratulated by the big-hearted Lynch with a hug and greeted by the sultry, once again Black Rose with a sleepy but exaggerated, "Hello, Da!" I went to Professor Tu's office to thank him for a beautiful test.

"No one has ever thanked me for my tests before."

"Because you make them miserable."

He grinned in agreement. "But you did really well," he said, his eyes smiling.

"Because you're a good teacher."

"Thank you. Oh, by the way"—he closed the door and leaned over— "the department is looking for a couple of good students to go study in North America."

"From my class?" I was stunned.

"This is a secret that I'm only sharing with you."

"It's safe with me. How do they choose them?"

"Grades," he said. My heart sang. "And politics," he added. My heart cried.

"Do I have a shot?" I asked meekly.

He smiled, put his arm on my shoulder, and squeezed me silently.

"No?"

"I did not say that. I'll see what I can do. But your class is full of people with powerful parents."

"What should I do?" I asked him.

"There is only one way to fight corruption."

"What's that?"

"Go back to your hometown and beg Buddha." He smiled his Buddha smile.

I left his office, excited and nervous. Heaven had just opened up a crack, and the sun was shining through, but I couldn't fly because I had no wings. His casual mention of Buddha somehow stuck in my head. *Home. I must go home.* Only the big fat Buddha could give me those wings so that I could soar. I was grateful to Tu for having leaked the secret, which by tomorrow would be known to all because, as Dad said, news this good never does well as a secret. Pretty soon everyone would be a candidate. Mud would fly and blood spill. But I didn't intend to be left out of this race. I needed my family, my pathetically powerless but enormously resilient family by my side to plot my victory. And Buddha was most effective when you could touch his toes and suckle them. I must go home. But where was I going to find that forty yuan for the train tickets? Dad could send me a ticket home, but he couldn't get me back, and I did not want to burden them any more.

I stopped by Hui's room, looking moody, woeful, and much in need of a good smoke.

"What's the matter? Aren't you happy our long semester is finally over?" asked Hui, ever the sunny southerner.

"I need money to go home," I said.

"Why didn't you say so. How much do you want?" He started to pull a wad of cash from his coat pocket.

"I can't borrow that."

"And why not?"

"Because the word *debt* scares me. It brings back bad memories. We used to sleep with debt and eat debt. Of course, in those days my grandpa had died deep in debt. Good thing Father was there to inherit his debt so that he did not have to have stones thrown at his coffin. Debts don't die with you. They live on forever and ever, give you nightmares, and blacken your family name, and soon your tombstones will be taken away. So fuck debt!" I ranted endlessly.

"Okay, okay, I got the point. That's fine, no debt then. I have another idea." His eyes narrowed.

"What is that?"

"Are you willing to make money?"

"How?"

He pulled out a yellow pack of Phoenix cigarettes and lit one for me. I sucked it hungrily. "Come on, spill it."

"You like the smoke?" He made a smoke ring and watched it rise above his head.

"Sure, every smoker's dream. It's a rare commodity. You can't find them in any market—"

"Except on the black market—"

"And with a criminally high markup."

"Now you're talking," Hui said, sucking in a long draw, letting the smoke linger meaningfully inside his lungs. "Listen, I can take you to the Friendship Store and buy one hundred packs. You take them home and resell them at whatever price you dare ask. Buy low and sell high. You won't have to worry about train tickets at all."

"Well, I didn't know you were such a merchant."

"My whole family were fruit merchants before the fucking Vietnamese came."

"But the Friendship Store is only for foreigners. How can I get in there?"

"You leave that to me," he said confidently.

The following day Hui concocted a guerrilla war scheme to sneak me into the menacing Friendship Store. It was owned by the government to skin foreign fat cows and run by the thuggish Chinese KGB to keep the Chinese and animals at bay. And they called it the Friendship Store.

In his room Hui, like the war hero commander he was, herded together a dozen of his dark-skinned countrymen and threw in a couple of skinny girls. They were all in green army uniform. In the middle of the crowd was me, the Chinese, whom they planned to smuggle into the security-laden mecca of fine goods and rare things.

In his native language Hui gave a serious and urgent speech to his soldiers, who shouted back in the same manner. One naughty young man chuckled, looking my way. Hui didn't like that and smacked the little guy on his cropped head. The boy ducked like a girl. I would hate to be one of Hui's foot soldiers. Then again, he looked commanding and incredibly purposeful.

When the drill was over, I said to Hui woefully, "I'm going to get caught."

"No you're not. You're going to wear my army uniform." He took out a green army jacket from the closet and draped it over me. "Now you fit right in. There's also plan B."

"Plan B?"

"Yes, I have asked Amee to do me a favor." He pulled a shy girl with big, staring eyes to his side. "She's going to accompany you as a special friend. You can hold her hand as you enter. Don't touch her anywhere else."

I nodded, smiling, and she gave me a reluctant nod, not smiling.

"How will that help?" I asked.

"Because it makes it believable. No Cambodian girl would hold a Chinese boy's hand, believe me. Look at her. Do you see her smiling? I had to give her a military order to get her to do this. Hold her hand only when necessary."

"When is that?"

"When crossing the entrance."

The store was the beachhead of a dry seaside town where chauffeured foreign tourists gathered in knots, sitting, standing, talking, and drinking. The babble of tongues tangled and untangled at this green oasis in the drab desert of Beijing. In the courtyard that fronted the four-storied white building, the smell of dollar was pungent. The fragrance of foreign perfumes danced in winter's morning light like frying grease in a kitchen. A world full of sensuous goods lay abundantly there for them to pick and toss away, while the world outside still lumbered along like an old freight train, puffing and dying in its rigid ration system—a system that only allowed half a pound of sugar and one pound of fatty pork a month; where a good down coat was filled with hard feathers; and cigarettes were made of chunky, foul-smelling tobacco leaves.

In colorful camouflage our uniformed troop lurked among the startled camels of foreign tourists, who wore cameras around their necks, sunglasses on their tall nose bridges, and fat pouches filled with crispy cash around their waists. Uniformed guards walked the beat, nastily pushing away and kicking Chinese who had knowingly or unknowingly stepped over the invisible demarcation line, while humbly bowing to the white feet of white men with white women on their white arms.

"You're going to be one of the very few Chinese making it through the door there," Hui said, checking his terrain.

"Thanks for the encouragement. But I'm not looking forward to being a butchered martyr. The security looks tight here." I suddenly remembered reading an article in *Beijing Daily* about a man being put away for trying to get into this place. The fear of being picked out as a fake gripped me.

"Walk in the middle," Hui ordered. "And you can hold her hand now." She was sweet, giving me her hand with a forced smile. I took it nervously, fearing her bite.

"You know, I speak some English," she informed me.

"You do? That's great!"

"So, you know how to be a gentleman?" she asked sternly.

"Yes. Please this, please that, pardon me and excuse me," I mocked with a leaky British accent.

She wasn't thrilled. "Be serious," she whispered forcefully. "And walk with me like that couple over there." She was pointing to a white couple, man in a suit and lady in a dress, striding gracefully up the steps. The man patiently waited for the woman as she picked up the hem of her skirt and, smiling, inserted her right hand into the crook of his left arm.

"Aha. I can do that. But we're not in the right uniform." I was trying to be funny.

"Pretend!" She bent my left arm, inserted her arm through it, and leaned on my shoulder while shoving me along with the force of a tiny giant.

"Are you sure this closeness won't violate Hui's military order?" I whispered into Amee's ear. She stepped painfully on my left foot in warning. Then she nudged even closer, and I couldn't help feeling excited, rubbing this loan of a girlfriend. But all sweet feelings vanished when a blue uniform barked rudely in our direction.

"Wei! Nimen shi nali laide?" Translation: Hey! Where the heck are you guys from?

"Cambodia," Hui answered proudly, cocking his head.

The guard narrowed his eyes, thinking.

Hidden in the middle of the crowd, I could almost see the guy's thoughts forming, then finally formed. *Where the hell is Cambodia? Is it a foreign country?*

"You cannot come in," he said. I wasn't surprised. In the minds of these snobbish guards, only freckled white Caucasians or the bowing Japanese were legitimate foreigners, all of whom had one thing in common: hard currency. If anything, Cambodians definitely took the bottom of this totem pole.

"And why is that?" Hui asked angrily.

"Because you fall under the category of refugees." He flipped a small book. "And this place does not take refugees. There is a big difference. It's in here."

Hui was fuming and waving his arms wordlessly, his Chinese all forgotten. I also felt my anger rising, hearing this nonsensical wordplay being imposed upon my poor friends, whose Chinese was at best lopsidedly effective and at times utterly unintelligible. Grabbing the slender waist of Amee, who was surprised by my sudden forcefulness, I stepped up to face the guard and said curtly, "A foreigner is a foreigner last time I checked my dictionary. You're insulting our national pride, and I'll report you." I contorted my already lilting Fujian accent with a dash of singsong Cambodian.

The guard stared at me with his murky eyes, those of an unthinking bulldog whose sole mission in life was that one magical word: bones. "You think you know Chinese, huh? But there are big differences among foreigners. And they don't spell them out on the pages of your fucking dictionary."

That did it for me. I felt like a rocket ready to launch. What a racist pig! What a fucking idiot! I could have punched the guy for insulting our civilization. "What is your name?"

"Why do you want to know?"

"I want to report you to Premier Li Peng of State Council."

"Li Peng, huh? Go ahead. Who the heck do you think you are? And your Chinese is terrible." He shoved his long chin at me.

"Your breath is no better. I happen to be the nephew of a very important Cambodian leader."

"And who might that be?"

"Well . . ." I cleared my throat, thinking, but nothing came up.

"The King Norodom Sihanouk," Amee said, thrusting her chin into the guard's chest.

"That's right, King Si . . . ha . . . nouk. Do you want me to give him a call now and get your ass fired?"

"And I will report this incident to the UN." Amee jumped in again. "You know what the UN is?"

"Okay, okay," the guard said. "But I cannot let that guy in."

"Which guy?" I asked.

"That one." He pointed to a short fellow. "He looks Chinese to me."

"No one here is Chinese," I said. "Who wants to be a Chinese?"

"I have to check his ID," he insisted.

"Give it to him," I shouted to the puzzled fellow, who fished out a picture ID. Though still unconvinced, the guard reluctantly let us all in, counting each of us with his angry eyes. We burst into victorious laughter as soon as we entered the hushed world inside.

"You did good, Da." Hui hugged me.

"We did good, especially you." I squeezed Amee, who pushed me away and said, "Cut it out. The job is done. No touching, okay?"

"Okay, I thought maybe we could . . . you know. . . ." I leered jokingly at her.

"There's no 'maybe' or 'you know.' She is engaged, you rascal!" Hui stepped in like a big brother.

"Hey, whatever you say. Thank you all again for the greatest performance ever staged. You even managed to look Chinese. Congratulations!" I patted the little fellow's shoulder. He wasn't amused.

The store felt velvety with the silent abundance of fine things, things rarely found in any Beijing store. In one corner of the rectangular hall, shoppers sat around coffee tables, drinking, chatting, and resting their feet so that they could charge back to shop some more. We, the green flock, roamed around in a group, afraid of getting lost in the big place. Some people smiled at us, while others rolled their eyes. We had the words *international refugees* written all over us—gaunt faces, sunken cheeks, narrow midriffs, and haunting eyes versus the world of big bellies, thick thighs, and terraced pagoda necks. But nothing could dent our joy. It was a voyeur's dream come true. We had climbed over the horizon and the other side of the universe lay ahead of us. Cigarettes, all kinds of them, packed the long counter in boxes, and liquor, in colorful bottles and jars, lined shelves that reached to the ceiling. Numerous precious brand-name bicycles displayed in all positions, begging to be had, reminded me of empty bike stores elsewhere. People had and would kill for them. The far end of the store was a meat market noisy with live chickens and ducks, chilly with frozen beef and lamb, and bubbling with cold beers. There were no lines, only attentive salesgirls who got paid for not doing much beyond knitting or chatting. This was shopping.

We went to the counter and I asked an ugly salesgirl for a hundred packs of Phoenix cigarettes.

"Foreign Certificate, please," she said without looking up from her knitting. FC, nicknamed "funny money," was routinely issued to all traveling foreigners when they changed their hard currencies into our local money. Only foreigners were allowed to use it, thus giving foreign tourists the privilege of buying things that ordinary Chinese would never have access to.

"I don't have funny money," I said, again with a tilted accent.

"Then I can't sell you any," she retorted.

"Wait a second," Hui stepped in. "We don't need to use FC."

"Why?"

"Because we aren't really foreigners," Hui reasoned.

"Oh, yeah? And I'm the British Queen."

"We're refugees," Hui explained.

"So what?"

"There is a difference between them, the white guys, and us, the refugees."

"Says who?"

"The guard showed us the book."

I watched silently, smiling. He was good.

"You really are?" She studied us from head to toe.

"Look at my scars?" Hui lifted his shirt, revealing a deep scar, which made her cringe. "And here, look into my eye socket." He pinched and pulled his right eyelid upward. His popper looked even bigger. "Do you see how yellow it is?"

"Enough, enough," the girl screamed.

"I've got hepatitis B," Hui continued. "It's highly contagious, you know."

"Stay away from me," the girl shouted.

"Well, now, if you hurry with this man's one hundred packs, you might be safe."

"All right, all right. Give me the money," she demanded, which I did. When the transaction was completed, she said, "Now get out of here," which we also did readily. We caught her running to the bathroom, covering her nose and screaming, while we sauntered through the thin crowd and returned to the real world again. Feeling happy and grateful, I treated

my friends to a *jiaozi* (dumpling) dinner in a stingy mom-and-pop store
hidden in a narrow alley. We celebrated the greasy meal with loud burps
and lingering Cambodian folk songs. A small crowd of curious children
gathered around, poking their fingers at the plastic window screens. They
started chanting with us, and soon the quiet alley echoed with quaint
mountain melodies in the darkening night.

Chapter Twelve

A returning heart is like an arrow leaving its bow, a poet once wrote. All that poetic stimulus sent the three of us—Hui, Abdullah, and me—spinning out of control, hopping from one leaky bus to another to get to the hopelessly choked Beijing train station. In the waiting hall, thousands of miserable holiday travelers sat on their luggage, chatting, dozing, and smoking, while others slept on the spittle-covered cement floor with discarded newspapers over their faces. Exhausted infants stared lifelessly at the noisy caged roosters, paying scant attention to their mother's dripping nipples; everything tasted sour after a three-day journey. Occasionally the shrieking of a distant train turned weary heads and made tired hearts leap, but it was just passing, not stopping, and the waiting must await another day's dying.

When we got to the platform, the train was leaving. Hui and Abdullah pushed me through the window, while the nasty passengers inside tried to return me to the moving platform. I fought with my arms, winning, and crashed onto the table covered with their food. Five pairs of hands gripped me like the coiling arms of an octopus before I made a leap to safety across the aisle. A fuming man closed the window, shutting out my friends, who were still shouting and waving.

"Open the window again, please!" I cried.

"No way, you have ruined our meals," a young fellow shouted.

"I'll pay you back whatever it costs. My friends are trying to pass a piece of very important luggage to me." I pointed at Hui, who was running parallel to the train with the box of Phoenixes wobbling on his head, and Abdullah trailing him, shouting.

"Can't do that!" the other seatmate pronounced.

"Please! Do you want to know what it is?"

"Don't care."

"It's Phoenix cigarettes," I told them.

A smirk came to their faces.

"You gonna share with us?" one asked.

"It's an investment," I replied.

"Sure. Let the investment grow on the foreigner's head. We don't care," one of them said.

The train was picking up speed now, and Hui was red-faced and breathless. Abdullah had long given up, having lost one of his sandals.

"All right! All right! I'll share. Open the damned window!" I cried.

Hui looked like a drowning man. A policeman was chasing him with a thick choke-stick, and the platform would soon end with a precipitous drop into a muddy pit.

"Quick!" I shouted at the man holding down the window.

"How are you going to share your precious goods with us?" he asked patiently.

"I'll give you two packs."

The man just shook his head.

"Three."

His head shook again.

Hui was dying out there.

"Six, one for each of you." I wanted to kill the man.

Slowly he slid the window up just in time for Hui to throw the box in, missing the fall by only a few inches. He would be all right with the cop.

The man hadn't broken any laws. Even if he had, his international refugee status should come in handy again.

Passing the smokes out, I mumbled, "This is pure train robbery."

"All right, all right, kid. We'll pay for it." The man smiled.

"You guys are okay. It's yours."

"Half price."

"Forget it."

"We insist."

I pocketed the money, wished them a happy holiday, and crawled into my seat after safely tucking away my cigarette box under my seat. I found myself facing a beautiful girl with the longest eyelashes I had ever seen. She was asleep. The shadows of her lashes reminded me of elegant reeds waving on a languid summer beach. I lit my first Phoenix, inhaling deeply, exhaling thinly. As the noise on this Orient Express faded away, a drama involving only two characters started unfolding in my mind, she, the sleeping beauty, I, her gnawing beast.

In the thicket of a thorny crowd, I caught a glimpse of my brother. He stood there slouching the way he always did. I picked him out in the tiniest fragment of a second because seeing your loved ones is like finding yourself in a faded group photo: there is no confusion. I rushed over, jumped on him, and he held me tight, then pushed me away to do his required brotherly inspection.

"You are stronger and taller." He patted my shoulders.

"Your mustache has grown longer and itchier. Did you put on weight?" I grabbed his meatier waist. He slapped my wrists.

"Good food would do that to anyone," he said, laughing. "Boy, I was so scared the day I said good-bye to you half a year ago."

"But you didn't show it at all. All I saw that day was your trusting look on me."

"I had to hide it. Remember the time I lost you in the city of Putien when you were a little boy? I had the same feeling going home that day. I wished that I could go and be with you."

I was choked with emotion. He meant it and I loved him for it. "But I'm here and fine." I drummed my chest.

"I'm very proud of you."

We laughed, and he continued, "Didn't you say that you weren't coming home this winter? What made you change your mind?"

"Well, I got some good news."

"Hold the good news for now. Let's get to the truck first. It's been waiting for us."

"What truck?"

"Our commune's truck is here to pick up some goods, and there's some
empty space in back. I thought we could save some money."

"I'm all for it."

We climbed into the waiting truck loaded with vegetables and the
famous Fuzhou rice cakes. We carved out a small space, just enough for the
much needed brotherly intimacy. When the driver, an important man in
our town, came over to apologize for the smallness of the space, I couldn't
help feeling a sense of sweeping pride. The Chen brothers had arrived. This
was the best vehicle of our commune. In the old days, they could have run
over us and we wouldn't have been allowed even to cry out loud. We
thanked him the Yellow Stone way, by giving him a pack of the rare
Phoenix cigarettes. Jin was quite impressed and even more curious. I tossed
him a pack and started spinning my tale about going to North America
and all. Jin nodded in approval and commented that Buddha was indeed
the only guarantee for such a task, but a small bribe would not hurt at all.
The big cities were just as corrupt as Yellow Stone, he added, pocketing
the Phoenix and whipping out his cheap smoke instead.

The road home was bumpier and narrower than I had remembered.
When we finally arrived at Yellow Stone, with its rickety houses lining the
only street, I was stunned by how small and slanting the street had become.
Not that I had grown or the town had shrunk, but something had happened. Maybe the beautiful memory of my hometown was just a creation
of my longing heart and fraudulent imagination. Suddenly Yellow Stone,
my lover, lay naked and ugly before my trembling eyes. I could not remember how many magical dreams had been woven from the golden glimpses
of this town, how many love songs composed from the sounds of the
rivers, from the colors of the mountains. Sadly, the lonely pagoda at the
head of the town looked shabby, its roofs shedding like a candle melting.
The old pine tree bent even deeper in the wintry wind; its leaves danced
a thousand dances, breaking the perfect afternoon sunshine into numerous
shadowy butterflies on the ground. The cobbled street looked uneven and

pitted like the naked bed of a dried mountain brook. It felt as if I had come from another planet or another century.

We thanked the driver and walked the Cousin Tan walk down the busy street, doing the obligatory waving, bowing, and smiling. The folks bowed and smiled back in a silent excitement reserved for someone important and unexpected. It was a dizzying walk worthy of Miss Universe. I stumbled along the uneven street, feeling happy and glorified, notwithstanding the three licking dogs sniffing my ankles and the half-dozen kids who dragged our coats and climbed our shoulders. Neighbors dropped what they were doing and stood by their doors, doing what they did best when excited. The stuttering blacksmith fumbled with words, the red-nosed merchant rubbed his dripping ginger root, the puffy-faced sugarcane man scratched his bald head, and the tanned fisherman hit his bamboo pipe against his own ankle.

Someone must have tipped off my family. Before I crossed the stone bridge, I could see my grinning parents standing on our front porch. Mom was wiping her hands on her apron as always, while Dad, smiling from ear to ear, threw away his smoke, readying himself to meet his two sons. Jin and I dropped everything on the ground and rushed over to hug them both in our arms. I could feel my tears of joy wetting their shoulders and theirs, mine. Then our three sisters shrieked excitedly and came to join our big hug. Homesickness suddenly seemed such a laughable affair as I once again returned to be the adored cub of this den, basking in its deep love.

This little house became a palace of love. And Dad was its tyrannical emperor presiding over the examination of his sons, making sure not a toe was missing or a feature frayed. He first frowned on Jin's new mustache, then said that though it added a couple of years to his age, it did make him look more authoritative. His mind was clicking along like an abacus, calculating the net worth of Jin's new status as a college man in the eyes of matchmakers. Come the New Year, ripe girls would rain aplenty like the drizzle of spring.

As for his young son, me, no one was sure if I was fatter or thinner. Standing before the court of His Majesty, I was still a sorry sugarcane of five-feet-seven with a reedy weight south of a hundred pounds. Two sisters argued that I had grown a bit, while Mom thought I had lost weight, thus giving the illusion of a taller man. Unconvinced, Ke was about to run and get a ruler to measure me when I begged her to let the matter drop. In the end, Dad passed his writ of satisfaction like a happy king, praising me for

having grown a bit stronger and wiser. But Mom still had to check one last
thing. She unbuttoned my collar and found them with delightful chirping
laughs—the monstrous rings around the collar, shiny and waxy. *You are still
Mama's boy!* I got the feeling she wasn't unhappy about them at all.

Sitting at the head of our dinner table, Dad's pipe dangled from his
mouth. His eyes smiled into two joyful slits. It was like sitting in the gentle afternoon sun, watching trees sway softly and birds sing lazily. There was
a rhythm in his smiling silence, a contentment at being surrounded by his
returning sons and adoring daughters. Jin and I, still smelling of the road,
talked with heavy doses of college jargon, which won admiration from my
three sisters and a shaking head from Mom. My brother, not a man of easy
jest, recalled some funny lines from the Hangzhou dialect and we laughed
our teeth off. But what my family wanted to hear most was my English. I
spoke a few sentences with the most tilting English accent I could manage, but no one laughed. It was only as I thanked them for listening to my
convoluted monologue with a bow that they laughed, loud and long, with
tears in their eyes.

"It sounded like you were swallowing chicken bones," said my younger
sister.

"But this is truly English," I insisted.

"We believe you, and I'm proud of you," Dad said, smiling with joy and
pride as if I were a one-year-old doing an imperfect somersault perfectly.
They loved it no matter what.

Then it was time for presents. For my sisters, I had bought the pretti-
est hair clips and pins that I could find in Beijing. They each put theirs on
and thanked me for thinking of them. For Mom and Dad, I had bought
each a pair of thick fur pants linings from the Mongolian mountains. They
were genuine furs, but cheap, handmade and badly stitched together without any attempt at style. Dad tried them on and they made him look short
and bandy-legged. He asked me why they cut pants like that with big
thighs and thin bottoms. I told him farmers there often sat with their legs
crossed, needing more legroom. So he tried sitting like a monk, which was
enough for another round of laughter. Mom refused to try them on no
matter how we urged her. I could already see her tailor's mind at work,
redesigning the whole thing into some sensible outfit, which she said
would be really good for Dad's rheumatism and her arthritis. But for now,
Mom demanded that Dad take them off before he ventured into the street

to show them off. Dad walked into the courtyard to test the thickness of the new trousers and came back to tell me that he hadn't felt a single thread of cold.

"A pair of hot stoves you bought here, son." He grabbed my shoulders. "Mom, you've got to wear them right away. It's your good fortune that our son could afford them."

"Good fortune is good, but I'll try them later," was Mom's answer.

"But how could you afford all this, son?" Dad asked.

I opened the box of Phoenixes and revealed its contents.

"Phoenix? A whole box?" Dad took in a breath. "Where did you get them?"

"With a friend's help, I bought them from the Friendship Store."

"*The* Friendship Store?" Mom gasped.

"Yep. And I'm counting on making a profit by reselling them to Liang so that I can pay for the train tickets and some gifts to bribe my department heads."

"What for?"

"They are picking two of us to go to North America." I dropped the bomb.

They all fell very quiet. "Now explain, son. And say it slowly," Dad instructed.

"My favorite professor, Tu, said that it's some sort of university exchange program. The problem is that most of my classmates have influential families."

"That we could never be," Mom said, wiping her hands nervously on her coat as if it were her apron.

Dad sat down solemnly and pronounced, "Don't worry, son." Like the visionary father he had always been, he continued, "We'll think of something. But I can't imagine how quickly opportunity has come your way again. Let me check your forehead."

"What for?" I came closer to him.

"Your facial features." He put on his one-legged, one-eyed bifocals, another gift I should have bought him, and wrinkled his nose to cushion the crippled magnifying glass while examining my face grain by grain as if I were a piece of old jewelry whose fate hung on the whim of its beholder. With much squeezing and positioning by his hands, I felt my blackheads being lifted from obscurity and my pores enlarging reluctantly into the

Three Gorges of the good old Yangtze. Dad was repeating his daily ritual of inducing rosiness for good luck, and he was determined to spot that particular color and bump in my face for any possible revelation about my fate in the very near future.

"Do you see anything?" I echoed the whole family, who were all silently and eagerly awaiting his diagnosis.

"Now that you are almost seventeen, your fortune line should be around your *Yin Tan,*" he murmured. *Yin,* official seal, and *Tan,* a hall, was the spot between one's eyebrows. "You have a full, broad, and shiny *Yin Tan,* which means you'll command the hearts and minds of millions with your power and position. All you need now for anything big to happen is the rosy color."

"I haven't slept well for three days on the train. There is no possibility of any color in me."

"Wait, let me look more carefully." He searched some more, pinching here and there, trying to squeeze some redness out of my pale face. But no matter how he kneaded, nothing came except for the fleeting pink from painful pinching. "Here."

"No, that's cheating, Dad," I protested.

"Nothing is cheating." Dad smiled his helpless smile knowing what I meant by that. "Hey, spring is the right time to try anything ambitious. You just wait. I'll think of something. For now, let's see what we can do with those Phoenixes."

"To the Liangs?"

"No, son. I want an auction. Do you know how things have changed since you left?"

"How?"

"Five more private cigarette stores have opened up, and I want them all to fight for this precious brand. This is the New Year."

"Should we be afraid that the commune will go after us for illegal trading?"

"Not anymore. Now that you're done telling us your stories, let me tell you and Jin about us." He gestured for both of us to sit with him and continued. "I'm the paid manager of our county's Fourth Artist Troupe. Ke is their *yan chin* player and is also a paid employee." He proudly pointed at my sister, who was busying herself with the preparation of food. "Huang is the true entrepreneur, running a brisk business, doing thirty heads a day as the hottest hairdresser of Yellow Stone. Show Da the sign," he told Huang, who went inside and returned with a billboard that shouted: *For High Fashion from Beijing. Huang Beauty Salon.*

"Where did you get the idea of Beijing fashion?" I asked.

"You are in Beijing," Dad said simply.

"I learned a lot from reading all those foreign magazines you sent us," Huang said. "My youngest client is a five-year-old girl, and the oldest is a toothless jewel trader who wants to stay fashionable in the company of her customers, Taiwanese visitors."

"Taiwanese? Aren't they forbidden to come here to the mainland?"

"Not anymore. They come through Hong Kong and are bringing a lot of cash to buy the best things they can lay their eyes on."

"Well. That's a huge change."

"And Si here is helping Huang run the beauty salon while waiting for her husband to return from the mountains to take up a job at the local lumber company. You know there is a construction boom going on here."

"A juicy job, Si, congratulations!" I shouted to my eldest sister, who had gone through a brief courtship with this big-eyed, handsome volleyball player whose first visit to our home had turned into a three-day stay ending with an engagement payment. They fell in love, and Dad returned the money to him so that they could start a new life without the burden of debt that weighed on the rest of the marrying and married men of Yellow Stone. Blushing, Si looked even more beautiful in love.

"And as for your mom, she will have to live with the fact that her old man is out there ready to kick ass again after so many years of being out of a job, begging for a living," Dad said, looking at a smiling Mom.

"I'm happy as long as you're all happy," she cried, wiping her tears. "Who could imagine the world would change so much?"

I stood up, came to her side, and whispered into her ears some happy words. She only cried louder. "All is well, all is well. You guys go on chatting. . . . I'm preparing dinner for you." She left the living room and entered her kingdom, the kitchen.

Dad turned to my brother, who had been happily and silently smoking. "Jin, did you get to travel home with that Fuzhou girl that you mentioned in the letter?"

"What Fuzhou girl?" I asked.

"Well, there's a certain girl that your brother thought was interested in him."

"Well, well, well. You have been hiding from me." I poked Jin with my elbow. "Leave no details untold."

Jin was never comfortable talking about girls, but he was pressured by the whole family to report any romantic moves he made because it was time that he got hitched. It was the tradition. If he had been married at fourteen, as some boys were in Yellow Stone, he could have been a grandpa already. Slowly Jin said, "She found an excuse not to come on the same train with me." He lifted his eyebrows, slightly embarrassed.

"But you invited her, didn't you?" I jumped in to help analyze the elements of the situation.

"No."

"How then can you accuse her of not accepting your invitation if you never invited her?"

Jin shrugged and lifted his eyebrows again. "I'd hinted."

"How did you hint it?"

"I had my best friend, a city guy from Tienjing, tell her about my departure time and location before she bought her ticket," he confessed.

"That wasn't very direct of you, was it?" I reproached.

He blinked innocently and said, "I guess I could not bring myself to tell her directly."

"Well, you should have."

"Get off his back, Da," Si said to me. "We'll find Jin a good wife no matter what."

"Time to eat, everyone," Mom shouted from the kitchen. And as we sat around the table, chopsticks fighting chopsticks, I felt that I had truly arrived home.

Chapter Thirteen

My plan to oversleep was disturbed by the first ray of the itchy tropical sun. It was a fine day, as fine as it could get in this melting winter. *Ma chie* birds were singing especially loudly. They wedged themselves into the snug forks of our flourishing *liu ju tao* flowering trees. The blooms here overshadowed the narrow bend of the Dong Jing River where a wooden bridge swung in the wind and squeaked at the touch of villagers' feet.

The flowering trees had been my grandpa's love because of their poetic name. *Liu ju tao* meant "willow bamboo peach." The tree had willow leaves shaped like a crescent moon; bamboo stems, knobby yet elegant; and peach blossoms with the combined exuberance of shy pink, a blast of gaudy white, and a shower of red. They had been fighting for their existence among the towering ancient lychee trees that colonized miles of the riverbank. Grandpa had planted those tender seeds squarely in view of our living room window so that at any given season of the year we could see the wonderful display of the resilient *liu ju tao,* which now climbed over the thick layers of lychees, reached way above the neighbor's canopy, and terrorized the undergrowth with their ever-enlarging roots. When the tide was high, branches dipped in the mirror of water, flapping in quiet but assertive currents among fish, shrimps, frogs, green snakes, and little river rats. When the blooms were full, they brightened up the whole section of the river with their rippling sisterly reflection in the water. Hatted old fishermen rafting by sometimes could not tell if they were dozing off under or above the blooms. They would dream on while their pelicans dove for fish in this wrinkling world of petals that gave off a divine fragrance of another world, another time.

The dog—our neighbor's old hound, half blind but vividly virile—was fighting in our barnyard with our mother swine, who had bred a noisy litter of thirteen. The runt had gotten squashed under her swollen nipples. Perhaps they were fighting over the little green snakes again. The dog liked the snake's crunchy head, and the pig its crispy tail. Sometimes they got the wrong parts, and they fought noisily as they were doing now at this ungodly hour of five. The swine squealed, and the dog barked. The swine had thicker skin, but the dog had sharper teeth. One was a guerrilla warrior, the other a born wrestler. Legend had it that the swine had poked the hound's left eye out, and since then the hound had taken the liberty of his half blindness by occasionally mounting the swine from behind. The hound and the swine lived in hate and love, in perfect harmony and utter contradiction. As they got older, they could be seen napping together facing each other, letting the afternoon sun soothe their souls, dreaming about youthful days and rowdier times. But that still left the issue of the green snakes unresolved. So the fights went on. I cringed, thinking of the outcome of such an unnatural marriage. Had any of their couplings been fruitful, what would their litter be called? A dig? Or a pog?

The musings came to a halt when Mom crept up the wooden stairs to my attic room. Her footsteps were lightened to minimize all unnecessary noise except noise itself. Then came her knock, her gentle but continuing knocks.

"Mom, I need to sleep some more. I haven't slept for days." I exaggerated in defense of my broken dream.

"It's six. The commune's wired broadcast already started an hour ago." She invoked another Yellow Stone common law that had long been the single most annoying aspect of our communal life. The commune had imposed the rule that every household buy from the headquarters a mini-loudspeaker that was to be hung on the wall of each home so that all the party's orders could be carried out instantly. At the crack of dawn, in the swimming darkness, the monstrously ceremonious song "East Is Red" was played. Its lyrics read sadly like a chanting prayer.

The East is red,
The sun has risen,
Chairman Mao was born in China [too bad],
He works hard for his people's [un]*happiness.*
Hu Ya Hai Ya [chanting],
He is the people's big savior.

"Forget 'East Is Red.' I'm West needs rest," I protested.

"Don't say that! The government still says the West is bad, even though we all want you to go there." Mom hushed me, invoking another taboo based on China's aversion to the Western world.

"Okay, okay. No more political education at this hour. Can I go back to sleep?"

"Yes I'll just do my morning prayers quietly."

I pulled my quilt over my head and decided to doze off and let my mom do her thing. Her prayers were the most important part of the Chen household. Buddha is above all earthly creatures, and this attic offered the highest point in our house, so it was where prayers had been done and would be done for as long as the Chens were still around.

She knelt quietly, her hands clasped, eyes closed, and head bowed, but slowly the prayer got louder as she dug deeper into her soul. She started out with her daily necessity list—health, food, safety, and prosperity. Then came her ever-changing wish list of the day. I stiffened the tips of my ears like the antennae of a snail and heard her struggling with the escalating pronunciation of Ar-Mei-Li-Ca, America. She said it again and again, trying to get it right but failing each time. I pulled off my quilt and caught her blushing a little girl's blush, not from her failure to make *America* sound right, which she duly and quickly apologized to her Buddha for mutilating, but for asking so boldly for what she thought would be the ultimate dream of her young son, Ar-Mei-Li-Ca. Finally she bent down like a little turtle hugging the floor, saying good-bye to her attentive Buddha.

The mention of America jostled me out of bed. Wasn't it the reason I had rushed home? There were many prayers to be said and kowtows to be slammed on this noisy floor. I whispered into Mom's ears, telling her that I'd be right back, and ran down the stairs, through the animal-crawling court-yard, down the stepping-stones leading to the edge of the river, and sat on a flat rock that Mom had smoothed through years of washing and rubbing our clothes on it. The water made wet kisses on the steps, swaying to the rhythm of the tidal sea far away. The air was pungent with not only the deepening scent of *liu ju tao* blooms hovering over my head but also the silent fragrance of swimming petals under the still water. The scenery stole my heart, and I was dreaming till a playful catfish leaped above the water, flapping its four slick whiskers before diving back into the river. *Oh, you criminal fish.* His gasp for air instantly crushed the twin worlds of flowers into lingering wrinkles and recurring ripples. In the ensuing chaos, perfection fled and the trapped flowery reflections bled. A perfect painting became cubically Picasso and nostalgically Monet. When the last ripple hit the grassy edge, waking a sleep-ing frog, calm was resumed and a perfect flowery imitation reborn.

Hurriedly I washed my face, swooshed my teeth with big gulps of cool water, and scurried back to Mom. I knelt down like a good son by her side, feeling again like a small boy and a destined believer. Buddha, in my mind, was Mom's parent. This was where she came to cry, laugh, beg, and thank or just to close her eyes and be wordlessly happy and silently content. We were all fatherless souls, she would say.

I mumbled, muttered, slurred, and stuttered many thanks and even more requests. The prayer of the day was one little thing called America. I slammed my forehead noisily on the floor, causing the little attic to trem-ble, and shouted, "I need to go there. I have to go there." Mom frowned in discomfort and whispered, "Ask modestly, but thank abundantly." I only banged my head harder and shouted louder. I happened to believe that one needed to lay bare his innermost desires to his supreme being.

"Do you think Buddha could hear me all right?" I asked Mom when I stood up, dusting my pants.

"He sure could, and so could the whole neighborhood," she replied, smiling.

"Was I that loud?"

"No louder than the commune's broadcast, so you're safe. Do you pray in school?"

"I do."

"Why?"

"Mom!"

"I'd like to know, if you don't mind," she demanded as I helped her down the stairs.

"Because you taught me to."

"I was hoping for a more intelligent answer from a college man but it'll do. It's my favorite one."

"Thanks."

"Dad and I thought you should pay respect to the Southern Shaolin Temple in the Hu Gong Mountains tomorrow."

"How would that help?"

"The monks there do magical prayers."

"That's great," I said excitedly.

"By the way, how did I sound when I tried the pronunciation of Ar-Mei-Li-Ca?"

"You sounded beautiful."

"I did? Maybe one day Dad and I could visit there as well."

"You will if I go."

"Good." She squeezed my hands.

"You know, Mom, it's the first time I've heard you daydream."

"It won't be the last time," she said confidently, "because you guys make me do that a lot lately."

I was all choked up. "Mom, I missed you and Dad so much."

"Oh, son, we missed you even more, believe me." She wiped her tears, uneasy talking this way with her baby son. "All right, enough of that. Breakfast is ready." The kitchen was her fortress and food her weapon.

According to the lunar calendar, December the twenty-fifth—around February in the new calendar—was a sacred day traditionally known as the "Sunny Twenty-Fifth." On that day, Mom never forgot to tap our shoulders, telling us children not to fight, curse, or lust. Buddha was on his way here for the Spring Festival, she would say, and he was all ears. Even the tiniest sinful thought would be detected by the Almighty, and punishment would soon follow. After being effectively scared, we would obediently sweep every inch of our old house, tear the trickiest spiderwebs from our roofs, and catch the fattest flying cockroaches hidden in the narrowest cracks of the kitchen walls to make the path clean for his big arrival. Yet no

mission was more sacred than fetching a pail of sweet spring water from
the old well and using it to make a holy dinner of stewed noodles called
Ming Go (messy noodles) with live oysters, diced tofu, glorious sliced pork
fat, chunky pungent leeks, handpicked tender *gai lan,* and sensuous
cilantro. The mere mention of its name made my tongue stand up on its
root and sing a watery aria. But the feast was for Buddha first. Mom would
scoop it into big bowls, stick incense in the middle of the noodles, and
pray. Only afterward did it become a lavish feast for the worshipers. It was
usually unbearably cold by this time of the year. That's why the locals called
Ming Go snot-running, saliva-flying, red-eyes-burning good. And I would
add throat-on-fire-and-mouth-aflame to it simply because the hot sticky
mess usually burned slowly down my throat before plunging into my
stomach. And no water could quench that internal and eternal inferno.

Huang Beauty Salon had been open for some time. The sign, painted with
a shock of golden blond hair, caught the brilliant rays of the morning sun,
dazzling that section of the street. The salon was a boisterous shrubbery of
dark and wet heads set in various stages of coiffure by the magical hands of
my sister. Two dozen dripping heads were waiting and watching, trying to
catch the orbiting shadow of Huang as she juggled with each of the flying
saucers in her small space. Under the colorful walls, pasted with an assortment of never-before-seen pictures of blond Western models, another
dozen patiently sat with their heads wrapped in plastic sheets that leaked
the smell of dizzying chemicals. Their heads might be cooking, but their
minds were thinking. The moment those wraps were lifted and the curls
touched by the whisper of Huang's fingers, they would be transformed
into immeasurable beauties.

I waved to Huang from our living room, which was attached to the
storefront. She could only wink back. Her lips held a bunch of pins and
clippers, and behind her ears was a brush of some sort. She was a professional in high demand, needing more hands to cut more heads. I was proud
of her. She stood a sexy five-seven with curvy contours. But more notice-
ably alluring was her carriage, the dash of authority in her voice to her
helpers, and a wheedling tone for the young and restless beauty seekers.
She was making money, a lot of it, and it showed on her. The rosiness that
my dad had looked for in my pale face was all over Huang's *Yin Tan.* Her

luminous eyes were full of life and youth. My sickly, big-eyed sister, who in my vivid childhood memory frequently leaned weakly on Mom's bed-post begging for medicines to cure her hacking cough, was a now a beauty by any measurement. I could not help shaking my head in silent congrat-ulation and a secret lament that one lucky man would get to have her sooner than I would think. She was too tantalizing a pearl to lie around unnoticed and untouched on the bare beach of Yellow Stone.

"Come in quick." Mom dragged me aside. "See that old lady?"

"The one sitting on the bench with a book covering her face?" I was curious about Mom's curiosity.

"Yes. She's not getting her hair done."

"Obviously." She still wore that traditional badge of womanhood, a severe bun at the nape of her neck.

"And she's been staring at Huang, watching her every move."

"What could she be doing? Spying for Huang's competition, checking out her latest techniques?" I speculated in jest.

"No, no, no, a woman with a bun?"

"True, but no one could be sure. It happens all the time. It's called industrial espionage."

"Nonsense, college man. I think she is here for one very good reason."

"What is that?"

"I'll let you boys know later. Why don't you join Dad in the living room? Ar Duang has been waiting for you."

"The merchant?"

"Yes, she has some news about the cigarettes."

Ar Duang was still her old shell of a leathery self, a living example of a woman wearing the pants, while her hubby, a hen of a man, hustled in the marketplace as she smoked her cigarette, drank her tea with my dad, and socialized the morning away. But today she came with a basket filled to the brim with yellow, hairy-stemmed *pi pa* fruit—loquats. Bees died fatly suck-ing the sticky juice from the bewitching fruit, and a dead man could be tempted to scratch his throaty thirst on it.

We thanked her for the fruit.

"Only the best for two of my favorite college men," she said, shaking my shoulders affectionately with her rough hands. "Let's talk cigarettes," she said excitedly. "I have good news for you. Five merchants want them bad. The high-est bid came from the new cigarette man with a fancy kiosk in the market."

"What's the price?" Dad asked.

"It's safe to say that you could easily double your investment." Ar Duang was good with commercial parlance.

"Well," I said, relieved.

"But with one condition, which I doubt will be a problem with a real Beijing man like you."

"What is it?"

"A receipt from the Friendship Store in Beijing."

"Why?"

"Authenticity. They've been fooled too many times. You know these puppies make the greatest bribery gift."

"Done. I'll fetch you the receipt now." I went to my attic, groped in my pocket, and ran down to give it to her. A satisfied look came over her face as she shook her head. "This is the very store where the red-haired foreigners shop." She studied it a few times, folded it carefully, and nodded at my beaming dad. "I'll be damned. I should have asked for an even higher price."

"We should pay you a five percent finder's fee from our profit," I suggested.

"See, a young man only thinks young thoughts." She pointed her knobbed and bent index finger at me. "Do you know I owe your dad a debt as big as the Ching Mountain? But I would take your five percent if you care to let me hitch you up with a rich girl."

"I'll marry someone for love only."

"Young men, young thoughts. Money can buy love sometimes, but not the other way around. If you ever come to your senses, let me know. There's this girl who is comely but rich with an even richer dad in Hong Kong. That five percent of the wedding fees would be something to look forward to, not this. This is for your dad." She snatched the bubbling water pipe from Dad, who immediately lit it for her. "What a great dad you have," she continued, choking on her first puff. "And you know what? He'd be an even greater dad if you married that girl. Then he'd be a living Buddha because men would kiss his toes just to smell the scent of money that would come off you. See, you won't smell it yourself, but others will. That's why you need money."

"Enough about money, Ar Duang. I intend to make my own money."

"How?"

"Going to America."

"Wait, wait. Did you say Ar-Mei-Li-Ca?" She turned to Dad. "Is that true, that this bundle of joy is heading for the land of the beautiful?" She rubbed her hands.

"He's thinking of it."

"If that's the case, I got an even better girl for you," she said.

"Do you have to top me each time I mention something?"

"Well, a man is only as good as the father of the bride he marries."

"No, no, no. A man is as good as he can be or tries to be," I retorted.

"Young man and young thoughts. I forgive you for that. But this girl is . . . oh, what should I say. . . ." The old lady began to draw a sketch of the invisible girl with her crooked fingers in the air. Somehow I wasn't convinced that this girl of unspeakable beauty could be so beyond Ar Duang's imaginative tongue that she had to resort to her ineloquent fingers. But I didn't have to suffer the torture of this mute admiration for long, because a loud noise of a unique quality was thumping its way from the beauty salon. It was the noise of annoyed excitement, resembling a swarm of bees in flight. I knew by instinct the cause of the commotion—Mo Gong. It had to be him, the most excitable of my sworn brothers. I bowed low to bid good-bye to the gesturing lady who had, in a stroke of her savvy genius, doubled my investment and ran out to the beauty salon. I knew that Ar Duang would, without being urged, continue to describe in the greatest detail what this girl's credentials were because Dad was just as big a gossip and nothing this good was going to be left untold or half told.

Mo Gong, indeed, was the excitement. I could always sense people's allergic reaction to him before he actually showed his face. As a kid, he was that fat, poisonous bee from whom all children ran away screaming. With chunky muscles bulging under his thin shirt and a bristly mustache under his nose, he was a half-grown, cockeyed brute with a full-blown macho sexuality. Each twitching smile let escape what he was all about—sex. He was always on the move, as he called it, and that showed vividly when he entered the land of screaming cuties in Huang's salon, a hungry wolf in the delicious company of tender chicks—breakfast, lunch, supper, and nightcap all in one. Mo Gong was having a mouthwatering invisible orgy when I stepped out just in time to stop his slipping tongue from dangling any lower.

"Did you see all those girls? I'd love to be a beautician," was Mo Gong's formal welcome to his long-lost sworn brother.

"Wake up." I smacked his head.

"I can't. The smell of their bodies, wet and warm in this crowded salon, slows me down. My head is spinning. I need to be dragged out."

"That's not the smell of girls, you nut."

"What is it then?" He inhaled another long breath of salon air and leaned on my shoulder.

"Chemicals that will kill you."

"Oh, shit." He rubbed his nose and cursed. "Would it really?"

"Yeah."

"So why in hell are these girls gluing that to their hair?"

"Because they want to be pretty and because it pleases men like you."

"Oh, sure, I like them pretty, but is it worth dying for?"

"It's so very damned good to see you, brother." I hugged him, and he hugged me back and took an inquisitive look at me. His mouth curled up. "You . . . you . . . you . . . you look like shit. You're all white now. What happened to the tan? And your accent! Don't you speak English to me."

"And you look great, mustache, new shirt, and all. You look taller."

"I got high heels." He showed me his inch-high heeled sandals.

"You woman."

"It is the fashion now."

"Who says so?"

"Just about every Hong Kong guest—HKG."

"HKG!" I was shocked at so much change in just six months, at the barriers that had come tumbling down after Mao died.

"Where are Siang, Yi, and Sen?"

"Still working, but they'll try to get out soon."

"You're not working?"

"I couldn't wait to see you," Mo Gong said, smiling.

"I love you, brother. I was just about to visit you guys."

"Let's go and wait for our brothers in a little diner."

"Let me grab some stuff and I'll be right out."

When I got on the back saddle of Mo Gong's new bike, Mom leaned out to wave good-bye, a worrying frown on her face. I knew her thoughts: *Please don't get into trouble.* And I wouldn't.

I threw Mo Gong four packs of the precious Phoenixes and he beamed. "I thought you'd share it with us."

"Who told you?"

"Every cigarette merchant in town."

"Some things will never change here."

"You're such a good buddy."

I lit one for him. He inhaled hungrily and let the purified smoke wash all over my face. "Now what else have you got for us?"

"Wait till everyone is here. Where is this little diner?"

"It's called Black Dogs."

"What is that?"

"It's the most hidden little restaurant in town."

After a maddening ride uphill, we arrived at our destination, which was named so because of the black hound with a burned scar on its butt that huffed and puffed its bad breath as it sniffed our ankles. Mo Gong, no animal lover, gave it a little kick, sending the animal plunging on its face into the sandy ground. A crippled dog!

"Why did you have to kick him?" I yelled.

"I didn't know he was so crippled." Mo Gong looking pained, squatted by the dog, and helped it up. "Now, you wait here, puppy." He ran into the restaurant kitchen and came back with a chunky bone with meat still hanging on it.

"I need the bones for the stock," said the owner, who had chased out after Mo Gong too late, for he had already fed the dog.

We went into a little wood cottage overlooking a pond of lotus with big fish flipping among the broad leaves. Crabs could be seen crawling on the clear sandy bottom of the pond, strolling blindly, counting their days, maybe hours, before a rich man came and claimed their lives on the dining table. "Here." Mo Gong stopped before a curtain that blocked access to a private room. "Please, come in."

I lifted the curtain and was shocked by the sight of the table full of food, steaming food, the kind only my friends would order—thick, chunky meat on top of meat, overshadowed by a long queue of liquor bottles. Before I could compose myself, three bodies came flying down on me, crushing me to the floor. It was Sen, Yi, and Siang. We wrestled on the floor, mopping up all the cigarette butts and spittle. Our heads clinked against the table legs and stone wall. We were laughing in a way I hadn't for a long time, screaming delightedly at the top of our lungs.

Wrestling like we were still a bunch of hoods, not caring a thing about the world, was the best reception I could have dreamed of. In our hearts we were that same bunch of losers, stealing fruit, killing roosters, and annoying girls who turned their noses up at us. There were tears in our eyes.

"Look at this table of food. Let me pay for it," I said.

"You shut up. You think we're poor?" Sen asked.

"Last time I checked, a big yes."

"Sen is loaded now. He works for the bank, and on each loan he makes, he takes a percentage," Siang explained to me.

"Under the table?"

"Do you have to ask? We're still a Communist country," Yi quipped.

"Take it easy with our little brother here. He's a little out of touch, that's all." Mo Gong jumped in.

"I'm so proud that you're as corrupted as your dad. How did you manage to fit in?" I grabbed Sen's head and planted a wet kiss on his oily forehead.

"Thank you for the compliment. I don't know. It just happened like that." He snapped his fingers. "At the beginning I thought I was going to die in a nine-to-five job. Everyone there was so high-class and fancy. I had to wear nice clothes, talk properly, get up early, and go to sleep early. I was miserable."

"It's true. He was dying out there," Siang said.

"I was about to quit and give the job to my other brother and rejoin our gang when one day an officer there asked me out to have dinner with some clients. That night I came home drunk and woke up the next day with a pocket full of cash, one thousand yuan in total."

"They bribed you?" I guessed.

"Sure. The client needed a big loan, and the officer wanted my signature on the approval."

"Why your signature?" Yi asked.

"The fucking two-signature system has been there forever to help fight corruption and shit like that." Sen was getting really animated. "But they didn't know that I was rotten beyond corruption. The officer said that it usually took a few dinners and at times some sexy girls to break in a green hand like me. But he was really glad that I was broken already. Now he hardly makes any loans without me on board. He approves mine, and I do his. We take a nice little equity in everything we do. It didn't take me long to realize that my skills as a gambler and street kid were invaluable as a banker."

"But be careful," I warned. "Sometimes they butcher the greenest chicken to scare the monkeys. I heard an anticorruption movement is just starting from up north."

"Don't worry, Da. All the bankers are equally corrupted there."

"Then a toast to corruption. Here, I got these for you all." I gave them each four packs of Phoenixes. They tore them open, and the room instantly filled with bulging smoke rings blown by five working smokestacks.

"Brother, I'm glad you did not forget us. Are these puppies really from the Friendship Store that we see in movies all the time?" Siang asked. He was, after all, the savvy man who knew the cities.

"They certainly are."

"Man, they smell heavenly."

I went on to tell my friends the adventure I had gone through to buy those cigarettes. They were stunned, with their mouths open and eyes droopy.

"Did you see any beautiful white girls with golden hair?" Mo Gong asked.

"The store was filled to the brim with them."

"Were they cute?" Mo Gong again.

"They certainly were."

"Forget blonds. Your story is too delicious. Let's eat."

We dug into the table of delicacies that only a true Yellow Stoner would fancy: crunchy pig tails, roasted pig stomach, a boiled pig's head, pig intestines stuffed with liver, pig kidneys diced and sautéed with garlic and ginger, and pig lungs lightly fried and tenderly juicy. Mo Gong mixed five different brands of drink into a large bowl, and each of us took turns taking big gulps. We went clockwise according to seniority. The drinks were dazzling. Before long, my four brothers' images were shimmering before me. It added a festive mood to our already festive reunion.

"Reading your letter made us want to come up to visit you," Sen said.

"Believe me, my world in Beijing isn't one-fifth as good as the one we have here right now. You don't know how many times I've thought of you and wished you were with me; we could have kicked ass over there. My first few months there were terrible. Everyone looked down on me and laughed at me."

"They did that to you?" Mo Gong asked angrily.

"The fucking city folks," Sen spat.

"Well, brothers, there's no cause for concern or anguish. First of all, I chose to invade their world. They're entitled to kick my ass. Secondly, I beat them in all subjects. I'm the best student in class now."

"That's fantastic. The best among city folks," Yi exclaimed.

"Another toast to you," Mo Gong offered. We drank like hungry puppies from the big bowl.

"Did you get yourself a girl or something? I heard it's pretty free-wheeling up there on college campuses," Mo Gong said. "Tell us about the golden-haired, blue-eyed lovers you keep under your warm quilt."

"Our Da is a serious knowledge man. He doesn't do that sort of thing." It was Yi, the old man, talking.

"Girls? You guys want to see girls?" I asked mysteriously.

"What girls?" Chopsticks were dropped and cups fell, broken.

I fished out from my bag four dog-eared adult magazines, courtesy of my friend Abdullah, and dumped them on the table. There was a deadly silence. Slowly I flipped open the first page of many beautiful pages to come. A pale-skinned blond sat naked on her silky bed with her bushy crotch open and glaring at four open mouths. Food was forgotten, though drinks were voluminously devoured. Each of my dear friends sank deep into his chair, his eyes sinking even deeper into the heart of each page. Mo Gong's head tilted to catch a special angle of a nude girl to the point of hurting his head. Yi no longer acted like a conservative old man. He flipped red-faced from one page to another with the same urgency and precision he applied to sawing the most expensive mahogany, turning each page in beat to his usual swinging of balls. Sen's nose was so close to the large breasts of a brunette that he could have sucked the milk out of them. Siang held his magazine with only one hand. As to where the other had gone, no one cared to know.

They all seemed to forget the food and me. Not only did they read the pages quietly, they also exchanged them in the most orderly manner, taking every precaution not to crease the magazines. The only time they looked up was to ask for more drinks, which I poured gladly. As they *oohed* and *aahed,* giggled and laughed, I snuck out to pay for the dinner and gave an extra yuan to have our wooden door latched from the inside so that no one in the dangerously gossipy town would know what these hoods were up to. If the cops even heard about these magazines, we could all be thrown in jail for a long time, and I took no chance on that.

When the sun set, we passed out in five different manners on the floor: Sen like an *L* against the wall; Mo Gong sprawling like a dog; Yi like a monk with his legs crossed; and Siang with one hand in his pants. God only knew how many times he had strangled his snake to death. I was the first to wake up, and realized that I had peed into my own shoe, thinking it was a night pot.

The night fell just in time to hide us in shameful camouflage. It would not be unfair to say that they would all have lost their virginity that day had they any virginity left to lose. In the waning light, Mo Gong told us about his secret romance with a married woman. For the last three months he had scaled a tall wall every day at lunchtime to nap with the lustful woman until one day her husband came running in with a knife. Mo Gong had been in hiding ever since. Sen, now a successful and marriageable man, was being hitched to a daughter of his father's old colleague. He was rather shy about it, but we knew that he was happy getting attention from a girl. Yi was also being matched with a flower of a girl with a ballerina's gait. She could sing and dance, they said, and he could now swing his balls in time to his future wife's dance steps forever. But all that didn't change the fact that now and again they would still consult those magazines under their pillows and let those paper blonds inspire many a wet dream, even on the coldest of winter nights.

Mo Gong still scaled the wall and enjoyed the noontime ecstasy. Only much later was he ordered by his father to marry the daughter of the shoe factory's party chief. Mo said later that it was his father who had wanted him to marry that plump daughter of the chief, a nice and dandy political alliance. Mo Gong's glee as a married man did not last long. The first day was sweet, the second day he felt drowned, by the third day, Comrade Mo Gong was heard shouting, "Give me a whore anytime. I can't plunge the same hole every day for the rest of my life." But that did not stop him from allowing his brother to marry his wife's younger sister. He said later that men got married much like a garden getting a fence. Good men stayed inside, while wild men like him roamed beyond, leaving the fence to contain only their wives.

To this day I regret giving those magazines to my friends. I had dented their granite souls with a poison that would plague them forever. Now and then they would still talk dreamily about those girls, identifying them by the page numbers they appeared on. So a brunette, the best pick of them all, was known as Page 99. A blond with a shapely ass was remembered as Page 87 of Book Two. Years later, I found those precious magazines sitting in Sen's banker drawers bound in hard leather.

When I got home that night, all Mom said was, "The Twenty-Fifth is meant for happy things. You went for the happiest, drinking." Mom was rarely sarcastic.

"You know my friends. They were happy when they saw me."

"You don't drink like that in school, do you?"

"No, not usually. Besides, I can't afford it. Mom, don't worry. I'm acting like this because I'm home. When in college, studying is all I do."

"You've done well, and we're proud of you." There was still some lingering doubt in her voice, but she let it go. My sisters were not that diplomatic. Whenever they passed me that night, they fanned their hands before their noses, saying, "You smell like a drunk."

"And I feel like one."

"Act like a real college student," Huang said.

"Even when I'm not in school and playing?"

"Yeah, because everyone in town looks up to you." She gave a sharp look that woke me up. Suddenly in the eyes of Yellow Stoners, I was different. They had imposed a different expectation on me. I should act more nobly because everyone thought of me that way. There was that tone in my sister's voice, the reprisal of a theme that befell me whenever I found myself straying away from my anchor as a college man. Don't become a droopy-eyed playboy. Don't waste your time. Don't do this, don't do that. Live within the construct of a frozen existence, happily. Even in my hazy state of mind, I understood her and thanked her for she knew hardship like no one else as a child laborer/slave/Communist farmer, earning more than her share of rations since age ten. She had almost died of starvation and dehydration in the desolate, cracking fields. The brightest glory in her life so far was the shining reflection coming off me. I felt ashamed from my thickening head to my unsteady toes, not because I had fallen and gotten drunk but that I would never ever be the kind of college man that Cousin Tan was. He was the perfect college man, one who knotted his eyebrows in a thorny thinking mold each time a question was asked him and nodded his nod of immense understanding. He walked with his hands behind his back, talking only after thinking, and talking only with a gentle whispering tone that was never above the hum of a mosquito. How I loathed all that, but now I was asked to act along that same dotted line. Anything less and I would be a half-cooked college man—a disgraceful one.

Chapter Fourteen

Sleep scraped the old paint of drunkenness off my head. I was a new man facing a new day, and what a pulsatingly exciting day it was. The Chens sat nostalgically around the small table in the backyard as in the old days, with feet fighting calves and knees clinking ankles as we awaited our breakfast of rice porridge, silky from much simmering and fragrant with the scent of the earth. These were not the grains that had sat in the warehouse but the very ones that we had harvested with bare hands from the field last summer. They tasted sweet with a bit of Q, which is to use a local word for it, chewy but not gooey. The Qness came from being alive and fresh, not like old, stored rice that broke easily.

Mom scooped the rice into six large bowls and one small one for herself, letting them cool so that they didn't burn our mouths. The steam caught the morning light, giving off swirling bits of color as it rose higher.

Laid in the formation of a square were some of the typical Yellow Stone breakfast dishes called *muie* to accompany the rice porridge: salted baby sardines with shiny scales and popped eyes; tiny red fried peanuts—tiny because the red mountain soil compressed their growth, making them deformed and compact with flavor; and thread-thin slices of jolly blind jellyfish, the kind that swam along the warm coast with tiny little shrimps on their noses as seeing guides. Then there was the fermented tofu, so salty that I wondered where they got the salt from. As a child, I helped grind soybeans into pulp in a stone grinder and strain the pulp into a pure, milky liquid. Mom then treated it with some recipe that transformed the mixture into the tenderest tofu. She sliced the tofu thinly and had the sun bake it into curled bricks, which she dumped into a jar filled to the brim with fish sauce. The jar was sealed with mud, and when the lid was finally lifted months later, I'd see cute little worms swimming in the salty brine, some penetrating the heart of the tofu, others just spinning and floating on the surface. Mom would cover her timid face with her hands and ask me, "Any worms you see in there?" Once I told her there weren't any, she'd open her eyes to utter the ugliest scream—a sound I'd never have believed my tiny mom capable of making. But the presence of worms was good. It meant the tofu had fermented—that magic moment that somehow changed the taste and feel of tofu. It was no longer tofu but a gift from Buddha that enlivened the bluntest appetite, thickest tongue, and waxiest throat. It was not just the saltiness but the subtle flavor of decay, of dying maggots packed together, that made it so magical that any Yellow Stone man craved it day after day. If one said he missed Yellow Stone, the feeling in taste would be that of the stinking tofu.

The last dish on the table was pickled cucumbers, lying rafted together with the intimacy of concubines. But home-grown cucumbers were no concubines. Their vines climbed up the stone columns, wrapping around those giants with stifling loops till they reached the curled roofs, then dropped into our neighbor's courtyard. It was there they bore the plump vegetables. Each time, Mom had to beg our neighbor for permission to fetch her cucumbers, and since it took away our neighbors' air rights, Mom was careful to share every fifth one with them with an accompanying apology. Mom called them the cheating vegetables.

The pickling juice of this dish had all the flavors—sugar, salt, rotten fish, wine, and more, the smell of stinking feet. That came from the fact that cucumbers weren't willing victims. Mom's feet stomped on them till the last bit of juice was squeezed out. Only then, when the vegetables were all hollowed and dried, would they soak in the flavors Mom imposed on them.

Elegance and simplicity were the essence of breakfast, not sumptuousness, Mom told us. Only a vulgar eater would be caught with big dishes in the morning. She added that the tinier the dishes, the more refined and civilized the household was. I joked that if these dishes got any tinier, we might have to nibble like rabbits. She did not take it as a winning joke. She demonstrated to us how one should eat the peanuts. Pick one up with chopsticks, dip it in soy sauce, and chew it with your mouth closed. Mom also warned me not to reach over the table to grab things with my hands. Why not? I asked her. Table manners. Why were we suddenly learning table manners? Because people are looking at you now. That was all she had to say. So breakfast was now the confined noise of fighting chopsticks and suppressed laughter with food in our mouths. Still, I giggled happily for it had been a long time since I had sat down with my family to a meal.

This morning Dad was taking me to Southern Shaolin Temple to pray for my chance of going to America. After that I was to go see Dad and Ke perform in another town near the temple. He was laughing delightedly, wearing the fur-lined pants I had bought him, whose ticklish warmth made him happy and silly. It was to be our first journey of worship together.

Our transportation to this temple of worship was the fanciest ride Yellow Stone had to offer, the famous Iron Cow tractor, a five-horse-powered beetle of a thing that jerked so much it was either good for constipation or really bad for diarrhea. One could count his coins in his pockets as they jumped and clinked with one another. To add honey to the joy ride, the narrow dirt road to the foot of Hu Gong was more of a ditch than a road, with muddy water splashing all over us. I shouted to the driver to dodge those uncomfortable puddles, which at some point almost threw me off the tractor. He shouted back, "This machine is too heavy to maneuver, and besides, if I change directions too suddenly, we'll certainly flip over." I believed him. The machine was a thousand years away from the magic of power steering. To change directions, the driver had to pull the whole thousand-pound weight of the tractor in order to nose away from objects unintended. The name Iron Cow suited it well, for it was as stubborn as a living cow and as lazy as a dead one.

Halfway there, we saw another one of the iron brethren capsized, with tractor intact but the hauled passenger compartment twisted, lying lop-sided. Four muddy wheels spun like windmills. The passengers scrambled furiously with mud on their faces while the driver begged his fares to help flip over the tractor and continue their journey. But the passengers gave him muddy middle fingers and walked away.

From then on, Dad and I coordinated our positions by shifting our weight from one side to the other to keep balanced whenever we were turning. Once the nose of the machine scraped the surface of a rock. Another time the front tire barely missed the collapsing bank of a river. But passing another one of these Iron Cows remained the biggest headache. It required all of us to climb down so that the two could kiss and bite each other's tires without falling off the road. At another junction, a little boy riding with us was tossed off when we hit a big bump. All the passengers shouted, but the driver could not hear us because the Cow's loudness drowned everything in the wind. Eventually I had to jump down to fish the boy up. Everyone was criticizing the young driver, who turned a deaf ear to us all.

"Don't do this again, you hear us? Otherwise we won't pay you when we get there."

"I can't promise it won't happen again. If you hold on to your bars, it'll be all right," he shouted back.

"Where are the bars?"

"Oops."

"Oops? What do you mean?" I demanded.

"Then hold on to the person next to you." He pointed at the old guy next to me.

"What does he have to hold on to?"

"The guy next to him."

"So when one falls, everyone goes down?"

He shrugged. "Hey, it really ain't so bad. Some young punks actually love the rough rides."

"Why?"

"Because if you're sitting next to a pretty woman, you could end up being tossed onto her lap and grab her breast. Get it?"

"Got it. And if you stop suddenly, I'll land on your head."

"How did you know that? It happened to me the other day. Boy, bad news travels fast."

It was a relief, to say the least, finally to arrive at the foot of the mountain. Feeling numb from being trembled and shaken like tossed salad, we got off the Iron Cow and paid the man, who was quickly loading up early worshipers for their return trip.

"Smooth ride," I wished him.

"Only Buddha could guarantee that." The engine started again like a furious animal.

Hanging on the frowning face of giant Hu Gong Mountain was the aged Southern Shaolin Temple. From a distance it looked like a small matchbox suspended from the formidable evergreen cliff. It was only reachable by a tiny winding path paved with thousands of slabs of whitish rock. The mysterious path hung like a spineless rope blown into a zigzagging swing by a typhoon.

On this sunny day, thousands of worshipers climbed the steps with quick feet and jerky gestures. Cartoonlike, they looked like tiny diligent ants in a lengthy food line. Their shouting and singing echoed loudly and belatedly in this empty, lush valley, making one wonder how such small creatures could make such loud noises.

"Well, Dad, how many steps do we have to climb to get there?" I looked at the dizzying height, dismayed.

"Thousands." He tightened his shoes.

"Why did they have to build the temple so high up there?" The lament of a lazy man.

"Test of faith. The young monks spend their days carrying hundreds of pounds of water from the wells down here."

No wonder they walked with bent backs.

"And guess what? No one has ever fallen off these steps before."

"Well, I'd better not break the record."

We blended into the flow of climbers in a toe-kicking-heel climb of ants. No rushing and no resting. It was like floating in the slow current of a dull river.

"Do you know the steps used to be rough, just raw rock, chunks of it, unpolished by masons?" Dad said, panting.

"The monks couldn't afford the smooth ones?"

"No, they knew that the feet of worshipers would wear them out soon enough. And hundreds of years later, they're smooth as silk."

When we climbed the last stone and stepped into the congested front yard of the temple, the sun was straight above us and the sea loomed only a short distance away. Gleaming rivers, rippling lakes, and grassy ponds all looked like small puddles of water. Old monks chanted with callused, burned heads. Ancient hairy trees leaned over the cliffs, further darkening the dark temple. The dense smoke of burning incense permeated and floated among the sweaty bodies of thousands of worshipers. Buddha looked benevolently aloof in the center of the temple, smiling his sleepy smirk. In the background, the yee-yee-ya-ya music of Chinese trumpets, bamboo flutes, er-hus, drums, and grandfatherly gongs filled the already dense air of worship with jarring noise, the thunder of Buddha with his mystical shrewdness. His toes hovered over my head as I knelt before him with Dad, who had found a small slot and was banging his head away as noisily as the next fellow.

The prayers were deafening. I seized the opportunity and rocked away for what seemed like an eternity of bending and kowtowing among a wave of heads and clasped hands. I had thought I was an extremist when it came to praying, but these people were ruthless and fearless. They sang their requests out loud, shouting whatever came to mind. Some were crying, even sobbing. One man's forehead was obviously swollen from too much head hitting. A woman was pulling strands of her hair loose while crying bitterly for her lost husband. Looking through the dense smoke, I sensed Buddha's transcending smile meant for all or none, his piercing eyes dragged down by drooping eyelids, seeing nothing and everything. That cool look seemed to be saying: *Everything will be fine, and if it is not fine, deal with it; it's called fate. If you got a raw deal this time, a better fate might be coming if you're good. If you're evil, you'll be born again but only as a pig, dog, or cat.*

I was hardly done with my petty requests and lengthy wishes, kneeling and smelling the toes of the Almighty, when an eager man rudely poked me out of my prime location with his nodding head, almost sending me tumbling under Buddha's bottom. I would have smacked the man's head with a wet leaf, but Buddha was looking. He would give him what he deserved. I stood up, dusting my pants, and there saw the most mouthwatering banquet laid in sacrifice on a long red wooden table with ornate carvings. A full pig lay blindly, painted red, its smiling snout pointed at the ignorant crowd. A little cow, boiled, was positioned as if happily plowing, looking hopefully into the distance. A set of ten of the most precious seafoods—monster crabs, monster squid, and monster lobsters—all lay garnished with green vegetable leaves on plates that were bigger than small tables.

I was wondering where the food would go afterward when Dad rose, breathing heavily from kowtowing. Dragging my hand, he said, "Hold your tongue and stop salivating over the food. Let's go see the head monk."

"Why?"

"For a special favor from Buddha, we have to see him. In fact, he's expecting me."

"You know him?"

"He's an art lover who often sneaks into theaters to see our plays. I've been giving him only the best tickets."

"A theater-going monk."

"He can sing a mean repertoire of oldies. Each time he sees a play, he comes backstage to ask my opinion about his style."

"Is he any good?"

"He trembles a bit."

"Like his chanting probably."

"Much so and with a high-pitched voice."

"That'd make a good female lead with a wig."

"That's all he sings, female parts. You know monks. This one had his balls chopped off in his youth."

"Really?"

Taking me to a quiet hallway away from the crowd, Dad knocked gently on a door. A crack opened and a young monk let us in.

Ben Chang was a miniature Buddha. The back of his neck piled up against his head like a turtle with a reluctant forehead. As was their custom, his head was burned to the roots with incense, with no hope of resurrecting its grass ever again. But his eyebrows grew boisterously like spring willow twigs swinging in the wind. When he saw us, he smiled, causing his hanging willows to arch forty-five degrees upward, making a *b* of his right eye, a *d* of his left eye, an A of his nose, and an O of his mouth. His overall face was a pot, with his ears the handles, utterly symmetrical.

"Oh, Master Chen." His *Oh* came out especially round because of his O-shaped mouth with meaty lips, like a mother hen's ass after passing an egg, still throbbing and contracting. "To what do I owe your presence?" He moved over gracefully with the dainty gait of a female lead in a traditional play. His feet were covered by the voluminous fabric of his velvety robe. His hips guided his walk, not his toes. I'd never seen a man with hips that round. His hands were slender and elegant like those of a well-kept woman who did no dishes. The hands moved like tongues, expressively, with his singsong intonation. I cringed and took a step backward upon seeing such a womanly man. Dad pushed me forward, and I was ready to be presented to Putien's spiritual leader.

"This is my younger son, Da."

"Daaa." He sang my name. "Prosperity, arrival, big and wide. What a fine name! Only a master like your dad could have bestowed such a name. I know a few Das in history who have made dynasties and ruined a few in between." He laughed.

"Well, thank you," I said.

"Names are like men's thirst. You know what I mean, aspiration and inspiration. But good names are not as important as good deeds. I wish the thousands of people in this hall would heed a hundredth of my advice."

I scratched my head to his piercing comment, which made me feel like a little thief in need of a bail bond.

"I can go on forever. Why don't you sit down here," he said.

We did as we were told.

The monk grabbed both of my hands, looked into my face, and smiled. "You came for a big thing, didn't you?" He kneaded my hands between his with his eyes closed, as if fishing under muddy water. Dad was smiling his mysterious smile. I was clueless.

"Your hands are as soft as cotton balls," the monk sang with a pained expression on his face. "Soft is good. Glory, noble reputation, wealth, and power all in one."

"Why?" I was pleasantly puzzled by this unsolicited fortune-telling from the wisest man in town.

"They are hands that were born to hold pens, not hoes or sickles."

I wished I had known all that when I was a kid.

"Once it's there it is always there. And if you are in college already, you are most suited to be a liberal arts major."

"Well, I am."

"See? You'll never be good at handling test tubes," he said, flooring me. He turned to my dad and poured some tea for us. I accepted the quaintly flavored tea with a worshiping heart, feeling that I was but an open book to him.

"You're absolutely right. He is a liberal arts major. But I brought him here to seek your wise advice on something else," Dad said.

"Wise man does wise things," the monk replied.

"Da's school is choosing two of them to go abroad to study."

"Oh, you're in luck. I have set up a special shrine for those ambitious few."

"You have?"

"In the far back, with a newer Buddha, painted in pure gold, donated by Hong Kong rich men. I consider that shrine my Foreign Affairs Ministry." He gave a wicked smile.

"Do you have to pray for different matters at different shrines?" I asked.

"You do if you want HIM to hear you better." He rolled his eyes upward as if his boss was right above us. "For the last couple of years there has been a rush to go to college, so I added a college hall, which is now packed with teary moms and disappointed dads. Lately, going abroad has become the rage here. Initially it was Hong Kong and Macao, but now Japan, England, France, and even America are in fashion."

"You're well versed in all the new trends," I said admiringly.

"One has to adapt to the new and changing world, as Mao said," the monk replied sarcastically.

"Can we see the Foreign Division?" Dad asked.

"You pay a fee for the entrance."

"How much?"

"However much your charitable heart wishes to give." He smiled his mysterious smile. "But of course the amount would vary from one demand to another."

"What would be your suggestion," Dad inquired.

"Hong Kong, the glitzy Paris of Asia, fifty yuan; Tokyo, seventy-five; and Britain, one hundred, because it's a great civilized country that has trained some of the greatest scientists in our land."

"How about America?"

"Is that where you want to go, young man?" The monk arched his brows again.

"Yes."

"One hundred twenty-five. That's the land of all lands. We don't call it The Beautiful Country for nothing. Dollars are everywhere, I heard. Chinese are making a killing there. I've never seen a bigger house than the one owned by a former restaurant owner who had retired from the Old Gold Mountain, San Francisco."

"One hundred twenty-five yuan? For what?" I whispered into Dad's ear. Dad pinched my arm, annoyed.

"I heard that. Well, I'll do the special prayer for you, and I'll also pull a verse to foretell your venture."

"Any guarantees?" I asked.

"Faith is guarantee enough," the monk said. Dad pinched my arm again. Frankly, I was surprised that this faith and religion thing had turned into a prosperous business enterprise. But the monk seemed to read my mind.

"I've got a Buddhist school to run with fifty students this year. The new religious freedom doesn't come cheap, and it's only as good as the donations are." He continued absentmindedly, as if counting beads in his hands. "Honestly, I'm tired of these steep stone steps. My bones are old. They also seem to have lost meaning for the young monks. That's why I'm raising a fund to build a cable thing like you see in the big park in Beijing. With that, I could be down there a lot more often to watch your dad's plays."

"Why don't you ask the county government for some funds?"

"They don't care about us. All the cadres want from us is free burial services for their families, chasing their ghosts, and praying for their special requests."

"We'd be more than happy to do our share," Dad said, passing the cash to the monk.

"A generous soul is a saved soul. Come with me." The monk slipped the money into a hidden pocket inside his right sleeve after a deep bow. We fell behind him silently.

"Isn't it a bit pricey?" I whispered.

"Never negotiate in the temple here," Dad whispered back. "You're buying a verse from Buddha, not the monk. He's only doing his job."

"He is doing a fantastic job. He pays no taxes and keeps no books."

"But he'll have to answer to his boss, and we do what we can. Shhh." We entered the tiny hall that had Welcome signs written in both Chinese and English. The monk asked us to kneel with him as he held incense in his hands and chanted unintelligibly. Then he put his hand in a jar and pulled out a slip of paper. All this I observed with one eye open while my dad nudged me in reprimand.

"Well, what a marvelous verse." The monk stood up and we followed suit.

"One thousand li of hard journey. You'll sing and dance at the rainbow's end." He read the verse in his singing voice.

"Is that good?" I asked urgently.

"You'll get there but only after a long struggle," the monk explained. "What wisdom!"

"Yeah, what wisdom," I chanted after him, halfheartedly.

"It's worth every yuan." Dad bowed to thank the monk.

"Da, you seemed disappointed at the verse," the monk observed.

"It's just not what I expected." Or had hoped for.

"The truth is always true. Maybe you're not ready for the journey to America. And sometimes, even when you think you're ready, heaven isn't. There has to be harmony of all elements before a miracle can happen."

"So you think the elements are not there yet."

"No, but I do keep a log of contributors here in this golden folder." He picked up a thick bound book. "And I pray for them every day and night. Wherever they go, they'll always have my blessings. And children like you who have big dreams had better check with me often, for I will give you wings."

"Wings?"

"To get there."

"Thank you." I was touched by his poetic encouragement.

"Thank Buddha. And remember, your deeds are always better than anything else."

"Even dollars?"

He chuckled at my petty sarcasm. "You know that of all the good deeds, giving has to be the crown jewel of them all."

"Why so?"

"Because it takes the deepest faith."

I left the temple, supporting Dad down the spiraling steps among throngs of believers. Good deeds, I repeated in my mind. Good deeds. The crowd was so thick, I wondered if I tripped and fell whether I would cause a chain of dominos to fall and put the myth of Southern Shaolin at stake. Carefully in the slanting sun, humming and chatting, Dad and I negotiated one step at a time, taking in the beautiful *feng shui* displayed before our eyes: the green fields, the lush mountains and distant sea looming on the horizon. The sun seemed to follow us down. The road home was filled with itinerants, pious and tired. A day spent in Buddha's palm was a day spent flying in the clouds of faith, a poet once said. I whispered that into Dad's ear, and he smiled silently with his tilting eyes looking thoughtfully at the pitted road ahead of us.

That night we rushed to Dad's show in Qu Jiu, a town in the shadows of Hu Gong Mountain. Dusk filled the town with grayish darkness. Lights from residential houses looked like little holes poked through the other side of a lighted world. In the shimmering darkness was one bright spot, the market square where Dad's show was gearing up to start. *Er-hu* strings were tightened as a flutist tested his breath. A *pipa* was plucked for its clarity and its drum screwed tighter. Actresses backstage were kicking and stretching their limbs to the thrilled delight of pimpled peeping punks. Children pulling the closed curtain made the tentative bamboo scaffolding squeak dangerously. Only local militiamen could keep the rowdy villagers from grabbing pretty actresses off the stage and devouring them in carnal embraces. Dad had negotiated for ten militiamen to keep the crowd at bay.

I sat next to my sister, who wound up her *pipa* strings and plucked away as Dad, the conductor and supervisor of the show, stood right behind the curtain giving out final instructions to the unruly cast before the opening number. Tension was high. The audience was an agitated mob sitting, squatting, and standing on the dirt ground and shaky chairs. They shouted rude gibberish and petty curses at the stage. Some were fistfighting, others wrestling, still others fought with their chairs and tables. The winners were laughing and losers sobbing while passersby cheered with robust encouragement. It was obviously an occasion for great celebration. Everyone smoked their thick mountain smokes, including tiny lads sitting on their fathers' laps. There were also the screams of "Fist Guessing," a local drinking game going on among the men as they downed large jars of liquor, wiping their mouths with the wide sleeves of their sweaty shirts.

"You take one, and I take your mom." One stuck out one finger.

"You take two, and I take your niece." The other threw out two fingers.

"Three, I down your girl thrice, and four she crawls back asking for more. . . ."

If one messed up the recital, he would be punished by having to down a bowl of hard liquor. Whoever got drunk first lost. Fist Guessing often led men to drink till they were senseless and had to be carried home by their angry wives.

Any moment the curtain would be drawn, but Dad was still shouting

and screaming. One boy was wearing the wrong hat, and a girl was running around with a princess's gown on top and jeans on the bottom, crying and shouting that she could not find her three-inch wooden-soled
shoes, a must for an ancient princess. Another boy's makeup was smeared
because he had stolen some food to eat backstage. Crumbs were all over
his nose and lips. Dad was mad as hell as he rounded up the cast. His ears
had picked up the follies of his orchestra: a few *er-hus* out of tune and a
flute that sounded too dull. Dad was anxious, excited, stressed, and drowning in all of the above. But his words remained authoritative and commanding, and they were listened to attentively and respectfully. Maybe that
made it all worthwhile.

Finally the curtain was drawn open by a skinny man. The audience
went wilder. Bricks and stones went flying. Militiamen were called and
heads clubbed. In the chaos, the music oozed out from the orchestra, barely
heard amid the din of the most unappreciative crowd I had ever witnessed
or cared to. The drama unfolded like a sticky umbrella. No big hiccup.
Only little hisses and hitches. When the drama ended three hours later, the
audience was unusually quiet. The drunks were asleep, and so were many
wild children.

Dad threw the script onto a table and let out a big sigh, shaking his
head.

"You did a good job, Dad," I said.

He gave a tired smile as we joined the rest for dinner. There were two
obvious cliques within the troupe. One was centered around Dad, the
other around the quiet and shadowy cadre.

"How strange," I said to my sister.

"He's a mean guy and is trying to take over Dad's title but not his
responsibilities."

"Why the empty title?"

"Higher pay. There have been some skirmishes between them, but Dad
brushes them aside as if they don't exist."

"Why is Dad killing himself with this job?" I asked, concerned.

"You know Dad. The Cultural Revolution is over. He wanted to go out
and make a living. But I think, more importantly, he wants to stick around
watching over me and wait for me to establish myself as a *pipa* player.
Otherwise he would have quit a long time ago. He constantly has chest
pains," Ke said quietly.

"Do you think he might like what he is doing?" I asked.

"Oh, he does. I've never seen him so happy."

"Well then, as long as our old man likes it, let him do it. And when he can't, I'll take good care of him."

"Don't worry, young brother. I'm watching his every step."

"Good."

That night I got Dad a bucket of cold water from a nearby river and dumped it over him, making him tremble and scream like a child. Dad never went to sleep without a shocking shower at the end of the day. He was the only man in Yellow Stone who took a shower every day, winter and summer. We shared a smoke while walking in the moonlit dirt road. Dad talked excitedly about anything under the sun, and I basked in his eloquent conversation. The night belonged to us, father and son.

It was way beyond midnight when we returned to the snoring crowd, in deep sleep on the floor of the village's high school classrooms. Dad and I lay down back to back.

"Dad, I had a nice walk," I whispered.

"I did too."

"You want me to rub your feet?" I asked, just like in the old days.

"No, too dusty. Let the mice lick them clean. Sleep now, son."

I nudged against his broad back and soon was snoring away like a baby.

Chapter Fifteen

Professor Wei's white house still gleamed in the glare of the morning sun while trees sang greenly their Western melodies. The red paper couplets pasted on their white entrance was the only acknowledgment that the Weis were indeed a part of the Yellow Stone Chinese New Year tradition, though their religious belief was a thousand miles away from that of the rest of the town. We thanked our Buddha. Did she thank her god on this glorious Spring Festival, I wondered as I walked the riverbank holding two noisy roosters with red bows? Mom had spent the whole morning thanking her various gods with sacrifices ranging from chickens to little piglets. Did the professor have to do all that as well?

Professor Wei met me at the entrance. She was a few wrinkles older, but her face was still a smiling flower. She hugged me, and I hugged her. How was college? How was everything? She wanted to know it all. Her eyes didn't leave me for at least five minutes as I babbled along excitedly in both English and Chinese about how I had done and what new things I had encountered during the first leg of my college life. She was like my grandma, hanging on to every word this new college man had to say. And I, the grandson, soaked in the honey of her love. She had tears in her eyes, silently looking and listening to me. My eyes also welled with tears as I admired this angel of a lady without whose efforts I would be nothing.

Today she wasn't alone. Her place was crowded with her Christian friends. They were there to wish each other a happy festival. She proudly introduced me to every single one of them. The dog was also there, except this time he was limping a little and his eyes were a lot dimmer and teary. His tail was no longer that stiffened poke but a sweeping broom between pained legs. I looked beyond and saw my Leader, the rooster that I had given Professor Wei as a gift. He stood proudly under a lychee tree on a piece of rock with his beautiful wings extended to their fullest display. His manners were like those of an easy and assured host, though his lobe was still half missing. His feathers, a flourishing burst of colors, shook as he stretched his slender neck to give a high-pitched crow as if to welcome me. Life must have been easier here with Professor Wei, for Leader looked well fed and seemed to have lost that edge from being a wild street chick. He had the contented look of a retired general that said the world beyond was the world forgotten. He looked at the two new robust roosters with lofty disdain.

"Now you really shouldn't have brought these roosters. You know I can't bear to eat them, they're too beautiful." Professor Wei patted one rooster's head.

"That's why they should be yours. They will be challenging company for Leader."

She shook her head, smiling.

"But I've got something else for you." I gave her the red English Bible.

She jumped like a little girl, grabbed it, and studied it hungrily, page by page, as if it were a long-lost treasure that had suddenly been salvaged from the bottom of an ocean.

"A red Bible in English? Where did you get this?" she screamed.

"From a Christian friend from Norway."

"Is this really for me?"

I nodded.

"How very wonderful. This is worth a thousand roosters. Oh, Da, you don't know how much it means to me." She held it to her chest.

"How much?" I teased.

She cried, shaking her head. "I almost lost my life trying to save my last English Bible that an ignorant Red Guard had taken from me. I fought to get it back, but he shouted that he would cut my hands off with a knife if I didn't let it go. I told him that I'd rather lose my hands than my Bible, and he cut me," she said, showing me the scars. Big, swiping, ugly marks ran across both her wrists. "I wouldn't let go no matter how many times that crazed man cut me. I was bleeding all over and didn't remember much else but when I woke up in a jailhouse, my hands were still there but not the Bible. That's how much it means to me. We have to share this beautiful gift with all my brothers and sisters." She dragged me into her living room where two dozen pious souls were gathered. "Everyone, look here. This is the first English Bible I've had since I lost mine some ten years ago. This is a miracle! Oh, thank God! Thank your grace!" All her wrinkles smoothed out as she looked upward, and at that moment she was young, vibrant, and sweetly in love with something far purer than anything my claylike brain could ever imagine or comprehend.

Mom's hunch was right. That mysterious old lady with the mouthful of gold teeth, who had sat in Huang's salon the whole day, was no customer at all. She was Mrs. Li of Han Jian, a far bigger town than Yellow Stone. And she was a desperate mother scouting for a suitable bride for her precious only son.

Word had gotten out that Huang was a pretty, righteous, hardworking girl of ripened and marriageable age from an honorable family. So the mother had walked four hours from her home just to sit and stare at Huang. Huang, being a smart merchant at heart, had let her sit there even though it was obvious that the lady wasn't there for a hairdo. Huang thought the lady odd, not doing anything, even rejecting a cup of tea and hanging around till sunset, but she had been respectfully nice to her.

Two days before I was to return to campus, a well-known matchmaker, Ar Ling, snuck through Huang's crowded salon. She was a small, hunchbacked old lady with a handbag looped around her wrist. She moved like a rat through tall stems of rice fields. One could see the rice plants part but

not the rat. Though cursed with the buglike existence of permanently facing the earth and defying the sun, she was a blessing in disguise, literally so.
She was a messenger who brought with her the promise of marriage and
maybe even love or romance. Though nothing was a certainty in this town,
least of all happiness, this four-foot-tall, elegant, ancient turtle garbed in red,
always red, was the nearest thing to the prospect of posterity, though not
necessarily prosperity. She was known for extracting murderously high marriage fees from the boy's side, from which the crab of a lady got her nice
and dandy 10 percent.

"Ar Ling. What took you so long to come by?" Mom greeted her dis-
creetly but expectantly, dragging the little thing into the innermost room
of our house, the living room facing the river. In the tradition of the
don't-call-me-I'll-call-you matchmaking business, her visit was sweet
honey for Mom, who had only married off one out of three daughters,
and no sons.

"Business, business, always business." The matchmaker had a natural
instinct to fake business.

"What wind has blown you here?" I could see Mom trying to conceal
her excitement, choosing her words carefully.

"Good wind, good wind." Ar Ling looped her bag once more. "And who
is he?" She pointed at me with her raised, painted brows. Her innate distaste
for boys who could not afford the merchandise that she had to sell was clear.

"My younger son."

"He is gonna cost you." The lady was mean like a bulldog. "I'm glad
I'm not here for him, thank Buddha!" She threw me another dirty look.

"Good, I'm not ready for you either," I retorted.

"You will be, soon enough," she barked, making it sound like a rotten
thing to be old enough for marriage. "Boys are only good for one thing,
and one thing only. I know that better than anyone else in town."

"For your information and to ease your soul, please strike me off your
client list. I intend to find my own love," I said, deliberately wanting to
annoy the tweedling old lady who saw from the keyhole of her crummy
business only the darkness of men.

"Young punk, talking like that is gonna cost you even more. Love is
never free. Wait till you meet the father of your dream girl. He's gonna let
his dog chase you and his sons beat you up if you try to steal anyone that
you *love* without payment. I've seen it happen before. It ain't pretty. The

greedy fathers will cut your lovy, drippy little ding-dong off if you try to dip it anywhere near her rotten knuckles. Tell him that, mother."

Mom squirmed uneasily at her vulgarity. "He is a college man, you know."

"Oh?" She looked up an inch, the most she could manage, then bent down again. "That ain't gonna change the way matches are made in this town. No pay, no knuckles, got it?" She spat at my feet. "Get him out of here. We need to talk serious business."

"I can't, he has to do his packing and this is the quietest room here," Mom explained.

"Not with him talking."

"You be quiet, Da," Mom ordered.

"I will be."

"Stay that way, for I have little patience with a slippery tongue like yours," the turtle warned.

Silently I shook my head as I bent over to tie my bulging trunk with thick ropes that would hopefully hold everything together for the long journey back.

"I come for Huang," the matchmaker said. "A few days ago one of the richest families of Han Jian approached me about her."

"How did they hear about her?" Mom asked curiously.

"The mother sat in the salon watching Huang the whole day."

"She did?"

"And she wants her bad."

"How about her son?"

"Don't worry about him."

"But he is the one marrying my daughter."

"His mom makes the decision. He lost his father, though not his money, if you know what I mean." She rubbed her two money fingers.

"But we still have to see if they even like each other."

"Oh, they'll like each other plenty. Buddha made her a hole and him a stick, hopefully a big one. She'll love him plenty."

"But this is the modern time. I urge my children to marry only if they love that person."

"What are you being so modern about? You don't think I'm modern already? In the old days a bridegroom never even got to see his bride till the wedding day. It was all about the price. I would see the girl, then the boy, talk about the price, and that was it. They were happy and never had any complaints. It all worked out well, better than these modern days. Do you know how many times I've had to return down payment to the boys' families just because the girls didn't warm up to the boys after seeing them? That's a curse. Girls aren't supposed to like men before they taste them. What is marriage, a movie or a play? You can't choose and change the cast. Buddha has it all worked out up there for us, you see." She tried to look up again.

"Well, I raised my kids differently," Mom insisted.

"How differently? Are you talking about not taking any marriage fees? If that's the case, I'm walking."

"No, no, no. Fees will be paid, but I just want to know what the boy looks like and what he does for a living."

"Handsome boy, big eyes, big face, big everything. I tell you if I had a daughter, I'd have her marry him not once but twice. You know why? Because he could use two." She winked, making Mom uneasy again.

"And what does he do?"

"A jewelry trader, a family business for generations. They're so rich, I actually saw cash stashed in the cracks of their walls to hide from Communist eyes. You couldn't find a man like him with a lantern in your hands, looking day and night. That's how good he is."

"What is his education?"

"I never asked that question." She threw a look at me as if education were a curse. "Man is only measured by the money he makes, not by a college degree."

"What are you looking at me for?" I asked.

"Because you think you got it all, but you don't," she barked at me, then returned to my mom. "Now, mother, you ask too many questions. I'm only here to ask you for a price for Huang."

"Don't say it that way," Mom said sternly.

"Let me say it another way then. How much are you asking? With that info, I can go to the mother and set a date of engagement."

"I have to ask my daughter first."

"Forget that. How about five thousand? Or maybe even ten thousand now that the mother is so hot about her."

"What does Mrs. Li like so much about Huang?" Mom asked thoughtfully.

"That she's businesslike, that she's gorgeous, that she has wide hipbones that can bear litters of sons and daughters, and that she's able to handle twenty heads of wet hair all at the same time by herself."

"What else?"

"That Huang was nice to her, that she offered her a cup of tea, and when it was rejected, that Huang graciously smiled and never bothered her again, someone who wasn't a potential customer."

"That was a good reason."

"But I think the mother likes the fact that Huang would make a heck of a jewelry trader herself and be able to carry on the gold mine of a business that they do. And Mrs. Chen, you'll have a very rich daughter soon if you just let me handle things from here on before the boy is snatched away by another girl. Believe me, there are many suitors out there hot for him. You've got to strike while the iron is hot." Now she was quoting Chairman Mao.

Sensing that she was closing in on Mom and making her nervous, I interceded. "Don't let her do anything before Huang says okay."

"Hey, stay quiet. Why do I have to listen to him? Where is Mr. Chen?"

"My son is right. I have to ask Huang first," Mom said firmly. "They need to meet first, then talk terms."

"Terms first, then meet," Ar Ling argued.

"Why?"

"So they don't back out."

"They should be able to back out if they don't like each other," Mom declared.

"Terms first or I'm walking." The turtle turned to leave. Mom was about to grab her when I took Mom's arm and stopped her.

The turtle inched slowly toward the door and paused, hoping. But Mom didn't stop her. Ar Ling stopped and pulled out a deck of dog-eared poker cards from her handbag, flipping them till a card fell out. She picked it up, pretended to study it for a while, then sneered, "Today is your lucky day. I'm gonna walk the empty walk to Han Jian and arrange for them to meet."

"That's good. Thank you." Mom bowed.

The hunchback moved like a bug, slowly but surely out into the street. She paused to gleam and wink at Huang before she ran off along the dirt road to Han Jian. The sun would forever be at her back and the moon on her shoulders. She might not be the fastest messenger, but she was definitely one of the surest, this angel of love, this ambassador of a time long gone.

The fanfare of the New Year's celebration died down. Good food was eaten and money lost. The bleaching sun and wet rain peeled the red paper couplets pasted to the door frames of all the houses, and Jin and I once again lugged our things, heading for Fuzhou where we would take the train north. Everyone was there to say good-bye, including Mo Gong, who leaned over and whispered into my left ear, "Next year, bring me a doll."

"What doll?"

"One of those advertised in the magazines you gave me. The blow-up ones."

"You're sick. Why don't you just be happy with your noontime?"

"I'll never be, Da. You're to blame."

"I'll see what I can do, brother," I said as good-bye.

When Jin and I arrived at the train station, a notice on the wall read that all tickets for the train leaving tonight for Beijing had been sold. If I missed the only express out of Fujian that day, I would miss a full day of classes. That wouldn't sit well with the regulatory body of our college. It was a bourgeois habit not to be punctual, they would say critically.

Jin was a bright man. He found a distant cousin of ours, a city slicker in the truest sense, who promised to send me on the train in return for three packs of Phoenixes.

"Where is the ticket?" I asked the young man, whom I had rarely seen before. During the Cultural Revolution all relatives had broken ties with us, and only now were they slowly reemerging.

"Don't worry about that," he said. He rode his bike and carried me on the backseat to the station. Instead of going through the main gate, though, he pedaled me farther along the forbidding wall of the station for a good mile.

"What are we doing?" I asked.

"We're going to the end of the wall where it's much lower. Then you're going to climb over and walk along the rail back to the platform where the train is waiting and about to leave." He checked his watch.

"But I'll be arrested."

He smiled. "Probably."

"What?"

"Then you can talk your way onto your train, get it?"

My heart was at my throat and my hands trembling.

"Hey, I said I would get you inside the station."

"I've never been arrested before."

"You don't have any choice. The tickets for the next three days have all been sold. Everyone is going."

"Will they put me in jail?"

"Hell, no. They don't want you there. If you don't sweet-talk them, most they'll do is throw you out the door. Don't be a chicken."

"Okay, let's do it."

"Good. Now you're learning."

We threw the luggage over, and I climbed the low wall. Then I dragged my heavy belongings, too nervous to regret anything until a station security guard saw me. I dropped my things and raised my hands in surrender. The man silently took me to the station manager's office.

"What did you do that for?" the fat manager asked me.

"I have no ticket." I showed him my school badge proudly.

"Is that supposed to mean anything to me? You think you college kids can just walk in and demand anything?" he screamed.

"School begins in three days. It's very important that I make today's express, sir."

"What am I supposed to do when all the tickets are sold?"

"Standing tickets."

"All the way to Beijing?"

"I'll take the chance if you would just let me up there." The train was making the last round of announcements.

"Fine, one yuan."

"Thank you, sir."

"Don't ever do it again. Next time I'll lock you up for two days."

"It won't happen again," I promised.

"Just that you know, my daughter always wanted to go to that college. I heard it's a good one."

"Well, I'll personally take care of her if and when she comes."

"But now I have second thoughts about it."

"Why?"

"After seeing you and your dirty little trick." He leaned over his table and shouted, "Get your things and get out of my face, you little thief!"

I flew out like a chased rooster only to timidly return and ask him, "Where do I get the ticket?"

"On the train, you idiot. It's moving now. Run!"

I ran with the luggage rolling on my shoulders and barely made it through the closing doors. I lodged myself between two clinking compartments, getting blasted by the mountain wind. The platform started to move, and soon the rhythm of boredom, the breath of this beast, transfixed us.

Chapter Sixteen

In the south, spring was a rainy season when mushrooms shot up from every empty spot of rich land and every rotten tree slain by the wind. The whole region looked like a wet canvas, still dripping with chunky paints and misty strokes. Mold grew on everything, including the pillows we drooled on and the quilts we overslept in. Naked toes waded everywhere looking for their destinations, and pants were rolled knee-high, allowing little green frogs to jump into the folds for a ticketless ride. Little fish swam blindly in the mucky dimples of the roads sunken by footfalls. Mountain brooks rushed the rampant rainwater downhill, choking the rivers on the plain and flooding shallow furrows of the endless ripening fava-bean fields. Often farmers had to float in a wooden basket to pick the beans. They wore *jan nui,* raincoats made of shredded palm tree bark, looking like grass men appearing and disappearing between patches of fog and misty, low-hanging clouds. As if this wetness weren't enough, mountaintops hugged the soft breasts of pregnant clouds; had they been any more amorous, the whole south would have been submerged under the looming sea.

But spring in the northern plain was more crisp than muggy, more ethereal than real. Hollowing winds made snappy twigs whistle and furry birds struggle in urgent flight. The sky was dryly blue, the sun was long, and the days chilly. Bo told me that people wore cotton coats till early May. I could only sigh at that prediction.

Still, spring was filled with possibilities, and I was happier and more upbeat. The visit home had pumped me up again with inexhaustible energy. I felt I belonged right here on campus, and better yet, the shackles of homesickness had mysteriously unwound and vanished.

My first mission was bribery. Nothing worked until fuel was pumped into the right places in this oil guzzler called China. My potent weapons were the big *O*s and *L*s that I had lugged all the way from home. Oysters, raw or cooked, were good for turning a man's dead snake into a singing sensation, a nightly Pavarotti, while lychees rebuilt a man's *yuan qi,* basic energy, so that he could climb his wife's mountains again and again. I was planning to have a few old Commies walking around my campus with volcanic erections, the bigger the better, the longer the closer my chance at North America. As a Yellow Stoner would say, big *O*s shone your tool while small *L*s added to your fuel. The two worked hand in hand, never one without the other.

My first target was none other than the dean of our department, undoubtedly the man writing the ticket out of here. He seemed unusually friendly when he opened his door in his frayed, yellowish pajamas with his wife in tow, smoking up a storm.

"Come in," he said.

I thanked him and quickly stated the purpose of my call. "I'm here to wish you a happy New Year. I brought something from home for you to taste."

"You shouldn't have, but let me see what it is," said his wife, a big woman in every way. She shoved her man aside and took the small sacks out of my hands.

"Dried oysters and lychees. The best the sea has to offer and the juiciest that our trees grow," I told them.

"Nice. *O* for yin and *L* for yang. How very thoughtful of you to give these to an old man like me," the dean said, smiling with yellow teeth.

I cringed at the thought of them doing the yin and yang thing.

"But they certainly are small sacks," she said, shaking her head.

"Don't say that," the dean intervened.

"I'm just amusing myself, okay?" she replied.

"He is still here."

"Good, maybe he can bring us more," the wife concluded.

"I don't think he has any more."

The two went on shamelessly like two jaded hawkers. I was feeling terribly embarrassed and slighted. "Why don't I run and get another sack? I'll be right back."

"Don't bother," the dean said.

"Let him do it. He'll feel better if he does. Right, Da?"

"Isn't she something? Do you mind, Da?" he asked.

She certainly was something. A monster, I would say. "Not at all."

I lugged two more bags in a few minutes later, hoping to see the couple bubble with gratitude. The beefy wife took the bags impatiently and disappeared into her room, where the Peking Opera was blaring away on a radio. The dean laughed apologetically and shrugged. The two worked like a couple of thieves, and they knew it. They had done it before, thousands of times, I thought. But that wasn't the end of their ruse. Just as I was about to broach the subject of North America, the wife returned, holding a bigger sack of Os and showing me the one I had given her. "Your oysters look like babies compared with these suckers. You know these came from a Cantonese student."

"Well, there's always the next time. Right, Da?" the dean said.

I was shocked by their blatant rudeness. *There won't ever be a next time, you thieves,* I screamed in my head. "Thank you for the opportunity. I'll try to do better next time," I offered instead.

"You don't need to do that." The dean waved his hand for his wife to leave. But she stood her ground and said, "He'll need to if he's interested in this America thing."

"Well, I am."

"I know you are. So is everyone in your class," she said. It seemed she was more the dean than her husband was.

"Really?" I knew I was late.

"Our life is busy. Let me tell you something else. It's going to take a lot more, and I don't mean gifts," though that was exactly what she meant, "to get you selected."

"Like what?" I was glad she was spilling the beans.

"Political ambition, family background, and of course your academic performance, which will be considered in its totality."

The dean kept quiet, letting his wife do the talking. One got the feeling the Os and Ls would most likely end up in her gigantic stomach, making her the yang and him the yin. She on top and he a crushed sugarcane.

"Hey, one red heart and two preparations," said the dean, quoting a Communist cliché meant for encouraging those discouraged. "If you don't go this time, there is always the next time."

"Well, I would very much like to be considered for this chance."

"We'll bear that in mind, Comrade Chen," the dean said.

From that tone, I knew I had outstayed the welcome of my Os and Ls. It was time to beat the grassy path.

My next visit was to Professor Tu. The beaming teacher received me in his narrow hallway. We had a hard time passing each other between the two walls. Tu filled his apartment fully like a well-stuffed dumpling. His equally big wife did nothing to ease the fulfillment. They were a lovely couple with good hearts. They tasted the gifts in front of me and loved every bit. He told me the chance for the pick was very slim now because everyone seemed to be bribing and knocking on the back doors of the leading cadres of our school. A scandal seemed to be brewing, he warned.

"Why is that?" I asked.

"Whenever so many people covet one thing, no one will get it. That's a guarantee," Tu said wisely. That was his way of saying, wise up, waste no more, and study hard. I did, thankfully.

But school wasn't the same anymore. Tension was palpable, and friction among classmates sparkled everywhere. Bo often questioned my disappearances by saying sarcastically, "Not another bribing activity, I hope."

"It's all yours, my friend," I would say.

"It should be mine. I'm the son of two revolutionaries. That pedigree I can live on forever."

"Sure, live on it forever. I don't care."

Then there was Hong, who constantly claimed that he should be picked to go to America because he was also the son of revolutionaries and his dad had almost died on the battlefield. Perfect logic. Revolutionary father, American son.

The dean walked importantly back and forth across the campus, knowing that our eyes were following him. In his hands he held two juicy bones that he could throw to anyone of his liking. Girls flirted with him a little more. He was happy about that, laughing with eerie, jerky giggles. There was a lustful shine in his eyes, which I was sure was my aphrodisiac big Os at work. What a pity he was wasting the glow on those flirtatious girls and not on his elephant wife who, by the way, looked more in need of medicine than a sex appetizer.

For some unknown reason, nobody had yet been chosen even when the peach blossoms were all out and smiling by late April. My classmates then realized that there was only so much they could do to promote themselves and that a little bit of back-stabbing wouldn't hurt. Soon reports were being filed regularly, on everything from little deviations of standard conduct to invented moral violations.

One day the dean took me into his office and asked if I had ever disguised myself as a Cambodian student to go shopping at the Friendship Store. I was shocked at the report. Few knew about my ploy. It was a serious offense that might land me outside the campus wall. I denied it vehemently with big gestures and foamy mouth.

"That's a lie," I said.

"I thought so." The dean smiled.

I was relieved beyond belief. "I'm glad you believe me."

"I believe nobody anymore," the dean said. "Luckily your Cambodian friends vouched for you."

As soon as I was dismissed, I rushed to Hui's dorm and kissed his shiny forehead. I thanked him, and we hugged.

"But Da, you've got bad friends among your Chinese circle. You have to be careful. Come with us when our country is freed. I'd love to make a brother-in-law out of you," he said thoughtfully. "That is, if my sister is still alive."

"Hey, bring your sexy sister here and I'll be horny like a bull. And I'll personally make an honest wife out of her."

We laughed.

"Hey, I want to thank you for the Phoenix cigarettes."

"Oh, Da, you already thanked me enough with your bags of oysters."

"Is it working?" I asked.

"Haven't found a girl to try it on yet. But I've been making a taut tent under my quilt every morning."

"Don't tell me you also draw Cambodian maps on the quilt as well."

He just smiled with a knowing smirk. I loved the man.

Bo's nose was working up a storm when spring hay fever hit the leafy suburbs. His nose was rubbed red like young ginger roots, and his wet hankies lay everywhere.

"Why don't you get your leaky bellows fixed once and for all," I suggested one day.

"Don't worry. I'm going to see the best surgeon in China soon. You won't even remember that I once had a lousy dragon nose," he said lightheartedly.

"A little plumbing won't hurt anyone, will it?"

The day came soon enough. He was expected to stay a few days after the procedure, but he returned late that same night. He was very quiet and slept till the next day with a quilt over his face, missing all his classes. He wouldn't discuss his visit with anyone. Soon he grew more and more distant. In class he slumped in his seat, losing himself in deep thoughts and sighing at homework. He took long, dark walks around the campus when everyone was asleep. I soon took to accompanying him during those strolls, where we would just walk and talk little. When he did talk, he was vague and elusive. He seemed dimmed, not the shining, vibrant old Bo.

He told me that when he couldn't sleep, he would roam the empty dorm rooms previously occupied by foreign students who had left. Lazy housekeepers left them uncleaned. There were many treasures there, he said. One day he came back with a bunch of Japanese lighters, which he flipped on and off. Another time he showed me a set of silk suspenders, which he wore without any shirt on and plucked them against his hairy nipples. "I'm keeping them. They look neat, don't they?" he said. Other things he passed along to others as gifts. Each night he would visit a few rooms and come back with a lot of goodies. Foreign magazines would keep him up all night. And mint gums were good too, leaving him chewing vigorously every day.

"Bo, you've turned into a junkie," I commented one day.

"I don't need all this junk, but I just can't resist the adventure," he said casually.

"Be careful. If the security downstairs knew about it, you'd be accused of stealing."

"Isn't that exciting?"

"I don't see it that way."

"You're a scared little chicken."

"I am because I don't have revolutionary parents like you."

"No, you don't, pal, and I do. That's why I can do whatever I want to do and nobody can do anything about it." He shrugged.

One muggy day, a security officer with uniform and pistol knocked on the door while we were resting and chatting in our room after a heavy lunch. Bo was listening to his music while dancing and gliding on his feet with his nice pants held snugly up by the suspenders. The guards asked for Bo, but he paid no heed, still dancing and whirling. When the guard came in and slammed his recorder off, we knew it was serious.

"Follow me to the security office," he demanded.

"What for?" Bo protested with a sneer, amused.

"We'll interrogate you there."

"Interrogate what?"

"Come now. Bring all your watches with you," the officer said.

"All my watches? But I only have one."

"So you say. Come now and shut up."

Bo put on his shirt slowly, his eyes darkening with nervousness. He stole one last glance my way, then quickly turned without a good-bye and followed the man out.

That night Bo did not come back. The place felt dead without him. Our elite neighbors looked curiously our way, but no one seemed too concerned. Bo had done much crazier things before. He was once gone for a few days and came back with a totally new look, which he expected us to be thrilled about. He was always surprising. The day he ceased being so would be the day he ceased living.

The next day he didn't show up for any classes, but that was no surprise either. School had long ago lost its sizzle for him. He regarded it more like boot camp than higher education. He called himself an idealistic idealist, which meant that he didn't like doing any practical things to make the ideals materialize.

But by dinnertime, when I walked into the congested dining hall, people were gathered in knots and groups, whispering and talking urgently. Gossip was nothing new here and chatting a must. We were the language students. We had to yak at all times. But today, the ear-biting whispering seemed a lot fiercer. I chose a quiet table away from the crowd to chew my *mantou* while digesting lengthy new words scribbled on my flash cards.

After that I trotted home with a steamy hot shower in mind to cleanse myself of earthly dust and the nipping exhaustion of a day's work before plunging into another nightly study session.

But things were tense around our building. There were guards and security personnel everywhere. Something was going on here, I thought, though it didn't interest me enough to pause and check. My routine of doing things in an orderly manner was too important to be shaken by any trivial event of the moment. I saw curiosity as a weakness, a curse diverting one from his goal. I prided myself on this vertical focus of mind and horizontal attention to my conviction. I was a walking grid that took no bends or dips.

When I sauntered into my room, the secretary of the Communist Youth League was there. He was a badly taught former French major who had abandoned his studies of Balzac and his lilting Peking Man's French for a monastery job as a Commie cadre. He was smoking, sweating, and sitting at Bo's table, plowing his hands through everything in Bo's drawers. Our door was choked with a thick crowd. Only then did I begin to think that it might have something to do with me.

"Chen Da," the secretary said sternly.

I dropped my school bag and replied crisply, "Yes, secretary."

"Comrade Zhang Bo has committed suicide last night."

"What . . . what did you say?" I was thunderstruck. "Is he . . . dead?"

"Yes."

I collapsed weakly into my seat. A cavity bored instantly inside me. I felt that a bottom had fallen out and I was drowning in an enormous sea of sadness and stabbing pain. Suddenly everything in this room was infested with Bo's ghost. I remembered his lingering glance, the last one he gave me. How could that have been his last? It was a lousy good-bye. *You could have done better than that, Bo.* Now I wished I had stopped him and said something to him, even the simplest farewell. I didn't cry, but I felt petrified. His death was sudden thunder without lightning. I must have turned very pale because the secretary leaned over to ask with concern, "Are you all right?"

"No, I'm not all right."

"What can I do for you?" he asked kindly.

"I can't sleep in this room tonight. Too many memories."

"We'll find you something."

That night I slept in the doorman's office while he manned his night shift, smoking, humming Peking opera, and making fun of me, calling me a crybaby, a puppy, and a boneless jellyfish. He was a jolly old man with a round, meaty face. No one with that kind of face meant any harm. So I ignored him and spent the night crying, speaking to myself, slipping in and out of a clinging nightmare that would not vanish. I tasted death in my mouth that night and hated it.

Not till the next day did I come to know the way he had died. He had sat in a chair next to an electrical outlet in the third floor lecture hall with literature books laid before him. He had swallowed a bunch of pills, then plunged his open pocketknife into the socket. It must have been a painful death. The police said there were signs of him thrashing wildly on the dirty floor, apparently after taking the pills. But dignity had brought him to struggle up again and sit himself down properly before electrocuting himself.

What a fucking way to go. You damned idiot, why?

Some people had reported seeing him walking and dragging his bike along a dark lane lined by tall trees the previous night. He had been deep in thought, looking really troubled. But it was a lover's lane where people were too busy making out and where Bo could have been just another boy with a broken heart, walking the night away in dismay. And by daylight, everything would be fine; the sun would rise again. But not for this boy.

The campus was bubbling with speculation over the motive. The unofficial official reasoning was that he had been accused of stealing a foreign watch from a Cambodian student. Accusation was always conviction, and he was to be subjected to some sort of public humiliation. Bo was the last person in need of stealing a watch. But he had shown me a new foreign watch the other day. Had he stolen it, which I doubted, he would not have boasted about it and flaunted it before my eyes. There was another theory floating around that he was dying of a terminal disease, that he had cancer in his noisy nose. That would explain why he had come back without surgery, and why he would chose to end the pain sooner rather than later, in a quick snap instead of a lingering fight.

The dean announced in our regular Saturday afternoon political meeting, like an afterthought, that any memorial services would be prohibited on or off campus, because it was considered a disgrace to take one's own life. It was a waste of government money, and Bo was a traitor to our revolution. All human aspects of the tragedy were swept aside like garbage tossed into the shadows.

When Bo's father came to claim his body, he first went to his son and then came to see us. He was a big man with warm eyes reddened from crying. He shook my hand and took a long time looking at me before hugging me meaningfully and silently. He thanked me, and I thanked him. I cried, but he didn't. I wanted to tell him so much about Bo and how proud he had been of his father. Bo had talked about him all the time with longing and sadness. But words failed me. I wished I knew how to console this man. But what was lost would never be made whole again. Even as we exchanged our brief and sad pleasantries, he seemed to have aged a decade. He said good-bye and left, his appearance completing Bo.

In secrecy I asked the whole class to hold a memorial for Bo. Everyone was unusually agreeable. We all cried, especially those girls whose lives had been touched by his vibrant madness. We made tiny wreaths and told stories about him in remembrance. In a simple speech, I remembered Bo as a wonderful friend who had cared and opened up a country boy's eyes to the colorful world of the city. With tears I hummed the first shimmering bar of the glorious "Blue Danube" and recounted his amused look the first time we met, the sunny days of his energy and enthusiasm, the dark nights of his bottomless despair, the hopelessness of his cancerous pain, and that final heroic courage to stare back at the ugly face of his illness and spit between its evil eyes. *Bo, my friend, your pain, the only imperfection, perfected you. You are a hero in your own right.* I wished that he rest in peace and that his pain be forever gone.

Many a night I woke up mourning him and feeling guilty that I hadn't been brave enough to come closer to see him one last time when they carried him off our campus. I had only dared hide behind a corner of a cement wall, watching from a distance as Bo's body, wrapped in a deep blue bag, was tossed like a rolled carpet onto the back of a pickup truck. Leaves and dust had danced wildly in the trail behind the truck, refusing to settle long after he was gone, traceless. I prayed to him in whispers that I would always see him in his glorious youthful brilliance. Age would never be his problem.

Soon another rooming policy was implemented, luckily, and we had to move out of the building. His ghost still lingered in that corner room where his bed had faced the south. The hallway still echoed to his naughty laughter, and his curious shadow still lurked in those empty rooms, searching for things that he did not need, things that had finally gotten him into trouble. *Good-bye, Bo. You were a good friend.*

Chapter Seventeen

Bo was at peace now, but his death was no peaceful matter for the living. Behind all the anxious whispering and forced silence, there was a sense that something big had to happen to end Bo's tragedy. Someone had to be blamed. A chicken had to be slaughtered to calm the monkeys. After all, Bo's father was a big shot, an angry and sad big shot. Someone must have done something to Bo in that interrogation room that made him leap off the cliff. There were rumors of severe self-criticism going on behind the walls, within the department heads. The university president, who had walked Mao's Long March, took charge of investigating the matter. Some said there were weeping sessions. Others said they had taken to fistfighting and pointing fingers at each other. The subject of a stolen watch was dropped, and the hunt for an overpressuring interrogator became the issue.

A senior who lived in the same diplomatic compound as Bo's father reported that the man had refused to leave for his post in France until some action was taken against such grossly cruel persecution. That only added frenzy to the self-criticism. One day the public security office was under fire; another day the blame fell on our dean. The puzzle got bigger. We watched with amusement as those corrupted cadres got their asses burned for the first time and deservedly so.

The outcome was dramatically predictable. The leader of the Communist Youth League, the half-baked French major whom everyone called Mr. Monsieur, was officially kicked out of his cozy office and sent down to the Logistics Department where he was put in charge of arranging tour bus schedules for foreign students. Once again the weakest in the lot got blamed, and the matter was considered concluded.

But the condemned Mr. Monsieur wasn't altogether unhappy. The change of job worked out even better for him. He no longer had to read that obnoxiously boring *Communist Manifesto* fifty times a year to refresh his smoked mind. He no longer had to read us those incomprehensible "VERY IMPORTANT DOCUMENTS" with big words, which were made even more muddled and unintelligible by the meddling of his thick tongue. It had not been an easy job for him anyhow. No student was ever interested in the political studies he had organized and made mandatory every Saturday afternoon. No one understood those mind-purifying documents anyway. Jargon such as *bourgeois democracy, right-wing leftist, left-wing rightist, Communism Chinese style, Socialism the Great Wall style* left one running for the nearest liquor bottle.

Now every day Mr. Monsieur could be seen smoking and wearing sunglasses, acting like a lazy tourist guide, occasionally speaking his rusty French while accompanying those rich foreign fat cows on greasy Beijing tours. Ten-course lunches awaited him every day. The cigarettes he smoked now were foreign brands that he bummed off tourists. Gone was the cheap tobacco, bluntly sliced and coarsely wrapped in inky newspapers. All the Communist doctrine that he used to expound was now a fart whistling down the wind.

The more severe and devastating punishment, handed down from the Ministry of Education, was to cancel the two slots to the North American college, which had been the cause of all this hubbub, and to freeze all the exchange programs, because a representative of the student body had taken his life, and that spoke ill of our quality in the greatest quantity. Some of my classmates cried for the lost golden opportunity. But I was still too numbed and deeply hurt by Bo's death to really care. My only regret was that my oysters and lychees had been blown and wasted on the dean's limp member. School reluctantly went back to its much needed placidity.

Chapter Eighteen

I thought I was dealing fine with Bo's death. I managed to swallow all the pain and bury all the stress that persisted in my soul. I simply told myself that he was gone and that was it. No good-bye was necessary—we were big boys.

Life became as smooth as the dark, silky night, and Bo was forgotten till mid-June when I suddenly began to feel sick. My stomach revolted at the oily surfaces of our dishes in the steamy cafeteria. I could puke at the mere mention of any meat, and run dry heaves just thinking about the pork knuckles on display. I felt an unusual knot choking my heart and rubbing the top of my stomach.

Like a true southerner, I went back to my dorm and made myself a pot of hot strong tea, the best of Fujian tea, those light green baby leaves from the heart of the tea tree. I sloshed down the whole pot. To help the mystic tea do its work, I smoked two dark cigarettes in one sitting as Dad would have done to dispel any discomfort. What could be better than the combination of nicotine and caffeine, my favorite twin engines? But this time a dull pain followed immediately afterward, rolling my stomach like a tidal wave. I tossed in bed like a baking frog for a good fifteen minutes before the pain receded, but it was not gone entirely. For that I smoked another cigarette, which to my dismay only propelled the pain from a slow needling into an urgent jab. The continuing pain shook my firm belief that there was no disease that a good smoke and hot tea could not cure. I didn't know what else to do to scare the pain away. Dad had fed me my first cup of strong tea before I could speak. Tea was king. It dried diarrhea, smoothed indigestion, cleansed wet lungs, strengthened weak kidneys, and sharpened one's soul. No one had told me that it could also drill holes in the stomach lining or scratch the fragile surface with its caffeinated long nails.

In fear, I sat weakly in bed, thinking of my family. Had my father been there, he would have smiled and asked Mom to cook something tasty, then walked across the street to the herbal medicine store where all the dried weeds and curled orange peels were sold by the pinch and measured on the dainty little scale. The old medicine man would lean over to listen as Doc Chen gave orders to his deaf ear, and he would "catch" a few ingredients as a prescription, as if those herbs were alive and kicking. By the time the herbs were brewed, Mom's food would be ready too. Medicine first and then food, Mom would say. I would frown but obey because I was a sick boy. The bitterness of the herbs would be swiped clean when the food was eaten and soup washed down. But home was far away. Pain followed into my dreams.

The next day in class, one snob jokingly suggested that I might have contracted hepatitis B. I retorted with a chuckle that my liver was swimming beautifully, and only city folks like him would get such a thing. I, the buffalo, would never be the victim. Then I laughed weakly and drummed my sunken chest to show my firmness. But the drumming only urged another wave of dry heaves, and pain returned sharply, choking my throat. The whole class covered their mouths and noses hurriedly as if I were a stinking corpse passing by. Their eyes pierced me with daggers of a deadly prognosis: *you hepatitis B freak, get out of here!* A girl from Beijing spoke through her fingers, suggesting that I check with a doctor before the illness struck everyone there.

Doctor? What doctor? I never believed in doctors. Neither did I believe that I would ever need a doctor. I stayed cool and weak, believing that whatever I had would go away in a few days. I skipped all meals because nothing appealed to me. I sat down to write a letter home, using scanty language to artfully disguise a much more serious pain. After reading the pathetic letter, I tore it to pieces. What was the use of sending the letter anyway? It would take a month to reach them. By then the problem would be gone, and they would be stuck with empty fear and worry. Mom and Dad were the most worrisome people I knew. She would sit up all night, crying over this suffering baby far away from home, and Dad would pace up and down his sitting room, trying to figure out what to do.

Then I wished I could call home, or rather that I could afford to call home. It would cost an arm and a leg, and I would have to take a slow, smelly bus two hours downtown to get to the phone company, where long lines awaited. A call home in itself would be a triple-jump miracle because it had to be routed first to fuzzy Fuzhou, then sandy Putien, then finally to Yellow Stone if the only line there happened to be unengaged. The post-man there would put the call on hold and run like hell for a couple of miles to get to my home. Then my parents would have to negotiate the muddy roads with their shaky legs and urgent hearts to try to catch the call. The connection would be staticky as the sea wind plucked the ropy wires like a *pipa,* and half the conversation would be barely understandable. Ultimately I would only frighten my parents and solve nothing.

I curled myself into a shrimp and fell asleep.

The next morning a class leader ordered me to stay out of class.

"Why?" I asked. "You're kicking me out of class?"

"No, you need to see a doctor," he replied, "and yes, we don't want you back here till you're clean."

"Fuck you, pal."

"Fuck you, too."

The school doctor had quite a reputation with girls. Had I a choice, I wouldn't have gone within ten feet of the octopus. Luckily, his scrutinizing wife manned his clinic, making any hanky-panky a near impossibility under her sniffing nose. Her eyes stared suspiciously at me as I stepped in. She had reason to be suspicious of girls coming through this door but why me?

"What are you here for?" she asked. "Not another pretense to skip political studies, I hope."

"No, I think I have hepatitis B."

"Are you a doctor?" she snapped at me.

"No."

"So be quiet and stay here, and my husband will examine you."

Contrary to his bad name, the doc was a charming man. He looked at me with his reassuring stare and ready smile, then cleared his throat, betraying a soothing baritone. He shook my hand and slapped my back. I felt healthy before he even opened his mouth. No one was safe with this man, I thought.

"Lie down," he commanded gently.

His voice brought chills to my spine. Had I been a girl in the close company of such a man, I would have felt like a bad girl already.

He poked at my tongue and checked my pulse. His hands, warm and solid, were acutely knowing and eloquently telling. The hair on his fingers was macho and the veins manly. He never let his gaze leave me. I felt warmth oozing from him, and I trusted him completely. Who wouldn't? He studied and listened to me some more, then lifted his stethoscope off his neck after taking off his gloves.

"You don't have hepatitis."

"Are you sure?"

He nodded.

Silence was gold here. I jumped off the little bed and continued jumping in celebration of my tremendous relief. Had I had the disease, I would have had to go home until I was cured, and my future would have been delayed, if not ruined. Now I was free. I shook his hand gently and wanted to hug him in gratitude but stopped. He reached over and patted my shoulders, rubbed them softly, and smiled. That was the best hug and the only hug that a man could and should have with him. Anything more, I would leave the clinic a withered flower.

"You have a slight case of upset stomach, that's all," he told me.

"Thank you, doc." I turned to leave. That was when I saw the two hateful eyes of his wife staring piercingly through the cloth screen that shielded the examining bed. She stared at me with not a word spoken, and I smiled, thanking her.

"Wait," the doc shouted as I was leaving.

"Why?"

"Are you limping?"

"I've got something on my big toe."

"Let me see."

I sat down again and took off my sticky shoes. There, glaringly, stood a growth that had been hurting badly lately.

"Lousy leather shoes cause corns, you know that?"

"Yes, but they're a gift from a friend. Besides, they're my only pair of shoes."

"I understand. But stop wearing them. Find something softer," he advised. "I'm going to write you a prescription to have the corn removed free of charge."

"Surgery?"

"A simple one."

"Funny thing, I came here for hepatitis but am going home with a corn."

"One should always be so lucky."

He passed me the slip, and I left after bowing to thank him again.

The clean diagnosis made me happy but not well. When I celebrated the good news with a smoke and a cup of tea, the pain crawled back instantly. Ignoring the jabs, I bravely smoked another cigarette, firmly believing the doctor's words. But the pain was sawing with blunt teeth now. I lay in bed puzzled and miserable for two more days before Hong, a clumsy caretaker himself, summoned enough courage to ask if he could be of any use. Nothing, I said. He stood silently by, wondering what to do for a sick roommate who was getting sicker.

The third day, a chubby and sincere female classmate named Peng giggled her way into my room and cooked me much needed rice porridge. Silently we sat looking at the simmering pot.

"It will make you feel better," she said.

"I hope so. Thanks."

"Don't thank me. It's a pleasure." She kept her eyes on her knees and fanned the steam from the pot.

I was moved.

"Must be hard being sick away from home," Peng said, her big eyes searching.

Tears rolled from my eyes.

"Sorry," she whispered.

"Thank you."

"Stop thanking me."

"How can I repay you?"

"Silly."

"Think of something."

"Dance with me at the New Year's Eve Ball."

"I will."

She was the only one in class who had offered to help. I felt even more touched that she had done so in such a silent manner. *Yes, girl, I'll dance with you till daybreak on that distant promised night.*

The porridge soothed my tummy but did not dispel the curse that had caused it all. The pain continued to appear like spring clouds, unexpectedly and sporadically.

It was with dull pain that I took the bus alone to another hospital to have my corn removed. The surgeon was a jaded city hotshot condemned to peeling my petty corn.

"Will it hurt?" I asked, lying down on the dirty table.

He shrugged. "It depends."

"On what?"

"On whether you take pain well."

"I don't."

"We'll find out, won't we?"

What kind of doctor was that? He tied my foot to the table and then injected yellowish fluid into my calf that made my toes numb. In he went, a bloody incision. I felt the knife slicing my toe. My foot jerked in protest.

"Keep it down," he shouted.

"I can't. It hurts."

"You won't feel a thing soon."

"But I do now." It hurt like hell.

He wrinkled his nose. "I've put in enough anesthesia for a cow." He continued scraping away at the corn.

"I'm not a cow!"

"I'm almost done."

I felt the knife digging deeper and deeper. I screamed in pain. He didn't care. He seemed driven to end the job quickly so that another injection wouldn't be necessary, a frugal Communist with a big knife.

When it had become almost intolerable, he gave my foot a slap and pronounced dryly, "Done." He walked out, leaving a nurse to clean and dress my throbbing toe.

"Will it still hurt when I go back?" I inquired.

"It depends," the nurse said.

"On what?"

"How you take pain."

"Not too well. Can I have some painkillers?"

"That also depends."

"On what?"

"I don't know. Go ask the doctor."

I stormed limpingly out. Same questions, same answers. Everyone thought, talked, and acted the same.

That night when I limped back to our campus, my foot had swollen up and I had no painkillers. The only thing available to moderate the pain in my foot was the dull pain in my stomach. Pain killing pain. It was perfect.

I stayed up all night, trying to stifle the waves of pain ripping from my toes to my thigh. Each step I took to the bathroom down the hall reminded me of the knife that malpracticing butcher had inserted in my toe. I wished someone could carry me back and forth until the pain and swelling were gone, but Hong was home for the weekend. Only the silent night accompanied me till the next morning, when Peng appeared again as silently as before and changed the dressing for me. The simplicity of her in her army uniform touched me. I couldn't think of any reason why she would help me. We hadn't talked that much before.

"Why are you helping me?" I finally asked.

"Because you are a kind person."

"That's it?"

"Yes." She smiled broadly, open and simple. "And I'm a good person too. Good people help each other."

"Who taught you that?"

"My dad, an army general."

"He must be a good man. I like your army uniform."

She opened up like a flower. "I can get you one if you like it that much."

"I surely do."

"It's a deal."

My illness died a sudden death one evening when a nosy Japanese major stuck his head into my dorm and inquired, "Did you just move your bowels in the toilet?" His glasses were all fogged up on his refined nose.

"Yes, what's wrong with it?" I had never liked the guy. He was a big snob from Shanghai and played the cello for our school orchestra.

"A very serious matter, I must say."

"Why?"

"I was right behind you, and I saw your black shit."

"It's none of your business."

"You Fujian fool. What have you been eating?"

"Nothing."

"Nothing black in color?"

"No, why would I eat anything black in color?"

"I'm just asking."

"Stop asking. In case you don't know, I'm having severe stomachaches, and I have very little patience for a nosy fellow like you."

"You have been having pain in your stomach?"

"Yes. Are you happy now?"

"You have internal bleeding," he said seriously.

"Rubbish."

"Rubbish? You don't want to listen to me, fine. Bye." He left, but not before saying, "You'll die soon if you don't take any medicine." Off he went.

His parting shot struck me like thunder. I got up and chased after the little man. "I'm sorry. Hey, could you please say it again?"

"You're bleeding to death. That's because you have an ulcer some-where."

"How the hell do you know? You aren't a doctor."

He stopped in the middle of the hallway and took off his glasses. Taking his time, he blew a puff of steam onto the lenses, then picked up the corner of his shirt and polished them carefully, looking this way and that, unsatisfied. A little speck stayed in the middle of the glass. He scratched it with his dainty cellist fingernail, and spat on it. When the deliberate ceremony was finally completed, he asked absentmindedly, "What was your question again?"

"Could you be so kind as to tell me how you came to know so much about internal bleeding?" I asked, humbly this time.

"Huh! When you have been sick long enough, you become a doctor yourself."

"I've heard that one before."

"Good. My first ulcer came at age fifteen when I lost my first cello competition in a citywide match, the second one when I lost my virginity to a woman who did not love me, and my third while studying for a college exam. Bloody stools and internal bleeding, you name it. I could have died many deaths, but no. I've got the magic medicine right under my pillow."

"And what is that?"

"Yunnan Bai Yiao." A white herbal powder from Yunnan Province in southern China.

"But that's supposed to cure a cut on a leg or an arm."

"It does the same thing inside."

"Are you sure?"

"That kind of tone is not going to get you anything here," he said angrily.

"I'm in pain, can't you see?"

"Okay, okay! Bad temper too. I'm gone."

"Thanks anyway."

"Yeah, yeah, yeah."

"By the way, where can I find the medicine?"

"Nowhere," he shouted back, his voice echoing in the dark hallway. "Unless you're a big-shot Commie leader."

I was elated and limped back to my bed. The pain was cut in half already, knowing there was a cure right here. I'd heard of the unspeakable voodoolike medicine that was extracted from a rare plant and could only be fetched by monkeys from a suicidal cliff. I'd seen it work as a child. A little pinch on a bleeding cut and the blood instantly clotted up. It left no traces and even fewer scars. My *Yunnan Bai Yiao,* you precious potion!

Where was I going to find some tonight before I died bleeding? Before I could finish the thought, pain attacked again. The roaring pain made me tremble with waves of dry heaves that left me leaning against the hallway wall and limping toward the smelly toilet. The place was dead, classmates having gone home for the weekend. I grabbed a slippery sink brim filled with leftover food, flies, and bugs, and puked and puked for a good five minutes. My head was buzzing with golden insects as I leaned over the sink regaining my composure. In the dark I saw the cellist standing by the door, one hand pinching his nose, the other holding a tiny bag of powder.

"Take it," he said. "Please."

"Really? How much is it?"

"The price is small, but it's worth a lot. Here, my gift to you."

"Are you sure?"

"I don't want to see you die, comrade. You're too young for that."

"Thank you, my friend. I'm sorry I was so rude to you."

"Yeah, yeah. The city versus country mentality. I understand."

"Good, but how do I take it?" I stood shaking against the door.

"Let me help you with that."

I opened my mouth, and my new doctor dusted the whole bag into it.

"Good man. Results guaranteed," he whispered.

I swallowed it dryly. The stuff tasted bitter with a little thread of sweetness to it. I thanked him again, and he gave me a curtsy to cheer me up. A dear friend was made then and there.

The pain subsided as he had predicted. I slept soundly till noon the next day. Had it not been for the knock on my door, I would have slept all the way through the night again, so weak and tired was I now that the pain was gone.

Peng and the cellist came in.

"Are you all right?" the cellist asked, looking really pale.

"Yeah, the pain is all gone." I smiled.

"Good, good." He sounded concerned, rubbing his hands.

"Da, this man could have killed you," Peng declared.

"Why?"

"He gave you way too much powder."

"Wait a second. Am I still in the dying zone?"

"No, don't worry. If you haven't yet, you won't." My cellist friend waved his hand like a fan, relieved. Some color had returned to his face. "You know, I did not sleep all night thinking about it."

"Don't worry, I was fine then and am now. You're a hero," I said. "Look, I'm smiling now."

"But you will still have a little lingering problem," Peng said expertly.

"What's that?"

"You'll not be able to move your bowels for a long time. All the stool has solidified by now."

"How do you know all that?"

"Because I grew up in Yunnan as an army kid. This stuff comes from there."

"What should I do now, you two?"

"I don't know," Peng answered.

"I don't know either." The cellist rubbed his hands again.

"That's great. Now the pain is gone but my intestines are cemented," I said. "What's going to happen next?"

"It will explode." The cellist nodded dryly.

"Fix it!" I said to him.

"I don't know how. That's why I asked her." He nudged Peng.

"I'll make you a very delicious soup with loads of lard in it," Peng suggested. "You'll feel diarrhea coming."

"Diarrhea?" I cringed.

"Unless you have some other options," Peng offered dryly.

I was surprised by Peng's assertiveness when it suited her.

"Make the soup, Dr. Peng. Make me the biggest waterfall ever," I joked.

So vegetable soup was cooked with half an inch of fat gleaming on the surface. Drinking the melted lard was worse than eating cow manure. The icky sensation crawled slowly down my throat, made a slippery plunge into my stomach, and swam in there briefly before sinking to the bottom. Within five short minutes, my whole digestive system began to grunt and rumble with angry gusto. The cellist was ready to help. "Hurry up." He lugged my right arm and dragged me toward the toilet.

"Take it easy. I won't go in my pants."

"Yuck!"

I won the race and was squatting above this windy manhole ready to let go of the torrential outburst when my friend advised, "See what color the shit is, okay?"

"You have to help me with it. I can't wait."

"All right. All right."

Without any effort at all, out shot a sword of angry crap. What a relief! What a release!

"What color is it?" I asked the poor fellow.

"Dark at the beginning and green at the end. You are cured. There's no more bleeding." He smiled, his glasses all fogged up. "God, it smells."

"You have really good eyes."

"I'm a cellist with a penchant for the raciest Paganini pieces. This little piece of shit is nothing." He wiped his nose.

Peng was happy to hear all that too. "You want another soup?" she teased.

"No, thanks. Hey, you guys would make a great couple."

"Us?" The cellist smiled, looking at Peng.

"Yin and yang. Powder and lard."

Peng studied the little man with fake interest. "You're too bony."

"And you're too meaty," the musician retorted.

Within days, I was eating again. My gigantic appetite came roaring back. But at any mention of melted lard, I still felt the urge to head for the nearest toilet. *Thank you, my sincere friend Peng, who was a shy bud waiting to bloom. And thank you, my deft cellist; you are not so deft a doctor. And Bo, my friend, for any loss in our lives, we all have to pay a certain price, if not in sorrow then in pain.*

Chapter Nineteen

During my sophomore year, Dad wrote me one day and told me that lots of changes had taken place at home. Brother Jin had received half a dozen decent proposals. The most flattering came from Ar Duang, the merchant, who had a beautiful granddaughter named Lan. A facial fortune-teller, Dad loved the good fortune written all over Lan's perfect face. She had a round face like a perfect moon to go with Jin's long face, and full hips that promised to breed fortune and posterity. Her earlobes hung heavily like a pair of round coins, the sign of a matriarch. Her nose tip drooped like a gallbladder hanging in reverse, which would help her man attain high office and maintain prosperity. He added that she did not have any of the womanly taboos such as a wide mouth that would eat her husband, sharp bony hips that sawed a family's fortune away, protruding eyes that would see her man's coffin young, or a mouthful of uneven teeth that guaranteed an early widowhood. Lan also had a nice state job along with a diploma from a two-year technical school, and was known to be a filial yet modern woman, the kind who cooked soft noodles for the toothless elderly, breast-fed her own cute cubs with her plump nipples, brought in the stream of a good state salary, and stood like a solid pillar supporting her man's success.

She was also a grateful friend's granddaughter. If anything went wrong in the marriage, her feisty granny would give her a fierce lecture behind closed doors, where all the wrinkles would be ironed out. Even better, Dad was counting on her to be the anchor to bring Jin home; his school would be much more likely to give him a job back home in Fujian if he was engaged to a local girl. That way Dad wouldn't lose another son to the city. He asked me for my opinion. I was flattered to be included in the poll for approval.

Dad also said that Huang might be getting married soon. She would then become a citizen of Han Jian, which was high up in the sky for a girl from muddy Yellow Stone. The only problem was that she would end up marrying out of order, before her elder sister Ke. But it was modern times now, he lamented. Nothing was the same anymore. Dad knew how to use modernity when appropriate. I could only chuckle at his wisdom of being supple like water.

In the end Dad suggested, in his imperative tone and stern prose, that I return home again for the winter holiday. He wanted me to take part in Jin's bridal choosing and help with Huang's wedding, which he promised would be quite a big deal, for the Lis had only one son to lavish their money on. But more importantly, he wrote, he and Mom desperately wanted me home for some good rest. They had been worried sick over my ulcer episode and would not allow me to spend the cold winter all alone and risk further ruining my health. He sealed all my possible arguments by wiring the train fare with the letter. I bought the cheapest seat available, near the compartment where the locomotive furnace burned hotly. Even though the train ride was long and slow, I arrived on time for the important day that the whole family had been anticipating.

The morning after my arrival, Dad donned his new Mao jacket. Rosy color painted his *Yin Tan*, the spot between his eyebrows. "Sparrows are noisily singing *hiu-ji-jiu*," Dad declared happily, descending the stairs to meet us, referring to another sure sign of good tidings.

This was the day we were meeting Ar Duang's granddaughter.

"And I have thanked our Buddha for the messengers already," Mom said, referring to birds known as *Xian Zhi,* prophets who worked part-time for the big Buddha. She clapped her hands and looked to the blue sky.

"Doesn't Mom look good with her red blouse and little rose flowers in her hair?" Dad said, praising Mom's special ornaments for the occasion. She had picked those little thorny red blooms right off the riverbank. A touch of red rose, a slice of a happy heart.

Mom fluttered shyly under Dad's praise.

"She does," I agreed.

"Children are to be seen and not heard." Mom patted my shoulder. "Go wash your head in the river and put on something new. Otherwise I won't let you see your future sister-in-law when she comes."

"Right away, Mom." In their eyes I would never grow up.

My three sisters giggled like sparrows, adding to the cheerfulness of the day. They fussed over Jin, trying to get him into the shape they deemed fit. They whispered lovingly their advice and admonitions.

By noon, there was still no sign of Ar Duang, that crusty-skinned, raspy-voiced chain-smoker who came to sit on "her" stool in the middle of our sitting room every morning while chatting about the men in her life, her husband who sold his fruits too cheap, and her son who still struggled with a limp. Dad was worried, but he kept a smiling face. Mom just looked worried, and wrinkles clouded up her otherwise happy face. She wasn't good at hiding things, especially bad things.

At two a deflated Ar Duang dragged her feet over to our house and told Dad, "Ar Lan is not coming."

"That we know, but why?" Dad asked.

"She's been crying all morning. Her father urged her to come. Her mom dressed her with the newest nylon blouse, a light green see-through thing. And I was on my knees begging her. She just would not come."

"Does she think Jin is too old for her?" Mom asked.

"No. She likes everything about him from what I told her." She paused. "That *ya tou*"—a phrase that meant silly girl—"is in love with another man."

"Is she?" Dad was shocked.

Our ears perked right up.

"It's not the first time I've heard of that little fling they had," Ar Duang said.

"You heard about it before?" Dad asked.

"Sure, loving and kissing." She swiped her hand dismissively.

"Why didn't you mention that before, so we didn't waste our time planning this whole thing?"

"It's not important that she loves another man," she said. "Love is like water, changeable. Another man is just another eggroll; sooner or later they taste the same. Marriage is a different thing. Jin is for her to marry, I told her. Love will follow. See how I love my husband, letting him do whatever he wants to do with his business while I just sit back and watch him prosper and grow?"

I chuckled at her declaration of love for her husband. He had to be the most henpecked man in town, smothered mute by her choking love.

"I'm sorry to have caused any pain to her," Dad said.

"Don't say that. I'm here to say that she is still thinking about your son's proposal. Give her some time, and I'll work magic around her."

"How do you plan to do that?"

"Well, Ar Lan did not exactly say she would not marry your son. She only said that she would still love that other man. So I figure I'll take care of that by finding the man another girl, and the puzzle is solved." She smiled.

"She said she would still marry my son? Why is that?" Dad asked.

"Parental order."

"It is very kind of you to offer that, but we can't accept it. We don't do it that way." Mom inserted her head between Dad and Ar Duang.

"It is being done everywhere."

"They have to love each other," Mom insisted.

"What is love anyway?"

"It counts for something in our household," Dad agreed.

"You are too modern for your own good. You don't take marriage fees for your daughters, giving them all away free. Why are you so crazy?"

"Because we don't own them," Dad said.

"Of course you do. You went through hell to raise them. I was here, remember? And you, young man"—she pointed at me—"better take good care of your dad here, do you hear me?"

Dad and Ar Duang spent the next half hour apologizing to each other. In Yellow Stone there was a face-saving aspect to everything. Ar Duang thought she had insulted us with that little untold detail, so the next day she came back with a huge basket of tiny sweet oranges to mend the fence.

Mom kept telling her that we were flattered by her consideration, and that nothing was made, so nothing was broken.

Jin commented lightheartedly to Dad, "I guess next time we shouldn't start with the facial fortune-telling."

"And how should I start the search for your bride then?"

"Check the availability."

"Everything is available, you just have to have the heart for it. You don't seem too eager to find a mate. We're the ones doing the worrying. If you could just open your mind and your mouth—"

"And your heart," Mom jumped in.

"Yes, your heart, you'll find girls that way," Dad added.

"Okay, I will try."

Poor Jin, so much pressure to find love. In Yellow Stone, if you did not get married by your mid-twenties, you were called "the bachelor," the single stick whom all mothers of suitable girls would sniff around suspiciously for imperfection. As you aged into the graying thirties, the sniffing stopped. If you were lucky, you got some poking but only by grumpy mothers or dying aunts of some sorry-looking spinsters.

"How do you plan to try?" Mom zeroed in.

"I'll graduate first, then find one by myself in two years wherever I get assigned to a job," Jin declared.

"Sounds good. Your fortune dictates that you'll be wedded within the next couple of years," Dad added thoughtfully.

"I don't believe this fortune-telling thing, Dad," Jin said.

"I'm telling you that it works."

"So why didn't this Ar Duang thing work out?" Jin asked.

"Because she is not meant for you," Dad said authoritatively.

"Besides, I got pricked this morning by a thorn," Mom added.

Somehow Mom was always more convincing.

The Li family of Han Jian had been courting Huang ever since matchmaker Ar Ling's visit. At first Mrs. Li was quite troubled by the unyielding fact that Mom and Dad would not accept any marriage fees. They only wanted the two young people to meet first and get to know each other. A refreshing idea, but what for? A five-thousand-yuan fee was a lottery won. No father could resist that sum. In most cases it would be used immediately to pay for a son's bride. Neighbors were bubbling with envy for Dad. Two beautiful, ripened daughters could bring in so much dough he wouldn't have to work at all. And two sons who had college degrees could very well be matched up with any girl free of charge. Dad, in the eyes of Yellow Stoners, was already a man wealthy beyond imagination.

The only time that any Yellow Stone father had given his daughter away free was when one shrimp-faced fellow named Mon Siu let his retarded daughter, Ar Ha, marry a decent-looking cripple. She was treated so badly that she escaped twice from her husband. Her third year there, she was brutally raped, stabbed, and left to die in a muddy ditch. In the people's hearts, Ar Ha came to stand for the simple truth that it was sometimes wiser to have the groom pay for his bride so that he would cherish her more.

Mrs. Li had spent months snooping around, looking and talking to neighbors and the townspeople in a thorough investigation as to why in the world my father would not ask a single fen for his perfect daughter. Maybe there was something wrong with her? When Mrs. Li was eventually convinced there was no blemish, she couldn't wait to arrange the wedding. Coincidentally, the two young people had by now fallen madly in love with each other. Mrs. Li could only praise Dad for his foresight and modernity.

But the wheel of modern times only rolled so far. One could not pick just any day for a wedding. It had to come from above, from *Yue Lao,* the moon goddess. It was incumbent upon the mothers of brides and grooms to take a sacred trip to Southern Shaolin Temple to consult a monk. Even the date to make the journey had to be prayed for and bestowed upon one. Mom's way was picking a random number from her precious *Shen Shu,* a well-thumbed book of 384 poems from which you had to decipher hidden meanings from the archaic writing. Mrs. Li, however, had talked to her secret Buddha in her own manner. Different methods resulted in disagrements over dates and times. The Lis liked odd days—they stuck out, while the Chens preferred even days because they were even. After a bit of haggling, the two pious souls agreed on an odd day, but Mom insisted that it should be preceded by a full moon, an evenly round moon.

It turned out to be a bright and breezy morning when Mom smilingly walked midway to meet Mrs. Li. It always had to be midway, the Chinese way. The two women dressed in their happiest best, Mom in red, still proudly married with a husband, and Li in light blue, a symbol of heroic widowhood, with a dot of red rose on her head. They climbed Hu Gong's dangling rock stairs and nagged the monk for a heavenly date. A fee had to be charged before the good monk would pray for that inspired time. He studied the marrying couple's names and birth signs. Some names had the elements of wood, others water. A dragon avoided the water, and a forest avoided the fire. It got trickier when a Li, meaning "plum" in Chinese, was to marry a Chen, which meant "vintage," instead of a Chen marrying a Li. A vintage plum was good, but a plum getting old was a plum getting rotten. So the monk hit his shaven head hard and wrinkled his nose, asking for more money to make this little technicality disappear. He shook a bamboo tube containing all the thirty-one days in a month written on thick bamboo sticks, gave it a nice hop, and out jumped the blessed stick. All this meditation and heavenly offering came down to a toss of some slippery bamboo sticks. He crawled to where the stick had landed and read in a pious tone the printed date. It was after the New Year. Mom said it was no good because her sons would be gone back to campus then. The monk had to toss again. Out came another heavenly date. This time Mrs. Li had a conflict. The monk crawled again. On the fifth try, everyone was happy.

On her wedding date, Huang looked beautiful. I could hardly believe my eyes. She had always been a skinny, sickly little kid sister. Now she stood impressively tall, slender, and vibrant. Her eyes were bigger than those of most girls in town, a legacy from Mom, and the high, refined cheekbones came from my matriarchal paternal grandma. My four friends had long been talking about Huang in admiring tones that I knew would have been totally lewd had it been someone else. But to be the object of their admiration was a badge of honor all by itself. I had always been proud of her.

In addition to all the wedding preparation, Huang also had to wrap up her salon. The store was packed now that the town's hottest hairdresser was leaving. Everyone wanted a cut before she closed the doors. There was lingering love and an outpouring of affection from the young girls. Some of them cried, and others hugged her.

"Are you feeling bad closing the store?" I asked her.

"I had to. I don't think it's proper to stay around after the wedding."

"That's feudal crap," I said.

She was silent.

Mom was busy with a thousand things as always. But Dad was sitting alone, brooding. A pot of hot tea sat by him getting cold. He looked a little lost, and I knew why.

"This place will be very quiet when she is gone," I said, sitting beside him and pouring myself a cup of tea.

Dad nodded. "Yes, it will. *Nan hun, nu jia.*" Boys married in, girls married out.

"You missing her already?"

"Just a bit, seeing her grown from this little girl to today." Dad was full of nostalgia. "But she has to go, and I'm happy for her." Tears welled up.

"You're going to be lonely here with Si and Huang gone, and Ke on the road with her job all day long."

"This house will be serene. I'll be able to sleep till noon." Dad was not as emotional as Mom, but letting go of his favorite little girl wasn't easy. He was choking up.

"Why couldn't she work here after her wedding?" I asked.

"Because it's the tradition here. A married daughter never stays back."

"What's wrong with it?"

"It shows her parents' unwillingness to let her go or that our in-laws are beneath us."

"But this is the eighties. Come on, Dad. The Lis, in the modern city of Han Jian, might like the idea of having a successful hairdresser in the family. After all, it's only a half-hour bus ride from here. She can come in on the first bus and go home on the last of the day."

Dad tilted his head, one hand cradling his square chin, thinking. "You think that might work?"

"You want me to talk to Huang?" Dad never liked to be seen as the one begging.

He nodded thoughtfully.

I'd never seen Dad looking so old and vulnerable before. I could not imagine what he had suffered, seeing both of his sons off to remote cities last year. Now we were just migrating geese who flew down only to rest our feet.

I had a teary talk with Huang. She cried, thanking Dad for his generosity. We agreed that it would be something for her to explore with her new husband, and that it would not be a point to make an argument about.

Her wedding day was hollowing. I had always enjoyed other wedding days, even that of our neighbor's rotten son. People were nicer, and there was always laughter. But to be on the side giving away the bride felt different. There was a feeling of loss, of letting go of someone for good.

Mom, though busy, cried all day. Dad wore a forced smile as he received well-wishers from the town. Huang looked like a bride; her rosy cheeks were two shy blooms. The neighborhood kids and her fans had long climbed tall trees and dangled from the old pagoda at the head of the village, craning for sight of the bridegroom's party that was coming from Han Jian. Jin was drinking and smoking with his friends who came by for the occasion. I had also invited my four friends, but they would not be there till dark. By noon, our house was crowded with all the villagers there to see Huang off. People laughed and talked, sucking on the wedding candies and smoking happy cigarettes. Tea was poured and longevity noodles twirled. Close relatives gave gifts of money, mosquito nets, red fabrics, and pillowcases. Neighbors gave bags of peanuts or eggs. In return, they would be invited back to attend a banquet given in honor of the groom the following day.

Amid all this came the tortoise, Ar Ling. Mom was alarmed by her appearance. By now she should have been out of the picture. The only reason for her to be there was to collect unpaid agency fees. She shuffled through the crowd with her mean elbows, picked a little stool in the middle of the living room, and sat down. By the look on her face, Dad knew what she wanted. The bonus, a thing that only a happily served client would pay. She didn't need to open her mouth; all she did was curl her crooked fingers at Dad. When he quickly stuffed a thick wad of cash into her blouse pocket, she smiled for the first time and started to waddle away.

"Would you please stay for noodles?" Dad asked.

"Too busy for that." Off she went.

"Why did you have to pay her?" I asked.

"She would have followed the bridal party to Han Jian if she was not paid."

"Blackmail," I muttered.

"But I am happy that she did find Huang a good family."

Around three, a thin girl ran breathlessly to our door announcing the appearance of four brand-new bicycles coming this way. It was the tradition that the groom's family send their best friends to pick up the bride with their shiny bikes. The bikes had to be brand-new Phoenixes, decorated with red ribbons. Borrow them, rent them, or steal them, whatever the groom needed to do. The backseats had to be especially long and matted so the bride could sit comfortably. There was always a married aunt who came with the bikers as a chaperone.

When they arrived at our door, firecrackers burned noisily and rained

in a flourish on the ground. Hungry hens and roosters thought the dancing crackers were some sort of dancing food and chased them till they
exploded in their eyes, burned their mouths, and sent them running off,
shrieking and flying. Kids fought to stamp out unexploded crackers so they
could claim them as their own and burn them later. But the smoky ones
weren't really bad ones. They soon exploded inside the kids' pants, shooting them off with their hands covering their crotches.

Dressed in a burning red blouse, Huang tearfully climbed up onto the
backseat of a bike. Dad stood far in the background with Mom leaning
against his shoulder, surrounded by my sisters. It was a quiet good-bye, but
silently emotional. We watched in the fading sound of firecrackers as her
redness disappeared into the distant green fields.

Dad thought that I, his little boat, was drifting away slowly in the changing tides of time. Only a couple of years back, a college degree with a following government job would have been heavenly. Now that everyone was
going into business, any government job prospect with a limited fixed
income looked pale in comparison. A farmer with a garden of onions
could fare better.

Dad was concerned when I asked him, "What should I do?"

"Nothing. Stick to what you are doing. You're meant for great things,
not just good things. Great things, Da."

"How do you know that?"

"Look at your face. Your ears stand high, which means your name will
be known all over the land. Your brows are thick and dark; you will command authority. And your mouth is big, which for a boy is good because
it will eat the fanciest foods and most exotic delicacies that the earth has
to offer. And your nose, the lion's nose, means a lot of wealth."

"Dad, you have been telling me this since I was three years old."

"But it is true. So far, so very good. And today I want you to have your
fortune told by the most famous of them all, Old Mei, the blind man, so
that you don't feel insecure about your future."

"Why today?"

"It's the twenty-fifth on our lunar calendar, the best for such a thing
because the old man has his communication with the heavens then," Dad
whispered.

Old Mei's house was hidden in the deep pocket of a narrow lane. Roosters jumped with fright, announcing our arrival. The blind man blinked urgently as he greeted us with his repetitive talk. "Good morning, good morning. What a blessed day! What a blessed day!" Everything he said, he said twice. He used his hand constantly to touch the bed upon which he sat.

"I have before you my younger son," Dad said sincerely.

Old Mei smiled nervously. "I sensed his presence."

"How?" I asked curiously.

"The roosters usually don't make that much noise," Old Mei said calmly. "Now, rule number one: Don't tell me anything that I don't ask you," he said. "And rule number two: The result of my reading doesn't depend on the amount of money you pay. A widow, a while ago, kept shuffling money into my hands thinking that more money would buy her son a better fortune. The answer was no, I read as I was told. It is meticulous calculation, not speculation."

Dad told him the date and time of my birth. He frowned. His mouth mumbled strings of gibberish while his hands played with dice. We sat there quietly so as not to break his concentration.

He started with my childhood. Terrible! According to my chart, I had killed my grandpa. I cringed at that accusation. Then I killed my grandma. I was on the verge of crying. But that was not enough. I had to suffer a very difficult childhood, an exile—he used a classic literary term. I shuddered at the accuracy. Dad looked at me and nodded with approval. My third grade and the whole miserable elementary school years had been an exile, a very painful one.

When he came to the age of sixteen, he sat back and threw open his arms. "This child is on a higher level. If his face is round, he should be a young general, but if he has a long face, then a college man. Preferably a liberal arts major."

"Why?" Dad asked.

"Let me feel your hands," the blind man demanded.

I stretched them out, and he caressed them gently, smiling. "Soft like cotton. This boy will write for an emperor and be generously compensated so that he will retire very wealthy."

"Old Mei," my dad exclaimed excitedly, "you have been right so far. Very right."

"He is in college?" Old Mei smiled.

"One of the best colleges, studying English."

The old man's face lit up. Even his unseeing fish-eyes rolled in excitement. "English! What an achievement. May I ask who his grandfather was?"

"Su Chan Chen," Dad replied.

"A scholarly landowner." The old man knew my grandpa. "What a fine man he was. So this boy's great-grandfather had to be the one and only Yu Zhang Chen who was awarded by the last emperor the title of *Jin Shi,*" a title given to the fourth highest scorer on the national exam. "Am I right or not?" Old Mei asked expectantly.

"You are absolutely right," Dad said.

Instantly the old man stood up and came over to shake my hand again, trembling. "You know, son, your fate doesn't totally depend on you but a great deal on your ancestors. If they were virtuous, as yours were, you are blessed already. In fact, that is the seal of your fate." Then he paused and said, "I must brew some tea for you, my special guests."

"Special?"

"Yes, your great-grandpa saved my grandpa. You see, one day my grandpa, a fisherman, was found clinging to a fishing net when your great grandpa's official ship cruised by. The Honorable Governor ordered his boat to stop and saved my grandpa. Today I'm the bearer of that grace. I thank you." The old man knelt down before us. I didn't know what to do. Dad hurriedly helped him up.

"But fate still is fate. Your great-grandfather had to be assassinated by a feuding thief. We, the Meis, still mourn that tragedy even today."

"Thank you." Dad was moved.

Great-grandpa's assassination had been a dark curse on our family that we didn't talk about. The pain still lingered from a hundred years before.

"Now, happy thoughts." Old Mei sat back down and resumed his Buddha pose, counting his dice and whispering again. "As I go along, I see a third tier of most powerful position descending on this boy."

"Well." Dad looked at me, lifting his brows high.

"What is this third tier?" I was curious now.

"Well, the first tier is the emperor; the second, the *Chai Xiang,* the prime minister; the third tier are the ministers, understand?"

"I will be the third most powerful person of a nation?" I asked incredulously.

"Yes, you will if you stick to your goal and work hard," Old Mei said.

"I still have to work hard?"

"*Only* if you work hard," the fortune-teller emphasized.

"How about his lifeline?" Dad asked.

"He will live to his late eighties, possibly nineties," the old man said, after some counting on his fingers and much blinking.

Dad was smiling as he pulled out a big ten-yuan note and pushed it into his hand.

"No, I can't take it," the old man exclaimed.

"Yes, you must."

"No."

"Yes."

"In that case, you take a rooster with you," the old man begged. "I wish to honor your great-grandpa."

"Then who is going to report your customers' arrival?" I asked.

"Well put, Da." The old man smiled.

"Good-bye." Dad bowed.

"Work hard, Da. It is within you," was Old Mei's last advice.

Chapter Twenty

In my third year of college, everything was changing and everyone was hurrying. School wasn't the same anymore. There was guilt in doing exactly what we were supposed to be doing, studying. The new glory was in carving out your little destiny, any destiny beyond the ivy-crawled wall to connect yourself with the emerging money-driven society. Half the senior class were off campus acting as tour guides and getting paid for it under the loosely defined category of PI, "practical internship." They came back with fluffy goosedown jackets, colorful sweatshirts, and lots of foreign gadgets. Classes seemed such a bore and PI opportunities outside, the greatest adventure.

I visited the dean to see if he had any PI gigs up his sleeve to dole out. He was killing time picking his nose and rolling the snot into little balls, then dropping them off slowly in the rays of the afternoon sun. Shaking hands with him would be a mistake, but I had to. He wasn't too helpful. In fact, he was borderline spiteful about it. He first smirked, then laughed about my naïveté in coming to him for any juicy PI opportunity.

"You go find your own PI, and I'll grant you the approvals," he said.

"Where do I start?"

"The ministries where your English is needed. Anywhere but here."

I dashed off to the nearest toilet to clean my hands. Passing his secretary, I heard her say sardonically, "If you do find any gigs, don't forget to bring us some goodies."

I made a mental note not to forget.

On weekdays after school, I pedaled along Chang An Boulevard on a borrowed bike to see if anyone would hire me. I started with the red-pillared Tourism Bureau. A kind clerk confirmed the rumor that there was a shortage of English-speaking guides, but the assignments were usually given to schools, and the cadres there made the decisions.

The second day I headed over to the Foreign Affairs Ministry. It was a fortress of power as evidenced by the presence of statuelike guards with rifles over their shoulders. The act of dismounting my bike caused them to look my way with extreme caution, fingers on their rifles tapping uneasily near the triggers. It didn't seem like a place to drop by for a friendly chat. The third day I visited the Foreign Trade Ministry, which hid behind iron grille doors. The only things visible there were the gleaming ribs of shiny Red Flag limousines, the official vehicles of the government. Nothing could penetrate that iron door, including myself. I couldn't even get my shadow in sideways. The guard dogs chased me off with menacing barks, and I flew back to campus on my squeaking bike into a nasty head wind. I had fallen for an old Communist trick and become a Ping-Pong ball of ignorance, kicked around town.

Hong, my roommate, enlightened me that night. I had started out wrong beginning with the dean's visit.

"That far back? How should I have done it?" I asked.

"You've got to give goodies to him first, then follow that with a big promise of more gifts to come."

"Well, the greedy freak. I thought it was just PI."

"You idiot! Just think for a second. That dean of ours is a Russian major, which is no use at all in getting him out of this country. Who wants to go to Russia? He won't have any foreign goods coming his way at all, while others, English or French teachers, even Spanish teachers, have the means to modernize their homes and liberate their wallets. He is bitter and gets jealous if you do too well. That's why he sent you for a spin in the city, letting you make a fool out of yourself."

"Shit."

"Shit is right. You have to have connections, my friend."

"The backdoor policy, I hate that," I said.

"Why?"

"Because I don't know anyone in the city."

"Well, good luck then." He went off to sleep.

I wrote a long letter full of despair and disbelief to my brother, who of late had become my soul mate in understanding and sharing thoughts that were too scary to be known by parents: young thoughts, naive angst, rebellious inclinations, and even some prodemocratic ideas.

In mid-May, in his fluid writing, he wrote back telling me to contact a second cousin of his best friend's temporary girlfriend. The man, he said, worked for the Sports Ministry, and he might give me a summer job. I jumped for joy. Finally I had found a crack in this impenetrable monster of our government machinery.

So one day in July 1982, clutching my brother's letter, I boarded a sweaty bus and headed for the Sports Ministry. I was hoping for a brief meeting with this hotshot executive, who would at most take my name and tell me to wait for his call, at worst toss me out with my crummy letter. The closer I got to the building, the more my knees jerked. Why should this man of power see me at all? The link was so tenuous. And what did temporary girlfriend mean anyway? How temporary?

I was surprised to find the man a smiling and kind Buddha. He confessed to having heard of me through the same ridiculous web of relationships.

"Sit down, young man," he said.

"Thank you." I chose the corner of a large seat and sat down noiselessly.

"You won't believe it, but we have a big job coming right up, and I think you could be of help to us." He smiled.

"Well." I stood up, with the sticking sound of my wet ass tearing away from the damp leather, and bowed in gratitude.

"Sit again." He gestured. "In front of the foreigners you should maintain your upright posture and dignified poise."

"Oh, I'm sorry." I straightened right up.

"Even though we Chinese are used to bending and bowing and all that, you should refrain from that and act more like an American."

"How do you do that?"

"I don't have time to teach you now because they are on their way here this afternoon."

"Who are?"

"The American NBA China tour is arriving at four P.M. at Beijing International Airport. Is that a problem?"

"No problem, of course." I tugged at my shorts uncomfortably.

"Oh, that. You'll be wearing a uniform."

"I will?"

"Yes. You are now officially a government interpreter, and we take care of you."

"Thank you, sir. I don't know what to say."

"How about asking me what this NBA thing is all about?" He smiled.

"Oh, what is it?" I scratched my head.

"The National Basketball Association, the finest hoopsters in this world. Have you ever heard of American professional players?"

"No."

"You will soon. You're very lucky to be calling on me today." He waved a stash of résumés in his hand. "I got some of the finest students from all over the city wanting summer jobs, but I picked you."

"I'm flattered."

"So am I."

"You, why?" I asked.

"Because your brother's best friend is the son of a famous Long Marcher who is now the vice mayor of Tienjing."

"So he is a man of power."

"He *is* the power there. And I hope the son, that handsome devil of a college kid, will remove the word *temporary* from my favorite niece that he is supposed to be dating. You know what I mean?"

"I'll write a glowing letter to the very boy to change the title soon. I'm sure the romance will blossom."

We shook hands, his chunky paw nearly crushing my twigs.

"Oh, one more thing," he said. "The Uniform Department is over there down the hallway. The lady there will measure you up."

"I can't thank you enough, sir." I kept bowing and nodding.

He shook his head, smiling. "Stop that. Hurry up."

The uniform lady sized me up with a sneer on her drooping face. A smoke roll dangled from her parched lips and gave out a thin thread of blue smoke that bothered her eyes, making them blink miserably.

"Size two!" She threw me a gray polyester four-pocket jacket with short sleeves. Though clumsy-looking, it was a regular hide for any government agent. With a pair of sunglasses, I would have looked like the despised public security officers. I tried it on. The jacket hung near my knees. "Too big," I announced.

"Any smaller I have to go to the women's section."

"I was born skinny. I can't help it."

"Young man, it's a compliment. Look at your snugly behind." She smiled without losing her cigarette and threw me another, half a size smaller.

I tried that on and liked it. She had me walk around before her a few times, tugging here and there. I was out of her office like a plucked rooster in no time.

Crouched in the minibus with the Sports Ministry insignia, I was on my way to my first official function as a glorious interpreter. It had always been my dream that one day I would put my slippery tongue to use, rubbing shoulders with dignitaries. I would be considered powerful as well, the same way a dog would be by virtue of his master's vitae. But that thought did not leave any dent of insult or dismay on me. I was sniffingly gleeful. Only moments ago I was that pig sweating among other pigs, riding the tired and stinking bus that contained all the smells of the summer (and I don't mean the flowery fragrance), heading for a destination that would only sentence me to another meaningless place among this shrubby throng. Now I was among the able and the useful and the air-conditioned.

Our interpreting team of five was loaded into the minibus, which zigzagged among the dusty traffic and throbbed with lulled anticipation. Mr. Huang was quiet, sitting in a corner, playing with a cigarette. He was to be the chief mouthpiece who handled opening speeches, closing ceremonies, meaty banquets, and brewing cocktails in between. Occasionally he rubbed his throat like a boxer warming up in the ring. His Adam's apple lolled absentmindedly, and what an apple he had there. No wonder he was nicknamed the "Golden Bell" of the ministry. His shaved head reminded me of Yellow Stone's ancient bell that rang in silent sunsets.

Two young ladies—one in the twilight of her twenties, the other in the dawn of her thirties—sat together like a pair of chopsticks, gossiping like two squirrels nibbling at discarded nuts with mouths together and eyes everywhere. From bits and crumbs of their noisy feast, I gathered they were expecting lots of free giveaways. The mischievous lights dancing in their eyes when they glanced my way informed me of a less than rave review of my ill-fitting uniform, among other things. I couldn't agree with them more. It made me look like a young rooster just learning how to crow, stretching everywhere trying to make squeaky sounds.

A young bespectacled man, Mr. Li, was a borrowed barrow from the Foreign Affairs Ministry. He looked every ounce a cultural attaché: folders in hands, pens lining pocket. He adjusted his glasses every few seconds to emphasize his polite and apologetic manners. Mr. Li looked reasonably relaxed, stretching his legs a little beyond his legroom under the seat before him. I greeted him with a bowing head, and he returned the favor with the diplomacy of his smile. He was not talking, and it all had to do with the sixth member among us, a high-ranking ministry official by the name of Gao. One could always count on having a political figure in every bowl of soup. It was like the requisite slosh of soy sauce we relished in every Chinese dish. Mr. Gao was not a fat toss but a slender dash. He was thin and straight like a pencil. He sat in the only seat facing us five with his bony arms intertwined like twin snakes over his sunken chest, snugly and coldly hugging himself. His legs miraculously and impossibly crossed twice, his boneless right foot somehow managing to loop around his left calf like a supple rope—a tangle of a man. His speech only confirmed his circularity.

"The NBA China tour is a resounding victory for our battle in the international sports arena," Mr. Gao said, tapping his pencil at the ridge of the clipboard in his hand. "The American club ballplayers are the tools of capitalism. They are the victims of a profit-driven society gone hopelessly under. They are suppressed by the ruling class of capitalists and have to labor like slaves in order to entertain the bourgeois leisurism. . . ." He went on and on like the pine trees lining the highway to the airport.

I lost my thoughts to the green corn fields outside and wondered when *these* poor souls would be finally freed. *Say it, Mr. Gao, tell us that you too will enjoy the events. It's perfectly okay.* But he would not, because it was his duty to be that thready dark cloud that could barely block the sun. To prove his point again, I heard him ending the speech with usual extreme caution.

". . . and never take gifts from them, and no personal friendships are to be developed. Prevent any attempt by street people to reach our guests. If anything goes wrong, a seriously negative report will be at the desk of your leader preceding your return. This is a test of your loyalty, conviction, and reliability." Gao then swiveled his seat to face the road, coiling up his limbs as before. "Now Mr. Huang will give you the details of the mission."

Huang, the monkish lead man, was smiling, amused by the speech. His being amused amused me. There was an incorruptible quality to the man. That amazed me too. Slowly he opened his mouth and in a few sentences tore Gao's logic apart. "NBA basketball players are a group of superstars in a rich America. They're well paid, and some are very spoiled professionals who are highly regarded in that society. I say that not to contradict our political leader, Mr. Gao, but as a piece of candid advice. They expect nothing less than the utmost respect, and some might even desire worship." He paused because he heard Gao tapping his pencil, which he disregarded and continued. "They are used to being chased by the media and groupies because people regard them as heroes."

I sensed the pale, cold wind emanating from Gao five feet away. The coiled man was not a happy man. He cleared his throat but did not stop Huang.

"They enjoy high social status—"

Gao coughed loudly this time, making his warning scratchily audible.

Huang peddled away to another subject. "Okay, the tour group is two hundred people strong. Two players have been chosen from each of twenty-three professional teams. Others include wives, girlfriends, trainers, doctors, lawyers, and staff. This is your assignment: I will take charge of the main events, and all of you are to fill in the gaps. There will be confusion at the beginning when they crowd through the arrival gate, but that is inevitable—"

"The easiest way to keep the crowd from getting out of control is to keep the Chinese away from them," Gao jumped in.

"Mr. Gao is always a brilliant guerrilla war strategist. But if you ask me, that job belongs to the People's Public Security officers. Now back to our jobs. Rule of thumb, speak American English as much as you can. Young fellow, you." He pointed at me, the new boy. "Americans will laugh at your tight-lipped, half-baked British accent. Please drop that 'pardon me' stuff. Just say 'excuse me,' okay?" He went on to read off a list of club names. They sounded really funny to me. Lakers. Supersonics. Sixers. Knickerbockers. Heat and Jazz.

This was going to be great. I loved basketball and could dribble pretty nimbly along the rice fields and shoot some pretty mean hoops in our dirt basketball courts. Dirt or no dirt, I counted myself a hoopster and could recall a thing or two about the rules and regulations on the court. I mentally went over all the basketball words that I could think of—*dribble, pass, score, assist*—and congratulated myself on knowing *slam dunk* because I had been told of such a miracle by some American friends in school. When I ran out of that list, we were almost there, and Huang was ending his reading out loud of all the translated names of the players: Lanier, Mix, Robertson, Jabbar. My mind kept spinning the wheel of the "Yesterday I was out there, today I am in here" melody. The air-conditioned state of mind was humming. I was as excited and happy as a monkey about to pee. All the spoken words became a part of my blurred happiness.

This was my first time at the international airport. Its fumes could be smelled miles away. The jets zoomed in and out like a summer night's mosquito attack. The Beijing police were at hand as Huang had expected, doing their usual good job keeping the curious people away, slamming their disobedient toes when necessary. No one knew what was happening. No one, of course, was ever notified of anything.

In the waiting hall, we interpreters lined up like a leaky defense, six of us to tackle an offense of two hundred. Huang rubbed his hands, taking his shades off in anticipation, while chatting excitedly with Gao, the official greeter. I felt any translator's fear of suddenly losing his memory, of his tongue tying in the tangle of his emotional coil.

Then the gate opened, and what I saw left my jaw hanging for the next few long seconds. The fairy-tale giants that I could never have imagined appeared slowly, one by one, through the narrow shortness of the gate. Suddenly the airport looked small, and these men looked like walking columns supporting the lowering roof of the domed and possibly doomed waiting hall.

Mostly black—shining black—our honored guests lumbered along with the calculated nimble slowness of giants. Their heads rose above the onlookers like those of giraffes on an African safari, mindlessly watching the sky but not the pathetically startled Chinese afoot. Many of them hovered an average two to three heads above me, making my neck strain for recognition that was as hard in coming as the rare sunlight penetrating the thicket of the rain forest. I felt like a mushroom in a forest of ancient timber. Worse, a shouting ant climbing the mount of their toe callus. Where they began I ended. My sovereignty as a man remained forever shadowed.

After seeing my badge, a giant leaned over to talk to me, seeing me as a man of some use. "Hello, are you an interpreter?" he asked in a thundering voice. My ears rumbled with alarming vibrations but duty called. I stood up to my highest potential on my stubby toes but still barely reached the man's craning neck.

"Yes, I am, and welcome to China." A miniature welcome.

"Thank you." He looked around and beyond, way beyond. A flicker of puzzlement crossed his bronzed, heroic face. "Where are the media?"

"What media?" I asked in a small man's shouting tone.

"The usual press—newspapers, TV, radio." He gave a big shrug, and two mountains of massive muscle moved up and down. His long vines of sinuous hands dangled almost to his knees.

"Oh, we didn't bring them." I shrugged back, trying to be American.

"Do people know who we are?" He seemed a little upset. The *p* in *people* caused his spittle to rain all over me like a midday tropical shower. I blinked till the clouds passed and said, "Yes, American basketball players."

"No, no. NBA basketball players, the best in the world," came the thundering whisper, a lulling anger preceding the storm.

Everything about the man was magnified through the binocular slits of my eyes. "I'm sorry. This is a governmental affair that has nothing to do with the people," I explained.

"But we want to meet the people. They are our fans." He swiped his big hand before his face, leaving a gust of wind behind, and walked away with that robotic mechanical smoothness.

While the players slowly boarded our buses, a large audience began to gather around them with hanging jaws and enlarged eyes. It was like an episode from *Gulliver's Travels*. The giants had landed on small man land. The players were laughing and chewing gum, happy now that more people were finally looking at them. Kids hid behind their fathers. Some braver ones climbed up their dad's necks so they could get a better view of these tall men with their tall wives.

Hundreds of pieces of huge luggage in solid aluminum trunks were dragged slowly through the congested gate. Just as the last tall tree moved through, a group of really short Japanese farmers waddled through the gate. At the maximum height of four to five feet, they carried toylike little luggage and looked dazzled and lost among the watching crowd. They bowed passing us, and we bowed back in welcome. Courtesy was so much easier when one did not have to climb a ladder to say a tall hello.

I trailed behind those long shadows in the afternoon sun and climbed to my seat as the guide for my busload of guests. I forced myself to shake off this daunting reality of me the shrimp talking to a school of tired whales. Otherwise the job would be impossible.

I planted myself in the little pullout seat in the front of the air-conditioned bus. A microphone fell, dangling near my face. Behind me were my big guests with their loving and beautiful wives (I presumed). Under the bus's belly, aluminum trunks weighed heavily, making the tires grind and grump fiercely along the cement route to Beijing Hotel near Tiananmen Square. The ride would take a while. The stage was set, and I cleared my tangled vocal cords even as my back crawled with worms of fear—fear of opening my mouth, fear of making any sound.

With eyes closed, out came the monologue of my Beijing. The guests listened to my teetering chatter as their heads and shoulders jerked in uniform discord on the bouncing bus. Some had dozed off, others looked woodenly out the windows, where their mirrored faces merged with the face of this strange land. There was an unnerving quietness looming behind me where laughter would surely explode any moment at any mistake I made. But none was forthcoming. The cross-Pacific trip had blunted even the most curious soul. I was just another oddity being choked down by their filled minds.

A long arm reached over and tapped on my shoulder. "Can you please tear away some seats so that we can stretch our knees?"

I turned to investigate the situation. Most of the players had hung their long limbs all over the seat backs. I promised them that I would report the situation to our political leader. They laughed and high-fived.

When we arrived at the hotel, I immediately took Mr. Gao aside and told him about the legroom problem. He scratched his head helplessly. But beyond the seat problem, Mr. Huang thought of something else and called the manager of the hotel, demanding a meeting. The manager, a short-legged man, fat in every way, wasn't happy to be called for such a trivial matter. "What can I do? Our clients don't usually have such long legs. We don't have extra-long beds waiting in storage for giants to show up."

"But legs are a political problem that could explode into a diplomatic impasse," Huang said, tongue in cheek. "Do you want the Americans to go home with their legs numbed? Do something, even if you have to saw off some Ping-Pong tables."

"Who are you to talk to me like that?" The manager was annoyed.

"I might only be the lowly interpreter, but I have the ear of the sports minister."

"Do you know this has never happened before?" the fat man said angrily.

"And will never happen again if you don't make some beds a little longer. Important people will not come if you let these famous guys sleep with their feet dangling, cutting off their circulation. They won't walk for days. Do you want to take the blame for that?"

The manager walked off frantically.

Before nightfall, a miracle occurred. Footrests were attached to lengthen the beds for those especially tall players. A cigar-smoking New York club owner came over and shook our hands. "Well done. You guys are amazing." He was a fast talker with a bouncing cigar on his lips. "Now, my players want to walk around Tiananmen Square before dark. Would you accompany them?" he requested.

Huang hesitated but said yes. The hotel overlooked the square, where thousands of residents were taking breezy walks and flying kites. The police would have a hard time keeping local moon gazers away from the sky walkers.

Huang took the request to a security head of the hotel, a big shot working directly under the national Public Security Ministry. The uniformed man almost jumped out of his chair. He hated the idea and severely criticized Huang for saying yes before consulting with him. "Do you know what kind of risk you run letting them out there in the square? How could you keep the people away from them?"

"Why do we need to keep them away from the people?"

"Because they talk to them. And I don't want that."

"The request was made by a very important club owner from New York, and the players' desire is well grounded. Why can't they go see our grandest square?"

"They can see it from their windows."

"Then our hotel would really look like a prison," Huang said.

"Very sarcastic, Interpreter Huang. You must have too much Western education. I have to take the crap and handle duty here. You give a nice little yes, and I have to summon my force. Get out of here. I've got work to do."

As we herded the players onto the square, a police ring was formed around them as if they were under quarantine. The players were more relaxed after a little rest. They laughed and joked as they moved in their impressive slowness across the square, drawing the attention of startled onlookers. In the setting sun of a long summer day, our visitors finally found what they had been looking for—the people. Thousands of Beijingers broke through the police ring and rushed to witness these greatest players in the world. Notwithstanding shouts of excitement in English and in Chinese, there was a ghostly hush among the moon gazers as if some science fiction characters had just landed in their city. They were curious yet cautious. What if they bite, some seemed to be thinking? Other foreign tourists surrounded them, begging for their autographs. The players soon found themselves drowned in the fighting throng.

When the sun finally set, our chief nudged us. It was time to herd them back to the hotel.

"What's the hurry?" one player asked me. His partner, an elegant lady, was leaning on his shoulder.

"It's time for dinner," I said.

"So we'll skip dinner."

"Then you will be starved the whole night."

"We can always order room service, can't we?"

"I'll have to check with the kitchen there."

"No room service?"

"I don't know."

Reluctantly the couple followed the group back to the hotel.

As a final safety measure, I carried a list of names and diligently checked off each one as they returned to the safety of the hotel lobby.

"Is everyone here?" Huang asked, looking much more relieved now. He had been frenetically nervous out there.

"Everyone except one." I tapped my clipboard with a pen. "Not bad for such a big group, huh?"

"You have one missing?" he asked urgently.

"Maybe he is coming."

"Who is it?"

"Kareem Abdul-Jabbar."

"Oh my, he is only the biggest star in the world! Go find him immediately!"

Hurriedly I ran back to the square. There I spotted Kareem standing like a seven-foot crane hovering over a thick, unrelenting crowd of a hundred American high school students who had just piled out of their bus. The crowd was screaming and clambering to reach him, begging for autographs. Some kids were so excited that they were crying, while others hung onto him as if he were a god. When Kareem moved toward me, smiling, the crowd got even louder.

In that brief moment, I suddenly understood how precious these players really were and how much they were loved by their fans.

Chapter Twenty-one

The venerable old Beijing Hotel had partitioned off a large portion of its restaurant just for our tour. Peonies reddened the windowsills overlooking the busy dusty street. Green lotus stems with pompous blooms sat on each table, still carrying traces of the morning dew. The pride of this land—the rare Mao Tai liquor and Zhong Hua cigarettes—were displayed prominently before each guest. A large pot of steaming tea sat brooding, surrounded by china cups. The waitresses all wore their special uniforms, dark green in color, which prompted the wife of a player to ask me, "Why are all the girls dressed like soldiers?"

"Because this is a special occasion," I said.

"What happened to the *chi-paus*, those traditional long silk dresses that I always see Chinese women wear?" she asked.

"Oh, those were abandoned a long time ago. Now the revolutionary women wear only revolutionary dresses with revolutionary colors."

"Which is army green?"

"Yes and no, because red is really our color, the color of hot blood." My explanation sent the woman's eyebrows higher up her forehead. She dragged her shrugging husband away as quickly as I could say good-bye.

Huang told me that my job was to herd all the visitors to the tables so that we could start eating on time. It sounded like the easiest job in the world. No one in China needed to be reminded of when to eat. If there was a banquet of this magnitude, one could count on having a long line waiting to get in, and if the doors were jammed, windows would be broken once people smelled the food. Yet that did not seem to be the case here. The Americans flowed in unhurriedly, couples hand in hand, men in suits and women in dresses, while I stood by greeting them still wearing the same sweat-drenched uniform. Food did not seem to interest them much, but eventually everyone arrived.

Along with five other players and their spouses, I was seated next to an old Chinese man in a Mao jacket. He seemed half blind and showed no interest in me or anyone around the table. His stony gaze hooked intently on the plates as if they might vanish any minute. He collected toothpicks, tore open the cigarettes, and poured tea only for himself. When I asked him for his name so that I could introduce him to the American guests, he waved me away with his crooked, freckled fingers and resumed his business of eating and drinking but not participating.

Tonight's banquet was given by the City Sports Bureau. The chief was giving an excruciatingly long speech, and we had to wait for him to finish before the food could be served. Each word spoken jabbed like a knife at my hungry stomach. Friendship, sportsmanship, leadership, all seemed such a bore. I could see the tall heads of the basketball players begin to dangle and droop and their wive's eyes roll backward at the painful wait. There was great relief and short applause when the chief finally bowed out.

I grabbed Huang and secretively asked him about all these Chinese faces surfacing everywhere like mushrooms after a rain. I was particularly curious about the nonspeaking old man making a mockery of himself sitting next to me.

Huang smiled and said, "Oh, them? They're called the 'Banquet Revolutionaries.' They don't speak English and have little to do with sports. They are old cadres, semiretired but still powerful enough to be invited to these glitzy events. Those seats are inheritable. That's why sometimes you see their children here as well."

"How should I address them?"

"Old fart or old revolutionary. What's the difference?"

My thoughts exactly. "Okay," I chuckled, "that's simple."

Before I could eat, I had to translate the menu, which ran a foot long—all delicacies of the mountain and flavors of the sea. Bear paws simmered rotten with rare ginger roots and palm-size mushrooms sat on huge plates dripping with gluelike juices. North mountain pheasants, served whole and complete with feet and heads on, stared with dead eyes. Live carp, still twitching, were covered with layers of spicy burning sauces. Side-walking crabs were cooked red in white fish sauce with green scallions wrapped around their bodies like sashes of honor. Pork shoulders rubbed elbows with Peking ducks. Ping-Pong-ball-sized fish eggs from the South China Sea floated in duck soup. Turtle heads lay on the edge of the plate, question marks in their fish eyes. Legs of lamb were chopped into meaty chunks and boiled in herbal medicine. Sliced pigs' tongues were sautéed hotly with ginger. And solidified cow's blood sat like bloody marshmallows, lightly fried with crusty tofu.

As I went along translating deliciously, tongues stuck out, heads shook, and eyes popped. They did not seem impressed a bit. In fact, there was a big show of disgust.

"What's the matter?" I asked a player from the American South.

"Well, it sounds more like a zoology garden with half-dead animals than a banquet."

"Since the emperors' time, we have prided ourselves on eating the rarest of animals and birds. They're very nutritious. Why don't you like them?" I asked.

"Please, Mr. Chen," one woman said. "We don't eat this kind of stuff in America. It just seems strange."

"But it is the best food in our land. We would never serve you second best."

My Banquet Revolutionary was extraordinary. He opened the well-simmered bear paws with his chopsticks. Like an expert, he sliced a few chunks and grabbed the biggest for himself. Everyone's eyes followed this shaking old man as he sucked the sticky paws noisily. He almost choked on the first piece, but that didn't deter him a bit. He helped himself to a second piece, but he accidentally dropped it and had to chase the slippery fugitive with his chopsticks on the table. Getting impatient, he finally grabbed the bear paw with his own wrinkled hand. Satisfied, he sucked his knuckles to rid them of the delicious grease, a genuine hero.

Acting like a good host, I held back my gargantuan appetite and patiently satisfied the players' never-ending questions about the food. Come on, I thought, they were all-American heroes. Why were they so scared of some dead animals on a table, in a plate? They made the food sound like so much poison rather than this impossibly expensive rare delicacy that would make their tongues sing. They picked and poked gingerly as if they were walking in a minefield with forks and spoons. What was wrong with them?

"Do you know that the fish taste very fishy?" one lady asked, curling her little finger.

"Well, what's fish without the fishy taste? In fact, for most Chinese who cannot afford fish, they mix everything with fish sauce to make it taste fishy."

"Okay, Mr. Chen, enough talking for you. You work too hard. Why don't you eat while we watch."

I got the feeling no one wanted to hear any more about food.

It was all true, just like what I had read in some enticing books. Bear paws melted on my tongue, and fish eggs popped at the touch of my teeth. Good duck skin crumpled at the seal of my kiss, and the freshest fish meat was the whitish strip on a live fish belly. Indeed, no fish was fresher than the one just caught from the lake at the back of the Beijing Hotel. I wiped my mouth with the stiffly ironed napkin and managed a silent burp before I stretched my limbs with satisfaction.

"So how was everything?" the interested ladies asked, as if seeing someone survive a bloodbath.

"One could only taste it, not describe it."

"Very smart, Mr. Chen, but then what good are you as an interpreter?" another said mockingly.

I did manage to introduce my guests to the potent Mao Tai liquor, which sold at the price of three hundred yuan a bottle. Even at that price, you had to kick down some back doors to buy the real thing, because the black market was flooded with fakes poured into the genuine bottles, the same way many medications were forged. It was after a thirsty taste of the fiery drink that my guests really began to enjoy themselves.

That night I was instructed to stay in a hotel room. The smooth humming air-conditioning was only a whispering reminder of the miserable heat out there in congested Beijing in July. I was too excited to sleep, looking out of the window with the city at my feet. The separation was only paper thin, but the distance seemed immeasurable. In here were sofas, telephones, and toilets, the flushing type that I dared not use until Huang showed me its power. The bed was soft and the pillow white like snow. The sheet was tucked tight at the end of the bed, and I had to climb into it when I finally decided to sleep. There was a small refrigerator in the room filled with all kinds of drinks. I was told that I could drink anything I liked and it would be charged to the Sports Ministry.

A night like this was too good to be spent sleeping. It was to be relished and savored every second. I felt that I had arrived in some way, but didn't know exactly how. In the dead of night I could almost hear the hooves of Yellow Stone buffalo stepping into muddy fields on a wet July day, and feel the earth searing in its own hot throes. But here I was, cool and chilled, smoking foreign cigarettes, drinking the limitless supply of bubbling sodas. Room service was only a phone call away, and I was about to sleep only a pillow's throw from the Forbidden City where the emperor used to make his lustful dreams. I drifted off in a daze, in the unfamiliar comfort of starched linen and feathery pillows.

Around one in the morning, I was suddenly awoken by one of the basketball players. "Come on, Mr. Chen, I have severe diarrhea," he shouted through the door.

I opened the door and helped him in. He rushed into the bathroom, leaned over my sink, and vomited thunderously, gasping for air, with his wife right behind him, apologizing to me again and again.

"Don't worry, I'll call the doctor now," I said, smelling Mao Tai in the potent mix.

Within minutes a hotel doctor was there. His diagnosis was: "Food too greasy and the air-conditioning too cold. You should be fine by tomorrow. Don't eat or drink anything but tea."

I ran downstairs and got him a pot of tea. The poor guy must have stayed up all night drinking that bloody green tea. Not because he liked to but because he had to. The man looked miserably gaunt and dead pale the next day, but his diarrhea was all gone.

I crawled back into my starchy bag after the room was cleaned. But my serene slumber was broken by the unimaginably cold air-conditioning. By three or four in the morning, I found myself hugging the thick blanket. My nose was all clogged up. I fumbled in vain, looking for the vent to shut the thing off, but couldn't find it. Fetus position, I bent myself into a little worm. By five, the toilets upstairs began to flush angrily, sounding like a dam bursting. The cheap wall shook each time a load of water was let go. As the sun rose, showers started to run in the rooms surrounding me. I sandwiched my head with two pillows to gain temporary tranquillity. When my hands got sleepy and the pillows fell, the showers had raced to the end, though I could still hear the drips of showerheads making those annoying little plunges into the gargling holes—some splashy, others perfect 10-point dives.

Slowly the drips blurred and my snores resumed, only to be interrupted once more as doors slammed open and shut and elevators cranked up and slid down their hollow shaft. By seven, Mr. Huang was at my door, beaming and smoking while giving me the assignment for the day.

"You doing all right?" he asked with concern, seeing me wrapped in a blanket.

"It's freezing in here," I said through my stuffed nose.

"You cheap bone. I put you in the most luxurious hotel room and you tell me you are cold. Why can't you just adjust it?" He stepped in and showed me the knob under the cover of a vent.

"Now how do you like it?"

I nodded, feeling the chill freeze.

"If you're still cold, open the window." He snapped open the handle, and the smell of Beijing came rushing in. Within seconds, heat and chill kissed. I was happily neutralized.

"Now today, and for the next few days, I want you to take these players to work out in the Beijing Capital Stadium. All the players are going with their trainers and coaches. You stay there with them, take care of logistics. The players are very anxious to practice for the game with the Chinese national team."

Breakfast was "Western food." I adventurously ordered what everyone was ordering, sunny-side-up eggs with runny yokes, and chose the foreign coffee over my usual tea. The sunny side looked awfully cloudy to me, and the yokes ran faster than my fork. Nor did the salt and pepper enhance the flavor of raw egg. To save the perfectly rotten meal, I dashed soy sauce on it, making it unrecognizable horse spit, which I enjoyed to the amusement and amazement of my American friends. The coffee was overrated as a foreign import. It tasted thick and bitter, without the sweet aftertaste of good

green tea. Cream and sugar only muddled it up further. To rid myself of
such an alien taste, I poured into myself a torrent of iced water. I could just
see the raw sticky egg yokes doing a teary dance with the ice cubes that I
accidentally swallowed down. There was no surer recipe for uprising diarrhea. I quickly switched to the Chinese menu and soothed my entrails with
some homey hot porridge and crusty fried dough.

The demand for a longer and roomier bus was met quickly. Waiting for
us in front of the hotel was the longest bus Japan had ever made. The
Japanese embassy had stepped in and readily donated its bus service to us
during the players' stay in the city.

The day was bright, and everyone was in good spirits. The players had
been divided arbitrarily into two teams, Pacific and Atlantic, and they were
now wearing their requisite uniforms: big shoes, big bags. They high-fived
one another as they stepped onto the bus, which sank grumpily. The driver was a miniature Japanese fellow who came with the bus. The heads of
those players hovered ever high and tall while the driver shrank further
into his seat. It felt as if the bus was driving itself.

"Capital Stadium is the finest and biggest in China," I said proudly as
we arrived and I guided the team indoors.

"It looks like a shithole to me," someone from behind me said jokingly.
Others laughed. The coach was quick to apologize to me. I told him that
no offense was taken.

"You see, in the States, stadiums are usually much larger, and they are
finer," he explained.

"No problem. I just hope that this will work out for you."

"We'll manage."

I sat on the bench, watching the scene with tremendous curiosity. The
relationship between the coach and the players was somewhat different
than I would have thought. They joked all the time with each other; in
fact, the coaches seemed to have a hard time controlling these guys. In
China the coach was the strict head of the family. Any coach here would
have long ago asked the guys to lose the gum in their mouths. I still
remembered my high school PE teacher scolding me because I had done
a 100-meter dash with a flapping smile on my face. What are you laughing about? he had cursed. Sports were a serious challenge. I, of course,
never dared smile again while running and became quite a solemn-faced
athlete. But here, though the columns might not be the straightest and the

coaches' rules were not always followed, there was a sense of camaraderie and warmth.

After a brief warm-up, dozens of balls were thrown to them, and the players began to fly all over the court. They dribbled with amazingly casual skill, as if the balls were attached to their nimble, powerful fingers. They jumped high and slam-dunked like bees diving into their hive. A pickup game was loosely played between the two teams, and I watched in amazement. Jabbar's sky hook, on the Pacific team, was a never-miss.

At the end, the coach jokingly threw me a sweaty ball and asked me to shoot a hoop. I caught the ball and sat on it. In front of those magicians, I was no illusionist.

I said, "I don't deserve to play this ball ever."

"Oh, come on," Steve, a trainer, said and kicked the ball out from under my ass, leaving me lying on the floor.

On the way back to the hotel, Steve asked me, "Who do you think will win the game tonight?"

"The Chinese team," I said with a smirk.

"Yeah, right."

For reasons unknown, the first game against the Chinese national team had to be played in Shenyang, a Manchurian industrial city north of Beijing. A plane took us there in one hour. Monstrous Russian-style concrete buildings loomed all over the city. The green summer trees looked old, showing the gray of pollution in what once must have been a scenic town. A curvy river slithered through the heart of the city, with its piers and docks splintering the water. Little boats and large barges jammed darkly stale water, and the riverbanks had become junkyards with piles of industrial leftovers. People dressed in typical northern dark blue in the brief breath of summertime. The phantom of a Siberian winter was only temporarily in hiding.

En route to Shenyang, the coaches huddled with the players, strategizing and talking about the game with heavy doses of sports lingo that escaped my comprehension. The players laughed raucously, tossing a ball around inside the airplane to the annoyance of the coaches. This old bird was a small version of a Russian invention. I had the feeling that if these guys started rocking back and forth, the plane would take the form of a dancer in the sky and soon start a nosedive. Finally a coach, who had chased the ball from one player to another, caught it and suggested they discuss some more strategies, but no one was interested. He could only shake his head.

"You guys seem to be in a good mood today," I said to a player whose name I still found hard to roll off my tongue and even harder to remember. David something or something David.

"I always feel good going to a game. I'm a ballplayer," he said. "Besides, my wife is not here with me." Wink.

"Ah," I said. "Maybe your coach should have made your wife come with you so you won't be so naughty."

"Oh, she wouldn't come. She doesn't want to hear me talk about games. She's only interested in shopping. In fact, she's been asking me to find someone to go shopping with her and her girlfriends. You think you could take them somewhere, say a carpet factory or a vase store? You know, that sort of place."

"Well, I'd like to, but I have to ask our boss for permission."

"What permission? We'll pay you. All you need to do is sneak out. They'll get a cab, and out you go. Please. She's already getting bored with everything. She calls Beijing a ghost town."

"But it is our busiest city."

"I know. I'm in trouble," he said.

"I'll think of something when we get back, but are you sure you can trust me with your wife?" I grinned.

He let out a huge laugh. "Oh, yes. She's at least a head taller than you are, and she only likes big men like me. All her boyfriends before were big tall black guys. But if you try anything sneaky, mark my word, she'll toss you off the Great Wall herself."

"That's tough, good. You knew that she had a few boyfriends before you married her?"

"Yeah." He shrugged.

"And you still married her?"

"Yeah. She was hot and getting hotter."

"In China, a man would be upset about it."

"But not in America. You see, people start dating early, and they usually go through a few test-drives before hitting the right one. Girls do that, and so do boys."

"You had a few girlfriends before marriage?"

"A few?" He lifted his eyebrows, laughing. "How about many." He took a stealthy look around the plane, making sure others did not hear him.

"Oh, sure," I realized. "You NBA guys could have the world."

"Pretty much so. A lot of them were party girls. They wanted money and fun, big cars, big houses. But my wife is special. She is from a different world. I actually had to find her." He paused. "She teaches at a college and writes poetry. Want to hear something funny? Her former boyfriends were all professors, glasses and all. Anyway, now she writes poems for me, which got me interested in the whole poetry thing myself. That's why I'm taking a course she's teaching in poetry writing in my off-season, and I love it."

"Sounds like a great love story."

"Yeah, it is." He nodded proudly. "And I find it wonderful to come home to someone so different from my life."

"Thank you for sharing your story with me. Now that I know you both are poets, I will try harder to take the time to help you shop."

"Why is that so?"

"You happen to be in the land of poets. We revere them. The more they drink, the better poetry they write. They are national treasures and cultural icons."

"I have to tell my wife that. But how about athletes? Are they heroes too?"

"Not till you guys go out there tonight and show my countrymen what you showed me this morning."

"Give me a high-five."

Our hands clapped, his nearly smashing mine.

The game in Shenyang was no cliffhanger.

The Americans easily beat the Chinese team by 93 to 66, even though they had had little time to practice playing together, the Chinese team were taller than they had expected, and they had to use a Chinese basketball, which they found to be heavier and smoother than their own.

In the end, their finesse, their love for the sport, and their openness on the stadium floor, with their gum-chewing casualness, won not only the 27-point lead in their initial victory but also the people's hearts.

To a deafening standing ovation, they shook their counterparts' hands and exited the stadium. They might have passed through the city for the night only, but their spirits would linger in the people's minds.

Chapter Twenty-two

The next day I extracted permission from Huang to take a few ladies shopping. He gave me a list of the "right" addresses where foreign camels were allowed.

"Beyond these, don't take them," he warned.

"Why?"

"Because there are laws forbidding such excursions. Military bases are scattered all about the city. You really don't want to take any risk."

The ladies were waiting for me in the hotel lobby, among them the wife of a certain powerful New York lawyer and the poet's wife, Debbie. These ladies had figured out their destinations already. They did not want to take the taxi assigned us by the Sports Ministry and quickly rushed me to another one waiting at the corner. It all felt like a spy story.

"Where are we going?" I asked them.

"This man said he could bring us to a carpet factory beyond the military base," Debbie whispered, pointing to the driver sunk low in his seat.

"But it's illegal."

"You tell them you were kidnapped by us. Let's go," the lawyer's wife suggested.

Reluctantly I got in, and the driver was more than happy to tell me that what Huang had told me was a bunch of bullshit. "How do you know what the law is in this town?" he challenged. "I've been driving this taxi for ten years, and you'll be happy that you got on board this cab," he said in Chinese.

"Where are we going?" I insisted.

"That's not important, young man. I've got a profit-sharing scheme here. You hire me for the trips, and I will split with you ten, maybe fifteen percent of my money."

"I don't need your money."

"You won't say that if I tell you this: If these fat cows do make a big purchase, which you'll urge them to do, of course, the general manager there will compensate you. And he might give you a deal that you could not refuse."

"It sounds very, very problematic." I turned to Debbie and her friends and said, "We shouldn't go. He'll take us to some seedy place with greedy people running the business. You might get butchered."

"Literally?" Debbie asked.

"Figuratively," I replied.

"Don't worry, we have money. Besides, each dollar is worth ten yuan, which means that we can afford ten times more than in the States. We must visit the factory."

"You can't trust the driver. He's too greedy."

"I heard that." The driver apparently understood some English.

"Good!" I said.

"Stop fighting. I also got tipped off by an Australian journalist who said it's a must-see. They've got plenty of handmade carpets there," Debbie hissed.

"Are you sure?"

"Yes, and I think you have been brainwashed. Just come help us, please."

"Okay, then."

Forty miles west of the city, in the valley of some tall leafy mountains, we found the carpet place, which was run by the military garrison force itself. Soldiers with rifles guarded the door, and a big sign announced *Foreigners Not Allowed*.

But when our taxi driver whispered into the ear of the guard, he was waved in like a welcome guest. The manager, an army man, was right there to meet us. "Welcome, welcome," he said.

"Doesn't the sign outside say that no foreigners are allowed," I inquired.

"No bad foreigners are allowed," he qualified.

"How do you know who is bad?"

"Only those with cameras and pens. Reporters."

"But my guests have cameras and videos as well."

"Yeah? But they also have money." His eyes drooped impatiently.

"Sure they do."

"People with money are usually better than people without."

I had a strange feeling talking to this man in a respectable army uniform.

He continued. "To soothe your young and active mind, ours is what we call experimental capitalism. We do a bit of business under the red flag to save the red flag."

"I don't understand."

"They might close down the base. If they do, thousands of us would return to the country to dig earth. So I do thank you and comrade driver for bringing these fine ladies here." He winked. "You won't be disappointed."

The ladies went wild when they saw the carpet workshop. Hundreds of army women were looping colorful carpets thread by thread. Debbie hovered like a butterfly all over the floor, scooping up ten, mostly for herself with some for her sisters. The lawyer's wife followed suit, and so did the rest of them.

They paid in dollars, which was unusual then, to say the least. The price was so low that the ladies were giggling when they were ushered into the attached dining room for a greasy four-course lunch. The manager poured good wine for us, including the driver, and we chatted lightheartedly without any sense that this whole thing smacked of illegality.

"I love capitalism," the army man announced over the liquor.

"I think you love capitalists even more," I said, toasting him, feeling like a part of this den of thieves.

"Well put."

"Hey, when you graduate from whatever fine college you go to, go find a job with the Tourism Department. I guarantee you a certain sum when you bring fat cats into our compound. We'll grow rich together," he said in Chinese.

"I'll make a note of that."

All the way home I had one burning question in mind. "How could you ladies afford to pay one hundred U.S. dollars for each carpet, and you each bought ten?"

The lawyer's wife jumped in to answer. "First of all, it's ten times cheaper for the finest of quality. Secondly, Debbie's husband makes a million a year."

"A million dollars playing basketball!" I almost shot out the car's roof.

"Yes."

"You are a millionaire every year after year?"

"And her husband, the association's counsel, probably makes tens of millions a year," Debbie said. "How much do you make when you graduate from college?"

"Five hundred yuan per year."

"How much is that in dollars?"

I calculated. "Fifty bucks."

"But you are already better off than most youngsters your age, right?" Debbie asked.

"Absolutely," I said, using up my last thread of pride.

"I envy you."

"Why?"

"Because you are proud of yourself."

"That I am." I might have said that, but all the way through the dusty ride home, I kept trying to figure out the arithmetic difference between me and that tall, handsome black husband of Debbie's. A million-dollar-a-year black man, fifty-buck-a-year China man. Is he happier, or am I happier? I was happier until today. How do you spend a million? Why do you want to spend a million? The last leg of the trip I tried to figure out all the things that seven figures could buy: a thousand villages with coolies thrown in, a hundred pure water reservoirs, a hundred thousand heads of wooden-eyed buffalo with three pagodas thrown in, or ten communes minus the nasty cadres. But why would anyone want a commune if he had that much dough? Money really was a very bad thing. I started thinking some very bad thoughts only by sitting next to a couple of millionaires. Even the cab trip, a silent velvety luxury racing against the blurred heat outside, did not soothe me anymore. I was troubled by the figure—a million, the insurmountable pagoda. My last thought was that I should have taken the percentage.

Chapter Twenty-three

The team visited the requisite trio of Beijing tour spots—the barren Great Wall, the red Forbidden City, and the crowded Summer Palace.

The Wall seemed even taller in the shifting summer heat and the climb even steeper. It took those giants a breathless effort at a snail's pace to finally reach the top of the Wall. No one would have bothered with the sweaty climb had they not had to do a photo shoot for Coca-Cola and Disney, which had been paying for their trip.

The trip to the Forbidden City was no slam-dunk either. The curious and nimble made it through the mile-long hollow and haunting courtyards overgrown with weeds and grass to the back entrance in this sun-scorched, feet-burning marathon. The lazier and the comfy curled up and lay down on the first sloping marble surface they saw, silently guarded by stone lion statues.

"...And those pagodas were here before the royal court was built...,"
I pronounced authoritatively, reading from a tour guide brochure.

No one seemed interested.

"...This is the emperor's bedroom," caused a stir of interest from wives
who quickly dismissed it as being drab without any foreseeable comfort.

"That was the bed for your emperor?" one asked.

"Yes, the best."

"I would hate to be your empress then," joked another.

That evening the Forbidden City opened its most exclusive restaurant
to the American guests. It overlooked a scenic pond, capturing the shadows of a red pavilion and green willows that danced over a whitish
wooden bridge. A perfect royal garden for some thirsty and hungry guests.

Everything here was done according to the menus of the royal court
kitchen of our last dynasty. They used to staff the place with royal chefs
from the past, the last of whom had died only a few years earlier. When the
food arrived, it was at best interesting if not primitive. The appetizers were
miniature replicas of what ordinary people would eat at that time—tiny
mantous, tiny *wowotous* (cornbread), tiny this and tiny that. The emperor was
a young man, so the chefs had had to make the food fun to please him.
Tofu had to be fried in the shapes of goats, tigers, or dragons.

The head chef invited us to see him create one of the most exciting
dishes on the royal menu. He dragged up a big carp from the pond nearby,
rapidly scaled and dressed it, then let it sit in a bamboo steamer for only five
minutes before it was served. The tail of the fish performed a nice little
swipe, taking its last saucy breath before dying a delicious death in the bed
of a royal plate. His guests were honored by his culinary manslaughter but
quietly put off by the sight of a gasping fish in its death throes. The big blunder the chef made was poking the eyes out of the moving fish and offering
them to the tallest player at the table. "Eat them," he said. "It's good for sex."

"Why?" The ballplayer pushed away the staring eyes, disgusted.

"The twin eyes resemble the twin nuts between your legs."

"I don't think my wife will have any more sex with me if I eat them."
He looked at his adoring wife who had hidden behind him.

"Why don't you eat them up yourself and go make your wife happy
tonight?" she offered.

The chef sucked them in noisily and said, "My wife will sing her
Peking Opera tonight."

By the time they were driven to the Summer Palace, another long yawn of seeing nothing but old pagodas, most of them were tired and bored and could not wait to head straight for the expected ten-course lunch in the sumptuous palace restaurant.

That afternoon, as we cruised in a pleasure yacht on the palace's Kunming Lake, supposedly the most beautiful man-made lake on earth, some were dozing, and all my fancy talk was just another reason to continue napping.

The sightseeing ended with another banquet at the Peking Duck Specialty Restaurant, where the very first crispy Peking Duck in history had been roasted, and where the players drank Mai Tai as if there were no tomorrow.

There was no tomorrow indeed. They would be leaving the next day, and that in itself had to be celebrated by yet another, the most formal, banquet. This time it was held in the People's Hall, where state dinners were usually given. They met the sports minister and a new group of Banquet Revolutionaries as well.

I said good-bye to them at the airport the following morning and was surprised to be given a bag of romance novels by Debbie, who thanked me for having taken them shopping.

"How did you know I loved books?"

"From the way you speak. You use words carefully and thoughtfully and speak with wonderful rhythm, unlike a lot of Chinese whom we talked to. Read more and you'll speak even better."

Coming from a poet, it meant a lot. I waved good-bye to them as they disappeared into the terminal.

One of the Disney cameramen ran noisily by and grabbed me to ask if I would like to fly with them to Shanghai to continue their filming.

"We'll pay you really well," he offered.

"I'm afraid not. I don't have permission to go with you, even though I'd love to. My job stops here."

"Sneak out, man."

"No, I can't. I'll get into a lot of trouble." I shook my head.

"Come to America. Then you could do what you want without having to deal with this Commie shit," he urged and smiled his white teeth smile.

"Maybe."

I was praised for my hard work and alert eyes. My contact at the Sports

Ministry said there would be other opportunities for me because I had showed them how hard I was ready to work. A cash payment of two hundred yuan was given to me in an envelope. I jumped for joy in celebration of this whopping sum made while having the grandest time of my life.

Once again I returned to the summer heat outside, the hum of hotel air-conditioning only a memory now. The Beijing Hotel again looked intimidating and foreign, a world beyond. I could hardly believe that my stinky naked toes had once touched the carpeted hush of the vacuumed hallways and my farting ass had once spoken hoarsely into the echoing toilet.

The noon sun shouted hotly and the street started to burn my soles as I embarked on my sweaty journey home, humming a broken tune. Though I had eaten the emperor's food and slept on the bounciest and squishiest bed, returning to my dull life did not seem especially extraordinary.

Chapter Twenty-four

For most of my classmates, the final year of college was a year of semi-retirement. There was a sense that a great achievement had been made. We, the retiring seniors, were too hot to study anymore. Teachers were nicer to us, as if we had grown up. Some saw the teachers' leniency as a sign of their greatness, whereas I saw it as a spiteful dumping of self-conceited brats into a rotting society where they would soon come to the realization of their own pettiness. The sentiment could best be summarized by Black Rose's yawn of, "Oh, seniors, you're so full of yourselves!"

The seniors' haughtiness stemmed from a rooted belief that they were storming into a society, a needy one, that would offer them glamorous jobs that outshone those of their teachers. But by then, the needy society had disappeared. The graduating class of 1983 was the third one since the ending of the Cultural Revolution. Two big classes of high-quality graduates had been let loose before us and had filled most of the important positions within the state machinery. They soaked up rations and, most devastating, living space and high salaries. The big government got bigger. For the first time one felt a cancerous glut being developed that would continue as long as colleges kept spitting out unwanted graduates who would keep coming and coming till the end of time. It was a disastrous awakening. The well-planned society of Communism was about to run amok. What could be done with all these graduates? They needed jobs, fast. If they didn't get any, the hot-blooded youngsters filled with fancy Western ideas would riot and kill. But what jobs to give if there were no more to give away? It was into this bleak landscape that our class was emerging, and the sting of reality hit hard and filled us with worry.

Dad wrote me a whispering letter, inquiring about prospects of placement. I told him proudly that English majors should be safe. No small town could hold big fish like us. We weren't the mute and deaf English majors that they trained in some no-name, outlandish college where English was taught as if it were dead Latin. Those graduates, I wrote, would be perfect candidates to fill up the windy gaps in the rest of our uninhabitable lands. You're wrong, he wrote back quickly. His advice was simple. Do something! Dad proved once again that he was a visionary.

A meeting was called for the seniors one day for the general purpose of calming their nervousness. The dean's face was as cloudy as ever. He leaned over a rusty microphone, spittle exploding before words were uttered. "The government wants you to be mentally prepared," he said. "Some of you will be assigned to wonderful opportunities in places where you are most needed. Millions of high school children await your arrival to teach them."

English majors were dead. The rotten countryside was coming. I cringed in my seat. A roar of cheers rose from the French, Arabic, Spanish, Japanese, Greek, and German majors. They had always despised us, and now they could watch as we were sent off to the land's end.

"Don't they have enough mute and deaf English majors to cover those areas?" one English student asked anxiously.

"Well, you won't be teaching high schools yourselves. No, you're too good for that. You'll be teaching those mute colleges so they won't be mute anymore."

"They've been doing fine with mute English. Why bother?" asked another.

"The government wants them to open their mouths now."

"How about other majors?" someone asked.

"Some of them will be going to the countryside too. Remote regions have put in the most demand for tourist guide positions because foreigners are flooding to see those old relics."

Now the English majors were cheering. Go roll those foreign tongues to the mountains and the rivers. Resounding echoes were guaranteed.

The dean waved his mighty hands, calming down the boiling graduates, and continued, "However, there are still plenty of good and important positions in Beijing and the other major cities. We will assign jobs according to one's grades, conduct, and the impression of faculty, etc., etc."

Etc., etc. equaled extras and extras.

Translation: Time to fight, bribe, or die the miserable death of being kicked back to the country that I had fought all my life to get out of. Not ever knowing the sweetness of paradise is one thing, but knowing it only to suffer being deprived of it once again was too punishing. The silence of the countryside was the tranquillity of death. The gloves were on and the bell ringing. The fight was on, and everyone was in it.

The next few months I succumbed to the requisite routine footwork of ingratiation like a slimy snail. I sent for large dried oysters and prickly dried lychees. On each trip I felt like a bony, unwilling peasant paying his annual levy. I was always met with the dean's wife's "Leave it there."

The second official whose favor had to be curried was a shadowy female party chief named Lui, a leading scholar of Leninism—a label that destined her to neither an academic future nor intellectual stimulus. Her apartment boasted the portrait of a goateed Lenin, and her eyes gave off lustful lights at the mere mention of the man.

But that didn't lessen her in any way as a crooked cadre. It only made her a more cunning one. When the subject of bribery surfaced, as it always did in this context, she exited into her bedroom and let her wooden husband do the talking. It turned out the husband wasn't wooden at all. He showed me a picture of their two kids and gave me a written list of things that they were in need of—colorful clothes smuggled in from Hong Kong to the Fujian coast, and plastic wristwatches of the same origin. But for his wife, he demanded a particular Fujian *lao jiu*—liquor. And for all of the above, he promised I would be on the consideration list for a big city assignment.

I dashed off an urgent letter to my father with my requests. A man of vision and action, he responded quickly and with precision and sent the items in a many-layered package, which I hurriedly distributed to their recipients before the trees turned green and the campus blossomed with flowers. That probably took care of the material aspect of my life, but every day at sunrise I still crawled to my paradise, now bursting with weedy flowers and alive with thick layers of unspeakable creatures. Before the books were opened, I said my prayers to Buddha. Men were not to be trusted, much less the words of those who slept with Marx and Lenin. Buddha had been good to me, and so had the Earth God I had invited with me from Yellow Stone. I still remembered the tremor of fear my first days here. But now it was almost over. I hung on and studied hard, hoping to squeeze the last bit of juice out of this campus. Graduation was still months away, but a song of nostalgia had already started deep in my heart.

I stayed up late into the night preparing for every phase of the examinations and rose early to review everything. Though the efforts only drew sneers and laughter from my comfortable classmates, who had long graduated in their heads and flown off the campus in spirit, I persisted and tried even harder, for this was the time the battle could be won and won big. There was a confirmed belief that books were useless now and knowledge a waste of time because the only knowledge you needed to have was the knowledge of power, the knowledge of connection. And they had all of that. Only a fool believed in the weight of these final tests. They were only hurdles to prevent you from getting a diploma, not the launchpad to that glorious job. But I firmly believed in playing the defiant and dogged fool, for I had been working too hard to make any mistakes now. I wanted my final tests here to be my lasting signature. Besides, I had something else to prove. I had landed here at the bottom of the class, and I wanted to graduate at the top.

My classmates only studied within the limited scope of our textbooks. My territory went far beyond. I searched in our library for all the old tests that had ever been given, and even practiced on American language tests, which I had stumbled across in the darkest section of the library. These were the language proficiency tests given to anyone heading to an American graduate program. I was fascinated by how tricky and difficult they were. I chewed them as if they were hidden treasures. I also reviewed thousands of old flash cards that I had created during the course of the four years. Those dog-eared cards all smelled like my old socks. On them lay my nervous fingerprints and stained layers of my bitter sweat. I intended to read them all one last time before casting them away into the wind.

But writing a thesis for my world culture class turned out to be the most challenging task by far because I had few sources for references and even less material for research. I had chosen to write on the English usage of newspaper headlines. It was an ambitious undertaking considering that the only English newspaper available in the library was one badly written official publication called *China Daily*. And even for that, I had to wait three days for them to make the rounds of the professors before I could lay my hands on them. Again I had to resort to my own barter system. I had a nice chat with an old cleaning man, called Shi Fu, in the foreigners' building, where students tossed genuine foreign newspapers into garbage cans every day. I promised to help haul and dump these trash cans for the old man, and he in turn allowed me to pick up those soiled and drenched newspapers, from which I cut out useful articles with catchy headlines. I hid my loot in a plastic bag so the school cadres wouldn't know and placed them under my bed to dry. The combination of the dirty paper and my stinking socks and shoes scared the biggest rats away. Only in the wee wee hours of early morning, while Hong snored away, would I pull out these papers to study them. Slowly I composed these incoherent bits of headlines into a ten-thousand-word tome that I finally placed on my professor's desk. She praised me for my effort and demanded to see my supporting documents. I told her my story about the stinking newspapers. She shook her head in disgust and said, "I'll take your word for it." But she was proud of the fact that I dared take up a project that was more than just translating—the usual undertaking by most of my classmates—and rewarded me with extra points.

The finals took a whole week. I swam through all of them gingerly and gleefully, hardly believing that this was it. I had feared an ambush of thorny tricks. None existed.

"Weren't they really easy?" I remarked to a passing classmate when our last test was over.

"You didn't find them difficult?" she asked.

"No."

"Oh, well. It's no use doing well anyway. The jobs have long been assigned. Grades are useless." She threw her schoolbag into the air, and the pages of torn textbooks flew all over.

The results came out quickly. I was number one in the class. I was ecstatically happy. Hard work had paid off, and I had once again conquered. But I was in no mood to celebrate my book success and in less spirit to dwell upon nostalgia, for the most nerve-wracking part of our college career—

job assignment—had just begun. And the worst part about it was that there was nothing more I could do to help shape my future. It was all up to the big guys, department heads, gathered in dark rooms, playing us like little board pieces in a chess game.

A class photo was taken with our eyes blinking under a glaring summer sun. Trees left shadows on our scared faces as we marched in a single column to the foreigners' dining room to be served a greasy graduation lunch. From this cliff, life would plunge or fly, all depending on the whims of our Communist winds. I drank happily with Professor Tu, my mentor. In audacious drunkenness, he took me aside to a quiet corner, silently patted my shoulders and squeezed them, then smiled and left. I got his message. It was good, but he was not to tell me.

That night I slept little and was first to sit in the hallway of the dean's office waiting for my name to be called. The hotshot boys from Shanghai and Beijing all went in first and came out looking pale. One girl stormed out crying, tears messing up her pretty makeup, and another exited with a near sob. Disaster! Those girls were not only well connected but sexy too.

"What did you get?" one asked a boy from Shanghai.

"Fucking shitty job."

"I know, but what kind?"

"Some agricultural college." He ran off cursing, his footfalls echoing.

Hong got assigned to our library as an English cataloguer. He was in a state of bemusement but not elation.

My heart sank when my name was called. I went trembling before our dean, who was not smiling. I shook even more. All my dreams of grandeur came down to a small talk in a dark hole like this. Country or city, good job or bad job. Life sentence, death penalty, or the honeyed sweet life of paradise. All came down to this.

Come, Buddha, count me in for a thousand loud kowtows. No, two thousand, I prayed silently, when I heard the dean say, "After prolonged pondering, the party has decided to offer you the honored position of an assistant professorship here."

"You want me to be a teacher here?" I repeated.

"Not in this department but the department for training students going abroad. You're one of only two to be so honored," he informed me.

"Thank you, thank you." My head was hot and cold at the same time. It was not a bomb: no deep and rotten countryside. But it wasn't glamorous either. I had wanted diplomacy, journalism, foreign trade, America, London, Geneva, or even the Philippine embassy. But it was an honor that I could not refuse, a deep and long, shadowy tradition of honoring one's teachers by becoming a teacher. And they kept only the best for their incestuous breeding. To reject it was to insult the faculty who had voted for me. I stumbled out to a much anticipating crowd.

Word had leaked out.

"Well, you country bumpkin. Cornered the best job," one shouted.

"Did I?"

"Of course. That department is in charge of sending students abroad. You'll be out of this country in no time. America and England, you name it. You lucky dog." But lucky dogs got no congratulations here. Everyone hated me for being so lucky. And the unlucky got no sympathy either. Everybody despised everything and everyone. It was good-bye time!

On my way home, I was still thinking about the plump jobs of the Foreign Ministry, international tourism, or *China Daily* and lamenting the flat-chestedness of my teaching job. *I have failed you, Mom and Dad.* I felt sorry. They had hoped for so much.

I stumbled along the shady road, a gentle breeze dusting the unknowing leaves, but soon warm and grateful feelings began to rise. *Hey, cheer up, country bumpkin. You made it to one of the finest campuses in this land. Professor Chen this and Professor Chen that.* I smiled and ran home to tell my friends the wonderful news.

That night I dashed off a long letter to my family, the tone apologetic because I had not gotten that juicy job that they had all expected me to bag back home. I thought I had let them down. I went on to talk about a bright future here and the definite possibility—what an oxymoron—of being sent abroad someday to further my education. I was telling and comforting myself more than my parents. I knew they would understand and be proud of me, but deep down I also knew that it was far less than the kind of job Dad would have bragged to his pals about. Silently I asked for his forgiveness among the unspoken lines. Moments like this made me realize how much I was living not just for myself but for those who loved me.

Dad wrote back right away with glowing congratulations. You're a city man now, he shouted on paper. He had expected nothing less of me, because our great-grandfather had been a scholar, as had my grandpa, and he himself wasn't such a bad writer either. He had written ten plays and he knew a thing or two about books and brushes. The highbrow good name of a bookish family was cemented once again by my job assignment and my ancestral pedigree reconfirmed. I could see him going around town telling everyone what an honor it was to be the pick of the year and expounding on the nuances of that fine academic tradition. He had also found the name of my department, "Going Abroad," to be enormously braggable. That spirit came through brightly on his envelope with the extra-large Going Abroad characters finely choreographed on it so that there would be no confusion about its meaning or connotation. The postman would let the rumor loose, and outpouring speculation would bubble hotly among Yellow Stoners cooling off under the old pine tree. When asked, Dad would smile ambiguously and chew on his bubbling pipe, letting the whole town simmer in the tantalizing guessing game. Is or isn't it true that this golden boy of Chen's is heading abroad? Folks would press Dad, who would just smile. Frankly, I could do no wrong, because I knew that he knew that the next rabbit I pulled from my hat would be bigger, or at least he hoped so. For that, his bragging would go on, and the big characters would get even bigger till everyone in town knew that I was truly, definitely, and dangerously lurching in the vicinity of the Going Abroad movement.

Dad, oh Dad.

In the same letter he also wrote about Jin's job assignment. He was soon to be the assistant general manager of Nanping's aluminum factory, a five-hour train ride from Yellow Stone. Jin had realized his dream of having a managerial job near the nest of our home so he could care for my parents, and now the only missing link was a bride to love and a thousand sons to breed. In the end, he wrote that we should all be thrifty and save every yuan that we could for a rainy day, and that we were lucky to have a fixed salary to count on and a food ration to eat from. Better yet, that fate would be passed on to our children and our children's children. I could almost feel the dampness of his tears, happy tears as he jotted down those lines because the writing got jerky and the strokes lingered even more with sentiment. I decided that a portion of my salary would forever be sent to my parents for as long as they lived. We had shared the darkest desperation, so now we should equally split the happiness.

Chapter Twenty-five

At twenty, I became a college teacher, with no obvious qualification to speak of or the weight to carry it. I could hardly tilt a scale at 120 on a good day after a fat meal and stood a reedy five-seven with concealed high heels, a fashion with guaranteed discomfort. My ribs were still as visible as the stripes of a zebra, and my thin-hipped, wide-shouldered shape forever framed me in a gaunt portrait of a V. I was a perfect picture of a fishing lad, not a revered "Old Master," as all teachers were addressed and bowed to in our deferential language.

All I had was a B.A. degree upon which the president's seal was still drying and a growing beard that itched more than impressed. To amend my youthful imperfection hurriedly, I bargained with a departing classmate and bought the secondhand thick plastic-rimmed prescription glasses that he had outgrown and said I would grow into. The doctor, in the annual physical, had proclaimed me nearly blind in one eye. The glasses worked out dizzyingly well considering no optometrist was ever consulted and no pyramid of alphabets scaled. The first few days I stumbled along with slight headaches. Stairs became unfathomably deeper and doors enormously closer to my nose. Five wrinkled yuan wasn't worth as much as it used to be, but no one could beat the bargain. The going price for a brand-new pair had to be in the high sixties if not seventies. Counting my first paycheck, a whopping forty-two yuan a month, with two more yuan thrown in as a food bonus, I could not afford to be nearsighted or farsighted, not in one eye, not even in half an eye.

A few days before classes began, an old teacher rushed into my dorm and gave me a beginner's English textbook with teacher's guide attached. She was a tiny lady with a whispering manner. I served her tea and was excited about my first contact with anyone in that department.

"Please sit down and tell me about the department," I urged.

"I have to go, can't chat very much," she said regretfully. "It's all very simple. You go in and teach, and then your day's over."

"How do I teach? And what do I do after school?"

"You learn by teaching. As to what you do in your spare time, it's all up to you."

"There's no training of any sort or any classes given in this regard?"

"No, you're on your own, and soon you'll find it liberating. I've got to go. My bus is leaving to take me home, downtown."

"Thank you and good-bye."

I bumped into a few other teachers in the department. They were unanimously nice and polite but had the same mysterious chuckle of a laugh upon hearing that I had landed the job.

Miserably I crawled to my mentor, Professor Tu, who received me with a bear hug after dropping his daily chore of chopping his lunch vegetables. He led me through his narrow hallway.

"Teacher Chen, how do you feel?" he asked, beaming.

"Antsy and at a loss."

"Oh, you'll get over that in no time. Have a smoke." He gave me a filtered one.

"Oh, thanks. We can now smoke together."

"Yep. I've got to tell you this." He wiped his fat hands on his greasy apron and sat down, his smoke lingering over his choppy eyebrows. "You got lucky with the Going Abroad Department."

"I wish they had kept me in our old department."

"No, you don't."

"Why?"

"Your students are important professionals from important government agencies. You're at the hub of the hottest thing in Beijing now. Everyone wants to go to America. Everyone wants to study English at a school like ours. But only the powerful and privileged few are sent here from their companies. And they love their teachers. Within a matter of a few years, you'll establish a great network of contacts that you can parlay into things unimaginable. Teacher Chen, you hit the gold mine."

"I did? Then how come no one pays any attention to me?"

"It is called freedom. Breathe it."

I sucked in a big gulp of smoke, letting it shoot up to my brain for some vibrating dizziness.

"And you know who voted for your placement there?"

"You."

He nodded.

"Thanks so much." I bowed deeply and shook his hand again.

"I know what you are thinking. Why didn't I get this job or that job? Yes, they were thinking of giving you a reporter's job in the city. But soon the two departments started to fight over you after seeing your grades and everything else. The two deans were nearly fistfighting. The president of the college had to step in to arbitrate."

"Well, I did not know that."

"He said the English Department can always train more of their own, but the Going Abroad Department needed people like you who needed no more training and could jump right in. That's the full story. You should be very proud of yourself."

"I am, and I can't thank you enough."

"Just let me know how you are doing. And if you miss your old department, rumor has it that our dean is taking over your Going Abroad Department. I would be very careful with him. He wasn't all that kind to you during the job placement thing."

"Really?" I was alarmed.

"No details. But just that you know, he wasn't all that malicious either. Your future is in his hands, so steer carefully."

Leaving his house, I looked up through the thick foliage of eucalyptus, dazzled by the sun, and thanked Buddha for putting all those good people at the significant junctures of my life. Some classmates had been sent to tiny cities to teach technical English to technical students. They would be there forever, possibly marrying some dark, thickly built lathe operator. How lucky I was! This campus, this job. *Teacher Chen, Teacher Chen.* The label had a ring to it. It dinged and donged as I found my way for the first time to the exclusive dining hall open only to the faculty. The doorman sized me up and nodded, letting me in only after seeing my red badge with gold trim.

"Teacher who?" he inquired, to register it in his head.

"Teacher Chen."

"Come in, please."

I sauntered among some old faces and ordered my first professorial lunch of sliced beef with garlic stems.

The night before my first class, I slept three jerky hours, waking constantly to the nightmare of angry student faces chasing me until I dangled from my window, several stories high. I woke up in the middle of the night and decided to settle my empty fears by going over the drills that I was supposed to instill in those students and by memorizing the entire English conversation for that lesson. I talked into a mirror for hours, making sure that I sounded right and acted authoritatively. I tried an easy glide of a walk, then changed it to an assured stroll with hands behind my back, fingers holding the chalk like a cigarette. I thought of all the extraordinary teachers who had delivered their spittle of knowledge with a dash of performance—the tilting of a head, the throwing of arms, the tossing of hair, that sucking of air as questions were being asked. My thoughts revolved around the memory of Black Rose, who had truly been more of an actress than a teacher, more diva than educator, while Professor Tu, a lovable teddy bear, was truly no performer but more like a coarse farmer. I did this pose and that posture before the mirror, feigning hard thinking, faking thoughtful agreement and tasteful disagreement.

I tried to remember all the big no-nos teachers had accidentally and fatally committed in the course of busy teaching, but the sun had risen and I had to rush off to the dining hall to beat out others in the long queue and be in class before my adult pupils arrived. The student days of sneaking into class after the bell, yawning and scratching, were over. I was the beacon of light, the spiritual leader of the class now. The weight of duty lay heavily on my shoulders.

After breakfast, a kind new teacher, Rua, who was an alumnus himself, stopped me in the hall of the department building. A casual, big guy from the southwestern city of Yunan, he invited me to sit down at his desk in his bullpen office where all the young guns gathered, smoking, drinking tea before class, and resting their feet in between.

"Take it easy, Da. What's the hurry? Fifteen minutes before the bell."

"I want to be in class early."

"Mistake. Never early, always a bit late. Make them wait and anticipate and then—*tada!*—you make your entrance."

"Why?"

"Psychology. Eagerness sells you cheap. You're what—twenty, twenty-one?—and thin. You can bet the students have long dug out your green résumé. But you have to act old, act wise, and act assured without appearing cocky. You see, these adult students are not impressionable anymore. They are successful engineers, dentists, doctors, lawyers, actors, and film directors. You go there and show your fear and you're dead. They'll have no respect for you, and you'll have a hell of a year ahead of you."

"What should I do?"

"Well, let's see. Glasses are a good idea, though you could use a lighter frame to give your nose a bit of a rest." He was right. My pinched bridge was red. "No heels. You'll be very tired by the time you're done. They look nice, by the way. Where do you get them?"

"I'll get you a pair if you want."

"Good. We'll talk about that later. Another thing you want to do in class is blow them away. Don't ever stumble. Just walk in and start talking at your regular speed and go on for a good two, three minutes without a break, pretending that you think they understand you. Ask yourself questions and then answer them yourself, so on and so forth. Enjoy yourself while doing that, and then some student will stop you timidly and say in a tiny little voice that they cannot follow you because they are just starting the English class. Then you ask each of them in English if they understand you. They will confess their ignorance one by one, and you will have defeated them psychologically. They will remain forever at your feet."

"That sounds bogus, though good, Rua."

"You will appreciate my advice when you stand before the class trembling, feeling utterly naked and helpless. Now the bell has rung and I've got to go. Good luck to you."

That was both the most useful and least useful teaching advice I was ever given. I waited two agonizing minutes before I stepped into my class with the deliberate blindness of a busy professor, books under arms, adjusting my thick glasses. I tensely grabbed the edge of the podium, looking out at the looming two dozen dark heads but seeing nobody. I squinted my eyes, pretending to be dazed by the morning sun, and gazed on intellectually, desperately trying to think of the first line to utter. The class was very quiet. All twenty-four cabbage heads froze in the perfect stillness of tombstones. It almost brought a chuckle out of me. Nothing was funnier than seeing adults playing your pupils.

I rambled on about myself: my degree in English, Shakespeare, poetry, sonnets, Whitman, Jack London, Sidney Sheldon, *The Delta Decisions,* and the NBA. I had to be the worst salesman. I only saw a gorging fear rippling among those worried eyes and wrinkled faces. Where was that timid hand? I was running out of monologue material and was three breaths ahead of myself, but I hung on. It was a battle that had to be won. And then from below came a timid female hand. "Teacher Chen, we could not understand a thing," she muttered in Chinese.

"How about you?" I pointed at the guy next to her, a bald eagle engineer type, who shook his head; the next, a bifocal musician with piano fingers; and the next, with wooden features of an army officer. "No," he answered.

"And why not?" I might be insulting the son of the biggest army general, but I had to ask. The shy dancer type with slender limbs and fine calves sticking out of the first row was next. And then the leather jacketed, greasehead punk artist, who had already picked the strategic spot right next to the dancer, horny devil. There was one of those in every crowd. The next and the next. . . . One could see so much from this spot, it was amazing. I braked only when an older and wiser cadre type stood up and made the sweeping confession that I had long been waiting for. "We are here to learn from A, B, C, Teacher Chen. Your fluent English much impressed us, and we feel very proud to be here, but please no more English until we can understand it better. Thank you, and forgive me for being so forward with my words. I do speak for the class."

He made me feel like a jerk. I quickly changed my tactics. My humble self had been screaming to come out, and it was now safe to do so. The class was a fog that lingered on forever. All I remember was the desperate longing for it to end. I was nearly out of breath when the bell finally tolled. I dashed off to my office and drugged up my head with thick smoke.

"How did it go?" Rua asked.

"Very well."

"How well?"

"Well enough to have them asking me how old I was, whether I had a girlfriend, and if not, was I looking for one?"

"Then it did not go that well at all. You became their friend too quickly. They will eat you alive soon."

"I think not, Dr. Psychologist. I much prefer the non-Hitler tactics of being my nice humble good old useful self."

"Now I'm a Hitler," Rua said, laughing.

"I was joking. I'm still a nervous wreck from the torture. Come have a smoke, and what is your foot size? I'll write home to get you a pair of these heels."

"Thirteen wide."

"I hope they make them that big."

We laughed.

I found out soon that I had a passion for teaching, and I was told by my students that I was a good teacher. They were a group of kind and eager grown-ups who were willing to grow with me as I went along. I committed more than my share of follies before them, but they understood and rallied behind me. I loved my students.

On Autumn Moon Festival, I was invited to a party downtown to see some of my freshly graduated classmates. They were all excited about their new jobs. The radio announcer was bragging about his first stint, the tourist guide about her first expedition to Tibet, the aviation translator was talking about his miserable time with aviation terminology, and I was babbling about the varieties of adult students in my class. We danced and drank, and the friendship that had never quite been there was now born because we were no longer in competition with one another. Half of the people there were drunk. So was I, happily so. I slept a deathlike sleep on the party floor till the following noon, then stumbled back to my dorm room. About to unlock the door, I was surprised to find the door already open, and even more surprised when I spotted our dean sitting on my bed.

"What are you doing here, dean?"

"You don't know why I am here?"

"No." I searched my foggy mind. Nothing came out.

"Weren't you supposed to be teaching some class this morning?"

"Oh, my lord," I screamed. I had forgotten the classes totally.

"Four hours of classes untaught. It's an unforgivable blunder for a young teacher like you. Where is your discipline? Where is your sense of duty?" He paced urgently, babbling and shouting.

"I'm so sorry," I cried.

"You ruin our school reputation that way. In your class there is the daughter-in-law of the education minister, a general's son, and the most outspoken reporter from a major newspaper. How are you going to explain it all?"

"I can't. I just forgot."

"Never ever again," was all he said before stomping out.

My future here is over, I thought. I rushed to the classroom, trying to catch up with my students and apologize. It was noontime. They should all have gone to lunch by now, but when I got there, two-thirds of them were still there.

"Oh, Teacher Chen is here," they shouted.

"We were so worried."

"I'm so sorry, so very sorry. And I'm so glad you are here to please accept my apology."

"No, no, no." The wise old man explained. "Everyone was wonderful. No one wanted to report to the dean at all. We just closed our door and studied. It wasn't until the fourth period that some teacher walked in by mistake and found out about your absence."

"You have been protecting me?"

"All of us."

"Why?"

"Because you told us about the party that you were going to, and we thought what a lonely fellow you are, no family here and no friends on this holiday. We thought you just probably got delayed coming back home."

"Oh, you guys are so wonderful."

"That teacher was good too. She said she would not have reported it except that she was worried that something might have happened to you. That was why the campus police were called and your room pried into."

"We were so worried about you," a woman said.

"I got drunk and slept through the morning. I had totally forgotten about you."

"Apology accepted, and we want to write a letter to the dean not to punish you because you have been a wonderful, dutiful teacher who should not be less regarded at all for an isolated incident like this."

"Thank you, thank you."

*   *   *

I lost my last connection with my student life when the school asked me
to move from my old den to the young teachers' quarters. I lost both hot
shower privileges and doorman safety in one stroke. The new abode was a
five-story dump with hallways lined with diapers and cooking stoves. The
laundry room hung with dripping clothes, and even the stairways were
narrowed two feet by chunks of coal bricks that were used for fuel on
every floor. During mealtimes, everyone was cooking something, and the
hallway became a smelly and smoky food bazaar under dripping diapers
and drying clothes. No one seemed to notice, and nobody minded either.
Everyone chatted happily about their day as they sautéed sizzling dishes.
The word *ghetto* came to mind, though this was hardly a bad life.

My roommate was a short man named Lee, who carried his old bike
to the fifth floor every night for fear of its being stolen.

"Why?"

"We're outside the wall. Thieves are everywhere."

At night the wind howled, blowing the dust and sand into the lobby
and slamming the squeaky doors loudly. Lonesome windows wept with
them. The floors were dirty and sticky. The building was poorly main-
tained and had no hygiene to speak of. Leftover food and rotten vegetables
were everywhere, and the footprints of coal trailed from our building like
busy bean sprouts into other parts of the campus. And yet there was that
atmosphere of an early settlement, an incohesive living waiting to graduate to a higher plateau someday. But when and how no one knew. One
should feel very lucky just to have a bed there. At night the young faculty
could be found in their pigeon boxes illuminated by fifteen-watt bulbs,
playing poker, chatting, and studying; some loving, others fighting, and still
others daydreaming. It was a world all by itself, a world of temporary
migrants. But that was okay, I too was only passing through.

The light four-class-a-week teaching load left me lonely and wandering
in my plentiful spare time. I dabbled in the subject of linguistics and borrowed a copy of Noam Chomsky's definitive book in the field, titled
Generative Transformational Grammar. I found it incredibly dull and didn't get
past the preface. I went on to comparative literature. It took me a while to
figure out what I ought to be comparing, and I soon realized that one

could not compare Peking Duck with T-bone steak. They were both good. Later I toyed with the idea of strengthening my French, in which I had toiled with a teetering tongue for two years as a requisite second foreign language, but the damned conjugation was all too noodling and the arbitrary feminine and masculine left my feeble mind effectively gender confused. So I strolled onto the campus, hoping to reignite the sparks of my student life. I waved to some familiar faces from the lower classes, but they politely peddled away with that look of disdain and deference that said, *Teach, get lost, you don't belong here anymore.* I then turned to the easy temptation of joining other young faculty in their yawning poker games. But soon I was disfavored because I was one of the few uncoupled sticks who broke the squareness and evenness of a good four-corner game. I, the unattached bachelor, ended up pouring tea and lighting cigarettes for the players to fill my lonely nights with empty companionship.

One day, seeing Lee lugging his bike on his shoulder down the spiraling stairs, I asked where he was heading.

"My classes," he said.

"What classes? You only teach eight classes, as I recall, and they are all on Tuesday."

"Right, but you didn't count the other ten I'm teaching outside the school."

"Outside the school?"

"Yes, moonlighting."

"Well, how do you get invited?"

"By contacts."

"Is it allowed?"

"No mention, no trouble. Keep it quiet."

"How is the pay?"

"Let me put it this way. I make in five hours what I do in a month here." Off he rode, whistling, the rascal. No wonder I hardly saw him. And I had just thought he was having affairs with five different girlfriends at the same time.

The following day I let it be known among my students that I was ready for hire if anybody knew of anyone in the far-flung city in need of a good speaking teacher. I was surprised by a dozen invitations that came in a few days later, which included the Academy of Science—China's top brain trust, the Chemical Engineering College around the corner, Qinghua University, Iron and Steel University, and the Film Academy. I

wished I had ten feet and three heads. All offers promised long-term con-
tracts with good pay. I took the five top bidders within riding distance.
Eight yuan an hour, teaching oral English and listening comprehension. I
plucked the abacus in my head. That was two hundred forty yuan a month
extra. I would be filthy rich teaching only thirty hours a week. All I needed
was some rudimentary linguistic talent. No rules, no political meetings, in
and out, eight yuan an hour. It was better than prostitution.

So I began the sunny moonlighting phase of my life. I bought myself
a bike and wheeled around within a thirty-mile radius. I gave rousing
lessons to eager red-faced students with stars in their eyes. I was the angel
who delivered the unattainable classes beyond the wall of the gilded
Foreign Language Institute. Young lads with American dreams saw me as
nothing less than a messiah who was there to deliver the gospel. Older
folks saw me as a singing artist with an Englished tongue. I logged
mileage on my slender wheels and counted the instant cash that kept
growing in my pockets. Life was all about working, and it was gratifying.
I sent a bundle back to my parents. They were surprised by the large sum.
I told them that money was easy, enjoy it. Mom kept it in a box for my
rainy day. At night I lay quietly staring at the ceiling like my roommate,
Lee, exhausted from the nonstop talking and standing and riding around.
I was too tired even to take off my heels. Lee would bring home a drink
sometimes. We would swallow quietly, and he would ask, "Now you
enjoy the freedom?"

I would nod.

Money was good, classes were fun, but something was missing. The
future did not look especially bright for a young hustler like me. I would
read and hear about some classmates' great success in America or in their
jobs, and I would stretch out on my bed, staring at the ceiling, mind blank.
Stagnation stifled me like a thick blanket on a summer night.

"Why are you so anxious about things?" Lee asked me. "You teach, you
moonlight, you date a little, and in a year or two the department will get
a slot for you to go to America or England. You go there for a year or two,
get yourself gilded with a master's degree, come back, get married, have
children, and be happy like the rest of us lucky bunch. By fifty, you'll be a
full professor, and by sixty-five, you'll retire. Then you return to Yellow
Stone and enjoy the warm sun. Isn't that wonderful?"

"It sounds like a risk-free life sentence, Lee. I need to get out of here."

"Like those highfliers? Business school, law school?"

"Law school? Who is going to law school?"

"One of our classmates who was an Ivy League undergraduate. She is going to law school at Columbia University."

"Well, why can't I do that?"

"I doubt it."

"We'll see."

"I've got to sleep. Tomorrow is heavy, eight classes at three different locations."

"May your dreams be rich with coins."

"They are." He was snoring in a second.

One Saturday after a long and hard week of work, Lee invited me for a drink of Mao Tai, a rare brew for the average person in China.

"Where did you get that?"

"Well, one of the students tried bribing me with it, because only the best in his class of this technical school get to go to America, and he isn't the best."

"What are you going to do?"

"Nothing. I am a teacher and I have integrity."

"Good man."

"He did offer me a job with a nice trading firm because his father runs it. Foreign trips and great benefits, but I don't want to make one mistake and regret it forever. That reminds me to remind you of one very important thing you ought to be doing now that you're making a zillion yuan a month."

"What is it?"

"You see, everyone on our campus is very jealous of us young English teachers. They think we're cheating the system somewhat, though I disagree. Their eyes are red because we make obscene amounts of money, and they are just waiting for a chance to ruin us. They don't bother me very much, except our dean and one of the vice deans. See, our dean studied Russian in his youth, and I heard he's quite envious of us. He leads us but gets no goodies. You have to bribe him big to make him happy."

"I happen to belong to the same school of thought as you. I've been bribing him throughout my student career. You may call me a career briber."

"Good, smart guy." Lee's tongue was slurring. "There are many ways of bribing them, the worst one being that they fancy you as a son-in-law."

"I will not have any problem with that."

"You never know. Frogs have been known to be the object of pursuit before."

I hit him with a roasted peanut let free from scissoring chopsticks.

"Okay, so you don't have that problem. I did. I said no, and here I am, stranded. The guy behind me has gone to England for an advanced degree in linguistics. But what are you going to do?" He shrugged. "I still stand by the belief that one marries for love and not because he's the bending peon in a strategic chess game. It wasn't a bad offer, army nurse, powerful father and all. But that's beside the point, young fellow. The point is that they will ask you to help them with their children's English, high school cousins of theirs, college sons, graduate school daughter-in-law, etc., etc. You have to pretend to jump at any request, or hint of a request, and never ever say no because you'll officially be declared fucked if you do. Just think, that's their only hope, the next generation. Put that line in your diary and remember it, okay?"

"I will."

"Good, someone already put in a request for your services, a very important fellow on campus."

"You got me a request?"

"Yes, indeed. What's a good friend for? While you were out today, our dean came here asking for you."

"The dean?"

"Yes, he wants you to teach his son, a graduate school student of some sort, on Wednesday nights."

"I have an Academy of Science class to teach, my favorite students, diligent and smart."

"Okay, okay, okay. That they may be. Why don't you run over to his home now and talk to him."

I did that right away. The dean and his heaving wife received me this time with a smile.

"Is Wednesday any good?" The dean came right to the point.

"I'm afraid not. I have an engagement that night, but I'll be more than happy to teach him on Tuesdays."

"No good. Can't you change your off-campus activity?" The dean's eyes dimmed.

"I can't. It's a big class with fifty serious scientists," I explained, trying to persuade him with the pompous name of the top brain trust, but he still got upset.

Leaving for her kitchen, his wife mumbled, "What good are you if you can't help even this much?"

"Don't say that." He pretended to calm his wife.

"And you call yourself a dean. You can't even get him to change his time."

Another melodrama. It was time to be very flexible. "Give me a day or two and let me see if I can change the date for you."

"My son can't wait that long. He is a very busy man. I can always ask others to do the job."

I found it odd that I was the one doing the begging, but the reality was that in some way beyond my control I was already making him mad. "Okay, one day is all I need to change the time schedule so that I can accommodate you."

"Accommodate me? I am giving you a chance."

"How so?"

"So you don't corrupt your young mind with money and money all the time. You guys have gone too far with this moonlighting thing. Go now. And I need an answer by tomorrow."

Shock could hardly describe my feeling leaving there. He was worse than a bull. Lee was waiting for me when I returned.

"What happened?" he asked.

"I got him mad. I said I can't change the time that quickly and needed at least one day to change the schedule for him."

"Didn't I tell you never to say no? You should have said yes at all cost."

"But I can't leave my students dangling like that."

"Fuck them. What is the worst that can happen to you if you let them dangle?"

"A lot of things."

"No, eight yuan an hour. That's it."

"More than that. I have integrity and duty and responsibility, everything that a teacher should have. I can't just walk out like that."

"Now you are fucked. I told you so."

"What's going to happen to me, you think?"

"Forget going abroad. Forget promotion. Forget everything. You'll suffer till you die."

"I don't believe it."

"You'd better. Have you ever read the translated version of *The Godfather*, an American bestseller?"

"No."

"You should. It is so much like Communist China, I simply love it. The only difference is that the Mafia seem to have a little more heart."

"You're drunk, aren't you?"

"Yes, I am, and fuck the cadres!"

My sentiments exactly.

The next day I got up early to call the Academy of Science and managed, through much begging, to change the whole class to Tuesday. Then I trotted to the dean's office only to be met by his cold eyes.

"I could teach your son on Wednesday. When can we start?"

He was quiet and brooding.

"Well?"

"No, thanks. My son thinks that you're not good enough." He would not even look at me.

"Why?" I asked.

"You speak with your Fujian accent and all. He is now being tutored by a young, female teacher who said yes readily."

"Well, I'm pretty good with my grammar, and I'm free most of the time if you ever need me."

"You can go now. In fact, my son's grammar is probably better than yours. He is taking lessons from a full professor on that subject."

"Good for him. What else can I teach him now that I have canceled my class at the academy?"

"For your information, my son is one of the brightest graduate students in his technical college and is going to get a doctor's degree in America. Frankly, there is very little you can teach him. Good-bye," he said.

What a bastard! *Fuck your goddamned son and the hell with you!* I ran down the stairs, oblivious to my students' greetings. It was then and there that I uttered the words in the willowed garden, "I need out of here. The sooner the better." My shouts scared a few birds that took off noisily into the sky. I wished I could just take off like them, easy and free, but I couldn't. The government's job assignment was like a shackle you wore around your ankles, chaining you down forever. This was what you were, and more, what they dictated you would always be.

One afternoon the fashionable wife of a vice dean danced her way up our narrow stairway, heading directly to my room. This colorful social butterfly wouldn't be here for nothing, I thought. She was a well-known soprano who belonged to a prominent Western opera company in the city, vastly different from the yee-yee-ya-yaing misery of the Peking Opera. I had a confessed softness for those temperamental artists, and I wasn't going to anger another dean, half dean, or their wives as long as I had to breathe near this tiger's den.

Dusting the hateful traces of coal dust off her dress, she delivered a brilliant aria of an opening line. "You're not going to believe this, but I've heard you play your bamboo flute. It was breathtaking."

Breathtaking! Did you hear that? A top artist thought I was breathtaking. That took my breath away. I coiled like a snail in hot embarrassment, claiming that it was just my rusty old fingers on a moldy, rotten flute.

"But you are the combination of earthy tradition and the heightened pursuit of a grand Western culture."

"What do you mean?"

"What do I mean? You are the quintessential ideal contemporary youth. The moldy flute and a mouthful of fine-tuned, beautiful English. You are happening!"

"Oh, that."

"Oh, that? Is that all you have to say about yourself? You're extraordinary."

Her flattery disarmed me, and I knelt in happy surrender. "To what do I owe your presence, Mrs. Ga?"

"Oh, I almost forgot. A dear friend of mine, the most renowned philharmonic conductor in our land, has a daughter." She paused. "Married, of course. This is not matchmaking, by the way, you can breathe now."

I chuckled.

"She needs some private tutoring in English. Are you interested in helping her?"

"Coming from you, yes."

"Good. Now how much do you charge? Because money is no object."

"This is where you get me wrong. I love artists. I'll do it for free."

"Really?"

"Yeah."

"You won't regret it. And my husband thinks you are a wonderful, promising young teacher." She said all the right stuff at the right time, a superb performance deserving a standing ovation.

A few days later, Ms. Wen Nah, a flutist, and her husband, an *er-hu* player, showed up at my door. They were a great young urban couple who were eager to learn English. They too wanted to pursue their education further in America.

"What do you want to study in America?" I asked Wen.

"Computer."

"How about your flute?"

"You don't go to America to learn the flute. This is a leisurely profession that makes no money. Besides, the flute was a way of getting a job, my being the daughter of a well-known conductor and all."

"What would your father think of your change of profession?"

"He'd applaud."

"How interesting."

Wen was candid and straightforward without the pretense of a city slicker. Her husband was funny and witty, there every step of the way to support his wife in her new pursuit. We became instant best friends. As I soon found out, Mrs. Ga's claim that money was no object was ill-founded. The young couple had the same worries about their future and money that I did. Her orchestra had been disbanded after the Cultural Revolution, and she was now condemned to a lathe machinery job that promised thick grease and low compensation. Her flutist's hands had been bruised and blackened on the first day of her job. The dark factory wasn't her dream at all. Her husband, a happy-go-lucky guy, still hung onto his Chinese traditional orchestra, which was being revived lately, though it remained as uncertain a prospect as the next crop. His biggest fear and the cause of his orchestra's inevitable demise was the earthshaking rock and roll that was raging throughout China. "I like it. It stirs something in me. But I hate it at the same time. Now I have to learn how to play the guitar just to catch up," he confessed sadly.

"Too late, you old man. Better start learning English," his loving wife said.

"Too late for that too. All the nicotine and drunken brain cells aren't helping. It took me a whole day to remember the word *dictionary*. By this morning, all I remembered was *dick* something."

"That's also a word, a bad one," I said.

"Is it? Let me write it down. How bad?"

"Don't teach him the bad words. What does it mean anyway?" Wen asked.

"I can't say it in front of you."

"You men are all the same."

To compensate me, they invited me to see her father conduct the

People's Philharmonic Orchestra. As much as I worshiped the Westernness of Beethoven and Bach, they all turned out to be good dozing materials. They had to wake me up as the last notes were being fluttered away. They did not want their father to see their young teacher snoozing right under his sweaty baton.

After the concert, her father, a distinguished-looking man with a Mao face, asked me, "How did you like the music?"

"Resoundingly well," I said. "It was nice of you to invite me."

"You are doing such a good job with my daughter. Thank you. We should have dinner sometime at our home."

"I'd be honored."

"I heard that you're a flutist. How did you like the magic flute section of the performance?"

I had no clue. His daughter came to my aid in the way only a daughter can. "Dad, stop asking questions. He fell asleep during the show."

"Oh, never mind then. But coincidentally, the magic flute was supposed to put a golden youth to sleep against a haystack."

"So the magic of your music is still there."

We had a good laugh.

"I'm sorry, I just couldn't keep my eyes open."

"That's all right. You didn't grow up with this sort of music," Wen said. "It takes a while to acquire the taste."

"Are you saying I'm a simple-minded country lad who is incurably naive and hopelessly beyond help?"

"Yes, I am."

"Thank you, my friends."

"But there is nothing wrong with your taste in Chinese music," she went on to say. "Some of the pieces are beautiful."

"They are. And thank Beethoven. Now I love my native music more than ever."

Chapter Twenty-six

In the winter of 1984, I was late for the swearing-in ceremony for two young teachers being admitted as the newest members of the Communist Party. I was returning from a moonlighting job. No matter how hard I had fought the traffic, it had fought back. My bike got a flat tire and I had to carry it all the way back to school.

I missed the bogusly moving part where the two girls saluted the hammer and sickle on the red flag and pledged to spread Communism to the ends of the world. It always made me want to puke, listening to the testimony of new members. They were untrue and some downright fraudulent. I planted myself next to Lee, another snorer on fanfare occasions such as this.

"These girls must be true Communist believers," I said. "They're crying." The two were teary and hugging each other on the stage, making quite a show.

"Bullshit, Da," Lee whispered. "You just missed the part when the party chief, our dean, announced their chance to go abroad. They had been quiet and nervous till then."

"They are going abroad? But Yang"—one of the girls—"came later than I."

"I told you you were fucked."

"I'd better hand in my application for membership soon."

"I think the answer is yes. Even the fellow who came with you is now promoted to Youth League secretary. You also missed out on the chance to go to Guangzhou for a training session. All the guys who got ahead were the ones who sucked up to them. Do something before you fall any further behind."

"But I've been doing my job well, as my students have been telling the leaders."

He shrugged.

Not long after, I filled out a wrinkled party application and found myself at the chief's home.

"Comrade Da, what brings you here?" the dean asked.

"The beckoning of the party's light." I quoted a line from a smushy party song.

"Could it be the calling of an American dream?"

"No, not at all. I feel the urge to be a part of such a grand tradition, and I'm willing to make sacrifices to realize the Communist tomorrow."

"You want to go abroad, I can tell."

"Yes, that too. I noticed that two girls who came after me are packing to go now. It makes me wonder if I have been dragging my feet along the political road. I want to catch up with everyone."

"But you are not the type for the party."

"Why not?"

"You seem to enjoy freedom too much."

"What do you mean, chief?"

"While you were reading your foreign books and taking side jobs beyond your workload, which is fine with us due to the new economic reform policy, others like the two girls were studying Mao's collection of works. They turned in their memos and diaries of their thoughts after reading them, and didn't go out there and make money, which is also fine with us. They spent all their time preparing for the few lessons they had."

"But my students say I am a far better teacher than they are."

"That might be. But they are diligent and docile. They are punctual for all the political meetings, they don't drink, and they don't smoke. While you guys, I heard, have quite a loose lifestyle up there on the fifth floor, buying drinks to entertain other young teachers and corrupting them."

"We do drink once in a while, but others do too, including some senior faculty."

"They've earned their right to smoke and drink."

"How do you earn the right to do that?"

"By being old enough."

"I am in my twenties now and make my own money to support the habit."

"I told you money is no good. Had you just made enough like all the rest of us, you wouldn't be flaunting the new bike that you have or those bell-bottom trousers and heeled shoes that you are wearing now."

"What is wrong with that?"

"Nothing's wrong. It only says that you are ordinary material, not party material."

"Can I just turn in this form anyway to show my good intentions and my desire?"

"It won't be necessary."

"In case you change your mind."

"We'll call on you when we change our mind."

"How about my chance to go abroad? Remember, at the beginning of my job, you promised me that would come after a couple of years."

"Has it been a couple of years already?"

"Yes. Will I be the next one now that people behind me in the line have already gone?"

"Well, that's really not the order, Da."

"What is the order?"

He smiled mysteriously and said, "Be patient. The party will let you know."

"I just wait?"

"Yes."

"And the party will let me know?"

"Yeah." He said a yawning good night.

I ran down the stairs and angrily stuck my middle finger sky-high in the dark winter night. "The party will let you know" line rang in my head all the way home. I downed a tall cup of a strong local brew with Lee, who had been waiting for me expectantly.

"So what did he say?"

"That the party will let me know."

"I hate that line too." Lee tossed down another cup and said, "I hate to say it, Da, but you and I are officially out of luck with the going abroad thing."

"What should we do?"

"I don't intend to do anything. I am a patient guy. I'll date until I marry the right girl and I'll moonlight till the sun rises. And I'll outlive this bastardly reign of cadres, until new guys take their positions. Then I'll restart my career. I'm happy where I am, making ten times what my dad makes. I drink my own drink. Other youngsters like me have to beg for a drink; they can't afford it. And girls are plentiful out there. I'm seeing three at the same time, at different locations, of course, much the same way I teach classes. I don't bring the feelings from one to another. It works out well. As for you, the impatient fellow from the hot stove of a province called Fujian, you have to find your own way out of here."

"Like what?"

"Some sort of a ship, any ship—scholarship, fellowship—whatever ship will sail for America." He gave a blurry toast.

"But will they let me go?"

"They won't. You'll have to fight. There is one successful case where a girl got her own scholarship and then went, but only after much fight." He took another gulp and wrinkled his nose, as if telling an ancient tale.

"How much fight?"

"A lot. But get the chance first. Expand your search, do what you have to do, young man, and deal with the issue one step at a time."

"It's so hard out there. I don't know anyone in power at all, and all the universities I have written to never responded."

"You are not party material," he deadpanned. "That's why you deserve only a tough fate." He smiled wickedly.

"A tough fate?"

"Are you up to it?" He picked up the drink and poured me another one.

"I am." I could hear my own hollow echo.

While I was working on finding a way out of China, I became enthralled with an American couple who had found their way into China. The Walterses were disarmingly lovable, and they made themselves even more adorable by being so in love with each other. They held hands, echoed each other's laughter, and finished each other's sentences, smooching lip to lip as they parted for each class. In the land where loving intimacy was to be hidden darkly under the nightly quilt at home, the Walterses broke all the rules of social constraints. But they were readily excused because they were foreigners, and even more so, Americans. They were from the land of beauty, and everything they did was beautiful.

Bob was a musician, I could tell from the gentle smile in his eyes even before his face creased into a smile. Myrna was a psychoanalyst with piercing eyes. They charmed people with their easy and comfortable way. Their smiles lingered long after their greetings faded away.

As the newness of their arrival aged, I found myself standing before Bob one day, itching to strike up a conversation that was long overdue. I loved artists in any colors or stripes. I felt that they spoke to me and I spoke to them, even in those nodding silences in passing, as if artistry set us apart from the rest of the world as a unique species.

He had begun to have that I'd-rather-be-doing-something-else look that transported him beyond the window, over treetops, into the invisible green mountains, the absentmindedness of a trapped artist. It was time to save his soul. I felt I understood him like no one else.

"I am Da Chen, assistant professor here, as you have probably noticed," I said politely.

"Hi, Mr. Chen." A casual American "Hi," while extending his hand to shake mine.

"You remember me?"

"Yes, I'm not one of those foreigners who claim that all Chinese look alike." His humor was disarming.

"You have the vision of an artist then."

He lifted his eyebrows, provoked out of his boredom.

"What instrument do you play?" I asked.

"Sit down." He shifted in his seat to face me. "The viola. You're the first one in China to ask me that. Do you know what the viola is?"

"A bigger peanut than a violin?"

"That's it. You have a way of putting things."

"Would you like to meet other musicians in Beijing?" I asked.

"Why, yes. I have been waiting for someone to ask me that ever since I arrived. Do you know any musicians?"

"The most famous conductor in China."

He leaned closer. "Really?"

"Would you like to have dinner with him this coming Sunday?"

"Would I?" he said, smiling now. "I would be delighted."

"Please also invite your wife to come along."

"Thank you, we always go together as a pair."

"I noticed. I just have one more question for you."

"Shoot."

"What are you doing here teaching English, when you're a violist and your wife a doctor?"

"Well." He looked around. "We'd better talk about it somewhere else."

We went to an empty classroom where he told me that both of them were volunteer missionaries from a religious college in Lincoln, Nebraska. They were using their sabbatical year to do this.

"But you're teaching English?"

"Because your government doesn't allow us to come as missionaries. So we came in disguise, so to speak."

"Well you just gave away your secret mission to someone you barely know," I said.

"Someone I trust."

"Why?"

"Your eyes, that spirit, that openness. My wife and I were saying even the other night that you looked different from the others. There's something graceful about you."

"Well," I said. "Are you recruiting me already?"

"We look and listen for our Lord. If we see the shining spots in darkness, we try to find them, and sometimes they find us, much like you did. I think someone sent you here to meet me. A good someone." He looked above, out the window where the sky was blue.

I got that same eerie feeling I had when I first met Professor Wei, that rare Baptist back home in Yellow Stone. "I have met a Christian before."

"You have?"

"Yeah. And she is the kindest human I have ever met. In fact, she taught me my first English words."

"Very, very interesting. I think we have a wonderful friendship ahead of us."

*   *   *

In the early eighties, foreign visitors were few. And they were politely kept at the hotels and gatherings where their own species flocked. No one was allowed to bring any of these foreign camels home for fear that the aliens would get to smell the rat and rot of our system. If, for any godforsaken reason, a foreign guest could not be coaxed out of an interest in visiting a private residence, the party chief of the community of the target resident would mobilize his muscle and have all the best furniture assembled from the neighborhood and moved into the house as stage props for the visit. The face of Communism had to be saved at all costs. The house might look like a hodgepodge of a local theater with furniture that did not match or fit, but worse was the state of the house when the hurricane passed through and the real owners of the furniture rushed in to claim their property. A house could be ruined that way, and no one would be there to carry the old furniture back into the house, partly because there was no point in doing so. Usually by then the aged furniture had already fallen apart. To resolve that problem, some communities had set up model homes for individuals to entertain their foreign guests. The hosts and hostesses would try to pretend that it was their house, but it was hard to pretend when you walked into a closet thinking that it was a bathroom.

Mr. Nah, the preeminent conductor, sneered at such absurdity even though his next-door neighbors—also a director of the People's Philharmonic Orchestra and his mean wife—daily peeped through the cracks of their door to make note of their frequent unusual guests so that they could report to the authorities and get Mr. Nah into trouble. Mrs. Nah, a kindhearted society woman of another era—the old Shanghai—had long since learned to cook a handful of delicious dishes during their hard years. She loved telling of her first encounter with her husband, the man who had always managed to move his feet half a beat faster than the music on the dance floor. She said that only a conductor could do such a thing without veering out of rhythm.

The Walterses arrived in a taxi, dressed in suits. Neighbors peeped from behind their windows, and the kids in the compound shouted, "Foreigners! Foreigners!" A politically correct household would at least try to hide those guests and rush them right from the taxi into their door, but not the Nahs. They stood at the door, smiling and shaking hands with them.

The ladies went to chat noisily in the kitchen.

Seeing the full table of steaming food, Bob said, "It is so kind of you to have cooked so much for us."

"We Chinese know no other way of showing our hospitality."

"That's the same way with Italians like me," Bob said. "Civilization was built around food."

"In China, food is built around civilization," Mr. Nah said. "Food is heaven."

Bob thanked me for arranging the dinner, and Mr. Nah thanked me as well with his unique reasoning. "I only consider a friend a real friend when he brings his friends to meet other friends of his. That shows faith and trust. Da is wonderful. We owe a great deal to him for teaching our daughter English. And today I owe him another debt for bringing an artist friend to my door from across the Pacific Ocean."

A toast was proposed, and the two men never stopped talking, Mr. Nah about his early years studying conducting with Russian masters in the fifties and the hardship during the Cultural Revolution, Bob about his own composing and conducting and his job as a music teacher and chairman of the music department at his college.

"You conduct?" Mr. Nah was struck by the revelation.

"I do, but I only conduct a small orchestra in Lincoln, Nebraska."

"That's good. Can I see some of your compositions?"

"Absolutely." Bob came prepared.

Nah dropped his chopsticks and read the title. "Very good."

"In fact, if it ever gets performed, it will be the world premiere. It's never been performed before."

Nah put on his bifocals and picked up one chopstick, which he pinched between his thumb and index finger. Silently he read the notes. His eyes narrowed and his head waved. The Walterses stopped eating and watched the master, as did everyone else. Nah knit his eyebrows and tilted his head. The chopstick flew up and down, making invisible lines and dots in the air, weaving musical notes indiscernible to the rest of us. Then a smile creased his face, and the bifocals slid down his nose tip. Nah leaned on his single chopstick and asked, "Would you like to premiere your composition here in Red China?"

Bob was caught off guard and fumbled for words.

"Would you like to have your work performed here by the biggest orchestra in China?" Nah asked again.

"Yes," Bob answered.

"Better yet, would you consider conducting your own premiere with our orchestra?'"

"Yes." A more certain answer this time. "But why, maestro?"

"Because you are the first living American composer I've met who could conduct, and you are here to conduct it. If everything goes as planned, you will be the first foreigner ever to premiere his own work in China, an unprecedented event."

"Oh, my. I could not thank you enough."

"The pleasure is all mine," Nah said. "The long Cultural Revolution stopped all the cultural exchange. We have to start somewhere. And it is better with you, our friend, than others who might be coming very soon to our door."

On our way home in the taxi, Bob was quiet, thinking about what had just happened.

"Congratulations!" I said.

"I'm truly flattered."

"He saw your talent. Nah is known in China for going to great lengths to discover new talent for China. And maybe," I said thoughtfully, "this is your god's reward for your missionary work."

The three of us smiled. The couple giggled and kissed happily. There was a sense of incredulousness between them. They hummed and chatted all the way home like birds resting in a leafy tree.

Chapter Twenty-seven

Every day after work Bob would pedal his bike with me to the People's Philharmonic and rehearse with eighty-some of the finest musicians there. Among the busy stream of bicycles of Beijing, we were like lonely salmon making their leap of faith against the tide, swimming one inch at a time upstream with spawning urgency. I was the nimble one, guiding him in shuttling quickness, while he overflowed the pathetically narrow seat, pedaling slowly. Fragile, thin wheels constantly threatened to turn oval or go flat. At times, when the traffic thinned, I would circle back around to cheer him up, and he would heave up his chest and charge on. By the time we got to the rehearsal hall, he would be wet and laboring for breath. But that would change the instant he climbed up to the conductor's squeaky podium. A spirit of serenity, authority, and triumph would ascend onto his prominent gleaming forehead, and a conductor emerged. He would click his baton on the aluminum edge of the music stand. The musicians' faces would tighten, their backs straighten, and out would flow the magic golden yarn of his modern music.

I helped compose the promotional slogan that was printed on large billboards, touting Bob as a preeminent composer, conductor, and violist making his debut in China. I bullet-pointed a list of firsts: the first American, the first foreign composer, the first foreign conductor to conduct his own work, which was to be performed for the first time in the world, staged in the most prestigious theater. The billboards loomed largely everywhere we rode our bikes.

On the day of the performance, I assembled a TV crew from our campus for a thirty-yuan fee. They planted a camera in the audience and another camera backstage facing Bob. Bob also assembled a team of foreign friends with cameras all over their necks and rolls of film peeking from their pockets. I made sure the camera crew were happy and well fed, with enough cigarettes to stay awake.

On that moonlit evening in May, Bob's concert was the talk of the town. When the curtain was drawn, Bob leaped to life. His baton rose and fell, and music swelled and sank. He wasn't just making music; he was telling a tale of his land.

When his music ceased, flowers were thrown to the stage, and he picked them up with tears in his eyes. He was happy and threw his arms out to embrace everyone from every angle. The audience responded with deafening applause. The night belonged to him, and he belonged to the people of Beijing.

For days afterward, all we talked about was the concert and how he had managed to pull off something bigger than anything he had ever done in his life.

"Mr. Nah has gone to great pains to help me realize a dream. It is time I did something in return. Can you tell me how?" he asked me.

"You know, nothing is more important than helping his daughter get to America."

"Where is she in terms of application?"

"I think she has gotten an admission letter from an American language school to learn English."

"Good, so what else can I do?"

"Well, admission to an English school somewhere in Queens, New York, is not going to fly at the American embassy when she goes there to get her student visa. The Americans are very tight in giving visas out now that China is more relaxed about letting its people go. The situation used to be the reverse. She has an auntie who will sponsor her to America, but that only works against her, because the embassy is now thinking immigration—she'll never come back. So she'll never get her visa."

Bob thought for a second and smiled. "Let's wait and see. Maybe there is something I can do, but don't tell them yet."

"Okay."

"Now, you. You helped a great deal in making all these goods things happen for me. I'm working on something that will please you."

"Really? Like what?"

"Well, it's common knowledge that you are not party material in your department."

"How did you know?"

"My students, who are also your students, told me so. Everyone disagrees with that verdict, though. They all say what a wonderful teacher you are. And that gave me an idea. I think it would be great if you went to a place where people would appreciate you a little more."

"What do you mean?"

"I'm recommending you to my college in Lincoln, that you be given a fellowship to teach Chinese history, art, and language there for a couple of years. Then you could decide to do whatever you like for graduate studies. What do you think?"

I was shocked speechless. An opportunity to go to America. The idea hit me like a thick stick. My head began to swell with happy ripples.

"Are you okay?"

"Okay? I could kneel down to thank you forever."

"I found in you a great and genuine friend," Bob said warmly. "My life was completely changed when you entered our lives. We were strangers in a strange land, but you made that strange feeling go away. You guided us every way you could, wisely and appropriately. Life has turned out to be wonderful here. My wife and I could never have imagined that our China stint was going to be so much fun and adventure. We have cried and laughed so much, and we are closer than ever, thanks to God. We also discovered a long time ago that you are an unusually kindhearted young fellow, a hard thing to find nowadays, and extremely intelligent. You will go far, and we would like to help you go even further."

I was on the verge of tears. His kind words melted me like a lit candle.

"But now we have to pray for your fellowship. I have done my job instructing my wonderful and capable secretary to write letters to my college, to the president, admissions office, and everyone on campus to support my recommendation. The rest is up to our Lord in heaven."

"I don't know how to pray your way," I said.

"We hold secret worship services all over Beijing, one place a week, so that the police will not give us trouble. Why don't you come and visit us this Sabbath?"

I hadn't given much thought to religion since Robin's fellowships during my college days, but something about Bob and his wife made it seem very appealing.

"I'd love to."

Early Saturday morning Bob had me wait for him across the street from the Friendship Hotel entrance to avoid the suspicious eyes of the plainclothes police. I leaned against the lush trees that provided dark shadows, smoking and waiting. I saw him now, like a bear huddling over his thin bike, his viola case strapped across his thick back. He stopped his bike at the gate, gazed my way, and signaled with his head to the west. Then he pedaled into the Saturday stream of bikers. It seemed like a plot in a spy thriller: head signals, hand signs, tailing each other without giving the appearance of following each other, for the cause was sacred and the code could not be broken. Religion, under the glaring stare of Communism, took on an edgy spin. Bob pedaled strenuously ahead, not to lose me but to distance himself from me. He knew he could afford to be in trouble but I couldn't.

The May humidity unleashed the beehives of residents into the streets. Everyone seemed to be out on their bikes, with birdcages on handles and babies on the sidebars. Grannies with bound feet waddled on uneven sidewalks, pounded even by the roundness of their deformed feet. Kids flew kites that caught among the greening trees; strings broke, tears shed. Now colorful kites became butterflies pinned on trees. Little girls skipped rope amid food peddlers' steaming cooking stands, their ropes cutting the wholeness of the spitting smoke, their feet slicing the completeness of the delicious smell. Chicks, scared by the slicing rope, danced with the girls before landing on the stoves and stirring up a typhoon of dust, feathers, and smoke. Everyone in the bazaar screamed and shouted for the murder of the chicks.

The crowd might be thick, but Bob was an easy target, a head taller than most riders rubbing his elbows. I ground down on my bony behind and pedaled like a pro biker, standing up, left and right, up and down, and finally caught up with him.

"Can you tell me where we are going?" I asked breathlessly.

"An apartment near a Chinese medical college. One of our church members is a teacher there."

"But this is heading in the opposite direction."

"Sure it is. I'll take this route, cut through that little lane, then turn back. It's ten minutes longer, but I make sure no one is following me. I don't want my fellow members in trouble."

"What would happen to them if they were caught?"

"Lots of things. They would lose their jobs or end up in jail. See, your government covers one eye, letting private citizens meet to worship God. But when it involves a foreigner, it becomes a defiant act of treason."

"Why?"

"Somehow a foreign god is more dangerous than a local god."

"Do you know why?" I asked him.

"Why?"

"Because he has long hair and blue eyes and doesn't use chopsticks."

He smiled, clicking his bike bell, and turned into a narrow lane, navigating among residents who scattered in shock. Knowing that foreigners rarely invaded their dirty, meandering lanes, Bob greeted startled eyes with a smile, and fifteen minutes later, we were at the back entrance of the medical college.

A guard stuck his head out and stopped Bob with a nightstick. "Hey, you foreigner, what are you doing here?" he shouted.

"I'm here to see Dr. Lin," he said. I translated.

He looked at us suspiciously before reluctantly letting us in.

"Knowing how dangerous this is, why take such a risk? Why not wait until you return home to worship there safely?"

"This actually makes worship more meaningful. It has become a test of faith and the test gets harder and more trying by the week."

We climbed the apartment stairs where coal chunks lined the steps. The residents seemed to have divided up the common space to store the ugliest stuff. One neighbor hung smelly baby diapers over the railing. Bob gave the door on the third floor a four-plus-one knock.

A white-haired lady let us in after much nodding.

"Dr. Lin, this is Da Chen, the young man I have been telling you about." Bob introduced me, and I bowed and shook her hand. She looked too young to have such a head of white hair. Her eyes shone with kind and searching lights. A smile climbed up her wrinkleless face.

"You must be wondering about my white hair."

"How did you know?"

"Everyone calls it *qin nian bai,* youthful white. But the truth is also the truth of the Gospel. When I was in my thirties, I was arrested for hiding a Bible under my pillow. They sent me to a camp in the mountain. For four months I had little salt, and my hair all turned white, but I lived. I feel proudly that this white hair is a badge of honor from God. I have been telling everyone about it ever since." She let us sit, waving another handful of worshipers to come meet us. There was a busy exchange of warm hands and crowded bowing and nodding. Sacred secrecy shrouded this tiny living room whose window curtains were drawn for fear of peeping Commies.

Bob started the service by playing his viola. The worshipers sang along in uneven voices, some high, others low, some strong, others weak. They sang one hymn after another, not in a shouting chorus but in cicadas' chanting unison. Each voice represented a knowing heart, each sound a brave dagger into the noisy, careless Saturday afternoon. It was a tiny ten- by fourteen-foot room with old furniture and medical books lining the pale walls. But the joy evident in the gleaming eyes of those present was heaven high, as if each of them had found a love forbidden but one they could not live without.

I was the only outsider, taking a backseat. How could one be so feverish about anything that was so foreign to a Chinese soul, I wondered? But that wondering had no place in here. Their invisible god seemed to overwhelm us, making me feel nakedly ugly and insincere. I quickly stopped my secular thinking and clapped my hands together, mimicking their pious gesture. Then a thought came to me: I should beg this foreign god for foreign things like going abroad and gaining the fellowship that Bob had been telling me about. He had said that the rest was up to God. I slowly slipped down off my stool and knelt in silence. When the praying was over, Bob opened his eyes to catch a glimpse of me kneeling and smiled. I quickly replanted myself on the stool as though I hadn't moved an inch.

The service was testimonial. Everyone had a fantastic story to tell. Their torture during the Cultural Revolution had scarred their lives. One man had lost a wife who had hanged herself, another his hearing because he had been smacked endlessly until the noisy world was taken away from him forever. The youngest fellow was a steelworker who had gotten up at four that morning and traveled for hours after getting off work at midnight. He had heard the gospel on the shortwave radio broadcast from Hong Kong, and life had suddenly had meaning.

A simple lunch of a few vegetable dishes was shared by all. "I hope you will come more often," the white-haired doctor said. "There's always plenty of rice for a hungry young man like you."

I thanked the hostess with a deep bow.

"I saw you making contact with God," Bob commented as we headed for home.

"I prayed."

"That's wonderful," Bob said. "Did you feel His presence?"

"I can't say that I did, but I did feel at peace."

"That's a good start. Did you ask for what you wanted?"

"No."

"Why not?"

"I thought it would not be polite at our first meeting."

"Could there be some other reason for your shyness?"

"Like what?"

He suddenly braked, narrowly missing a child running across the road. "Like you are afraid of your Buddha."

I was quiet for the rest of the way home. He did not disturb me with other questions, just let me quietly pedal my bike, as if biking was such a thinking chore. Before we parted at the fork of the road, he straddled his bike with one foot on the ground, the other dangling. "Sometimes the best prayer is a silent one," he said.

"Yeah?"

"But He will hear you because I prayed for you."

With a mixed feeling of delight, shame, fear, and discovery, I rode home alone. I felt desperately in need of some earthly evils. Seeing me stumble home, my roommate, Lee, quickly poured me a tall drink. In silence we smoked and sipped, looking out our foggy window.

"What is bothering you?" he asked after drawing in a long lungful of smoke.

"A territorial dispute."

"How so?"

"I grew up in a Buddhist family, but I have just been to a Christian service."

"Religion. I can't advise you on that; I'm an atheist. I like sin too much."

"That's partially my problem too. I'm just as prone to sinful stuff as you are."

"Cheers."

"But I also worship the divine power."

"Bottoms up."

"What should I do?" I asked.

"Bottoms up again."

"Be serious. I need your guidance."

"Da, your struggle is the struggle of many great men. I gave up the fight early. The struggle itself is the winning spirit of a mortal man. At least that's what I've gathered from the writings of some great men. So relax and stop torturing yourself. It's okay to sin and love and worship one god or many gods at the same time. That's called faith. That's called love, and you are a lovely man."

"I don't know what helps me more, the smoke, the liquor, or you."

"We are equally bad for you."

Silently we drank up, leaving another philosophical problem unresolved.

Chapter Twenty-eight

Beijing in June was besieged by the grassy fragrance of ripe watermelons and damp armpits. Melons lined the streets like little mountains, some covered with leaves, others exposed. But armpits were everywhere, walking and spreading like death. Both tended to rot mightily in the slanting, fermenting afternoon sun. Sweaty men dried their armpits the manly way, using their hands; one wipe, two swipes, the final grab always the face.

But my fight against the white heat was the classic Yellow Stone way. I floated some cheap melons in the school swimming pool, then smashed them open on a tree trunk and slurped in the meat, letting the juicy shell wash my face. The coolness was a delight, and I burped with satisfaction. Then I let cool tap water run a shocking course through the hot rod of me. I wished summer would die in its own heat. Then again, I was likely to miss that hot spirit when autumn came. Oh, long summer days, short summer months, thou are the childhood of all seasons.

I was in dripping shorts, doing one of my coolings under a public water tap, when Bob came to see me with a smiling face. Foreigners were never forbidden here in the seedy residential quarters of my Chinese colleagues, but neither were they invited. I was surprised to see him. Quickly I closed the tap, but the dripping continued. I kicked once, kicked twice. The dripping stopped.

"You do know how to fix things," he said, amused.

"It's easy, that's the same way you fix everything in China. Who gave you the road map to find me here? You know you have gone way too far beyond the borderline," I joked.

"Good news couldn't wait." He waved an airmail envelope in his hand.

"The fellowship?"

He nodded.

I jumped for joy and my shorts splashed happy water. I ran over to grab the letter, but Bob pushed my hand away, admonishing, "You don't want to get it wet. It has important documents, an I-20 in here"—the official admission letter.

"Thank you, thank you. Please, you here wait," I babbled excitedly in Chinese English. "I change clothes and come back." He smiled, parked his bike, and sat down on a wooden chair painted red with its armrest missing and back broken.

I felt myself shivering, not from the cool shocking water but from the fantastic news. I flew up five flights of stairs in a 100-meter sprint, mopped dry my hair, and jumped into old, unwashed shorts that had three days of smell in them. Both feet tried to get into one leg. I fell, sitting on my butt. My head was spinning with the whirling good news. I-20! I-40! I-80! And my mouth was chanting, "America, Amelica, Amereeeca, Ameliiiica! Show me America, Bob."

Back downstairs, Bob said, "Sit down and let me explain the news. You are officially admitted into Union College's fall semester program. This letter says so. But the I-20 is really the important thing. See, it lists your major, business. I arbitrarily had my secretary pick one for you. Does that sound good?"

"You read my mind."

"The tuition comes from a few sources. One-third is from an achievement scholarship; they loved your grades and all. The other third comes from a tuition waiver, which applies to anyone who teaches at the school. You will be doing some teaching, by the way."

"What do they want me to teach?"

"Lectures on history, culture, language, calligraphy, maybe music. You will work it out when you get there."

"It sounds a little tentative."

"Wait till you hear this one. Another third of your tuition and your living expenses come from a donation."

"Donation? From whom?" I asked.

"Well, my wife and me."

"Oh, no. You don't make very much money, I know that. I can't accept that," I protested.

"Well, I knew you were going to say that. Here's the deal." He lowered his voice. "All I did was sign off on a required affidavit of financial support, allowing the college to issue you an I-20 with which to apply for a passport and visa."

"I see the wisdom here." I smiled. "Now what do I do after I get there to cover my living expenses?"

"It's a free country like they say."

"So I can go to work and make money to support myself?"

He nodded.

"But I heard you can't work legally without a permit?"

"But you have to live," he replied.

"Ah, I got it. It truly is a free country."

"I have the feeling you're going to do fine," Bob said.

"I will. I can't thank you enough for your help. You don't know what it means to me. It's a dream, an ideal, it's beyond description. It's like oxygen, freedom."

His eyes followed my words, as if words were physical shapes spelled out in the air.

"I want to run down the street and shout."

"But you can't."

"No, I can't."

"The real work is ahead of you. I heard it could be nasty," he warned.

"Nasty is hardly the word, more like deadly. The school thinks they own us, and they will do anything to stop us from going."

"I wish I could be here to help."

"You have helped more than enough. Are you leaving soon?"

"Mid-July."

"So I'll see you at Union?"

"I'm afraid not."

"Why?"

"I lost my job at the school. The new administration has appointed a new chairman for my department."

"I'm so sorry to hear that. Nothing seems secure in America. Here in our school, no one gets fired."

"But no one can leave the school alive either, as you will find out soon."

"Long live America."

"Indeed."

I invited Bob for dinner at the Chinese faculty dining room. Surprisingly, he accepted my invitation. Our government deemed the kind of local food served there inedible by foreigners.

"You don't mind eating there?"

"I'm easy to please."

The dining hall floor was sticky, and his big-toed summer sandals got stuck a couple of times. He wore an amazed look on his face.

"Have you ever seen a floor that could eat your shoes?" I asked.

"Never." He grinned.

"And have you ever eaten in a place where you have no idea what you are eating?"

"All the time," he said. "I like to be surprised."

He stood with me in the long line in front of the greasy windows. There were whispers and glances, but we ignored them all. We were too excited about our futures, mine an American dream, his an Asian dream. We sat in a quiet corner where ears were far away. Since he did not have anything to go back to, he said he might linger here in friendly Asia a little longer and perhaps secure another teaching job. He had been to Hong Kong once and he had loved everything there. I told him that he was one of the most ingenious men I had ever met. There should not be any difficulty that he could not resolve. He was a pearl that would shine anywhere he went.

The simple dinner was meant for celebrating our futures, but in our hearts it was a celebration of friendship formed a short while ago but destined to last forever.

That night I dashed off a long letter home telling my family about the good news. Mom would be in tears, rushing to the shrine to thank her gods, while Dad would stay up late, too excited to sleep. He would prod my dozing mom to continue the juicy talk of America. In doing so, he would bump into some great ideas. I asked him to write to his brother, my uncle in Taiwan, to let him know that I would be the second member of the Chen family to leave Communist China. What good news that would be for him.

My roommate, the permanent pessimist, was thrilled to hear my good news, which I limited to only a few very good friends because as a rule good news got no sympathy and even less mercy. He greeted it with a mysterious sigh. "Da, I don't know how to break this to you. But you could be looking at a piece of wastepaper here, your I-20."

"Why?"

"They won't let you go."

"But you were the one telling me to go find a fellowship by myself."

"Yeah, but you did not hear the end of the story."

"What is it?"

"You know that girl from our neighboring department who left for America?"

"The volleyball star?"

"Yeah, the long-legged, large-breasted girl."

"I got the picture."

"They let her wait for months without giving her permission to get the passport. Without that pink slip, you're not going anywhere fast."

"What happened then?"

"She used her weapon number one, tears. It did not work. Of course, she would have fared better with her bare legs and those plump knockers of hers."

"Go on."

"Okay, okay. She, of course, was not the type to sleep her way to America, the easiest way to gain a passport, which, by the way, you needn't try. Men are not wanted in bed. Women are, but not any woman, just pretty women. They get what they want anywhere they go."

"Stop your woman-bashing and go on."

"Forgive me for being a sad case. I was just dumped by all my girls on the same day. They got together and ganged up on me. It's a union. I'm finished!"

"Good for them but bad for you. Go on with your story," I urged.

"Okay, okay. So then she tried that last resort."

"What was that?"

"I wouldn't recommend it to anyone."

"Try me."

"Suicide."

"Are you kidding?"

"No. She was found unconscious from overdosing on some sleeping pills. They rushed her to the hospital, and the passport was issued the next day."

"And she was alive to use it?"

"Of course."

"Of course?"

A sly smile appeared on his face. "Rumor has it, unconfirmed, that she had written a letter to every cadre in the college who had played a part in refusing her the passport. She had promised, as a ghost, to haunt them and their offspring forever. That's why they let her go right away."

"Well."

"Then after she was safely in America, she was rumored to have written another letter to all those who had received her ghost letter. This one was a bomb. She told them that there had never been an overdose! It had been a fake suicide. She withheld the details but called all those cadres fools to have believed it at all. The letter ends with the 'he who laughs last' stuff. Now you know why I said you couldn't use that method, because they won't believe it's a real suicide attempt anymore. They'll just let you die. It won't work."

"You're not being helpful at all in telling me this."

"I'm not a cheerleader. I'm a problem solver."

"But you're eliminating all my options."

"No, I'm reducing your probability for error."

"What do I do now?"

"Start with the usual. Knock on the doors of all the big guys, and if it doesn't work, which will most likely be the case, then think of something very, very creative or kiss your dreams good-bye. And by the way, it takes a long time to buy plane tickets, assuming you have a thousand U.S. dollars. So you had better start tomorrow."

"Thank you, you just kissed my sleep good-bye."

"Then stay sleeplessly still. I need my eight hours before I can tackle my capitalist tasks tomorrow, eight classes, you know."

I had my first bout with the bureaucracy the following morning. I had slept little, oscillating between sweet dreams and nightmares. I looked gaunt without breakfast, for which I had little appetite. My eyes were circled with the dark rings of a night owl. I had prayed in Chinese to Buddha and to the new fellow called Jesus, then did both again in English. I was Chinese, trying to conquer the American land. This way Buddha would get used to the tongue-twisting English, and Jesus, the gut-wrenching Chinese. They had to learn how to work together, or should they work together at all? There was no time for theological debate of any religious significance. I needed a passport, and all stops should be pulled. Still, fear gripped me as I planted myself at the dean's door, waiting for his arrival.

"What can I do for you?" the usually nasty dean asked nicely. He must still be remembering the oysters, those devious, erection-building sea creatures.

I sat down, hands between my knees, holding a piece of paper, shaking quite a bit. "I have gotten a full scholarship from an American university, and I beg for your permission to gain my passport so that I can leave before the fall semester begins."

"Wait, one thing at a time." He swallowed his smile. "First of all, you have no permission to gain the fellowship from any university by yourself. Secondly, we have a policy of keeping our qualified young teachers for the growth of the university. Thirdly. . . ." He scratched his head. "Anyhow . . . there is nothing I can do here to get you the passport."

"Where do I get the permission, then?"

"The Personnel Department." The real sharks. Those guys were lifelong politicians good at nothing but playing chess games with people's futures. And he was sending me over to them.

"Could you please at least write a recommendation for me?"

"No recommendation."

"But I am doing what the Education Board rules specify. I have fulfilled the two-year period of working, and I have been a studious and diligent good teacher."

"That you are. That's why we want you to stick around."

"But I am only twenty-three and need to grow intellectually to serve our country better. From my work here so far, I find every day how little I know and how much more I need to know. I am pathetic. Four years of home-grown studies of a foreign language have only gotten me started. I need to go to the country where the language is being used like oxygen and water."

"You will have your turn. Just wait patiently like you do in the dining hall for lunch. We have a billion people. Lines are always long. You should know that by now."

"But people who came after me have all been sent abroad. I have a feeling that I am not going anytime soon."

"Well, they are members of the party, and special slots were made for them."

Nothing got me madder than hearing that line of crap, especially since he had told me I was not party material. I could feel my anger rising, which I knew was not a good thing when you were begging from their hands. I quieted for a second and tried to think of something meaningful that would break that fossil of a man's logic. Finally I asked, "What is the reason that you won't recommend me to go at this time?"

"You will never come back."

"It is my plan to come back to serve the college that has taught me everything."

"We need guarantees."

"Like what?"

"A wife, children. You are too young. You will lose your way in the corruption of the American culture."

At that point I realized that I had forgotten rule number one in deal-making here. Cigarettes. I fished out a sacred Marlboro smoke that I had saved, grabbed a few more, and laid them before the dean. He paused from all the serious talk, lit one, and continued. "You'll want to stay on and never come back. The temptation is too strong. That's another reason we are not sending you anytime soon. We want you to settle down here first."

"I can't settle down now. Our constitutional law dictates that men cannot be married until twenty-eight. I have to wait five years to get married. By then I will be an old man."

He smiled slyly, happy to see me see his point. "My recommendation to you is to forget about it and wait until we send you," he said in a steely tone, snuffing out his smoke as a not too subtle way of saying good-bye.

I had such an urge to cry. Tears rushed to my eyes, but I would not allow them to flow. Not in front of this hardened man. Tears were a waste with him. Logic. Hard cold logic. *Think!*

"I am sorry, sir, but this is a dream come true for me. I can't just forget it. If I go, I save our government money so that you can use my money to send someone else. Saving money for our country, why is it a bad thing?"

"Not all things that are good to you are good to me, do you understand? I've got a political meeting to go to. You could still try the Personnel Department if you like."

"I will then. Thank you."

"Don't feel too bad if they say no. Dreams are not that important. Reality is."

I could not find a sensible way to retort. I stormed out of his office, reduced to a human ball of thorns. The fight was still on, and I felt more than ready. Quickly I trotted to the administration building where the Personnel Department was. In a large room sat six cadres who had nothing better to do than read newspapers and sharpen endless pencils. A have-nothing-to-do cadre is the worst cadre one can find. You could just see mischievous looks come into their eyes. Another freak, they must be thinking. How should we torture this innocent creature?

"Can we help you?" a lady asked.

"Yes, I am Chen Da, and I am here to seek a permit for a passport."

All six pairs of eyes lifted up from their papers and stared at me as if I were crazy.

"Why are you here?" a fat man asked.

"Well, my dean of the Going Abroad Department asked me to come here."

"We don't give out permits until the grassroots unit, in this case your dean, sends us a written permit. Only then will we evaluate the whole situation and vote on a decision. You are really at the wrong door."

The rest of the five laughed and chuckled. I was no match for their slippery political savvy.

The fat man stood up and gestured to me to come outside into the hallway. "You are being kicked around here, okay. You have to start from the dean again."

"But he will not give me the permit."

"Then there is nothing we can do here."

"Nothing?"

"How many years have you been teaching here?"

"Two."

"According to the policy they should let you go."

"But they won't."

"The dean is a nasty man. He is probably jealous of you. You know he himself has been trying to go to America or England, but his major is not English and he will never be sent there. We might send him to Russia someday when relations improve. That is why he is giving you a hard time. You have to overcome him first."

"How am I going to change his mind? He has said no already."

"You have to figure it out yourself."

"Thanks."

"Don't tell anyone what I told you. I am not allowed to let you know the inside workings of the party."

"I know."

"Why don't you try the vice party chief of the department."

That was where I went next, but I doubted I would have any better luck with this turtle. She was one of those labeling me nonparty material, the ungrateful miser. I had oystered her before and possibly lycheed her husband as well.

"You are not married and too young. And without a party membership and the political ideology to grow healthily, I don't recommend that you go either, especially if this is a religious school," she said, like a Chinese nun counting fortune-telling beans. I instantly regretted letting her know the religious nature of the college. Now they had one more reason to dismiss me.

That evening, when I walked back defeated to my room, Lee grabbed my shoulder and stuck a lit smoke in my mouth. "Cheer up. There must be something you can do."

"I'll go to the president of the college and appeal to him."

"Wait, wait, wait. One thing you should never do here is overstep the ranks of power."

"I have been told by all the important grass snakes that it is a big *no*. What else am I supposed to do?"

"You can try, but it's not going to work. He is not going to do anything for you. You have to think of the consequences of what you are doing. What if you don't go at all? You will still have to work here forever and ever. You'll be buried here then. No one will like you anymore."

"It seems no one likes me here anyway."

The next day I went to the president's office and was stopped at the entrance by an imposing lady with a lot of dangling hairpins.

"Can I see the president, please?"

"And who are you?" came the insulting tone.

"An English teacher here."

"Do you have an appointment with him?"

"No."

"He only sees those with appointments." She pushed a logbook with dates and entries in it.

"Okay, can I make an appointment?"

"Why do you want to make an appointment?"

"Because I have some personal matter that I need his help to resolve."

"No personal matters. He only handles matters that are referred to us through the grassroots units."

The damned dean again.

"But it cannot be resolved at the grassroots level. They would not resolve it."

"Then we cannot resolve it."

"Where else can I appeal to?"

"You just did and failed again."

"I need to see the president."

"You can't see him if I don't let you. Besides, he won't be back for a few days. He is attending some central government political meetings. You know that our old enemy Taiwan is holding talks with China. There is talk of reunification. As you can see, that is the kind of problems that our president deals with, not your petty personal ones."

I saw no point in standing there haggling with this lady. No one seemed to be of any help when I needed it. For the first time the college looked a strange place. A place I had loved so much was now just empty buildings filled with strangers. I locked myself alone in my room, smoking and drinking tea. The old ulcer seemed to be kicking in again. A low dull pain pressed at my ribs, and I feared a recurrence of the internal bleeding.

One evening Lee found me in the fetal position in bed, trying to snuff my increasing pain. "Is this real or fake pain to get that passport?"

"I can't tell. All I know is that I can't eat and there is a big pain high in my stomach."

"Poor man. I wish I could help you."

"Let's have a drink."

"That'll kill you."

"I don't care. I need something to numb me."

"Cheers, then. You know, everyone was talking about your fellowship in the dining hall."

"I don't care anymore."

"Sometimes public opinion might help."

"Not in this case."

"Just a thought."

I decided to stake out the president's home, hoping to catch this wise man. Nothing else was working. I had heard numerous stories about the top leaders usually being benevolent guys who were kept out of the loop of everyday happenings. They were surrounded by feel-good men who filtered everything so that they were literally cut off from reality. I went over the story again and again, the fake conviction that I would return to this blasted college, the money-saving rhetoric, the two-year fulfillment, the validity of the central government's desire to grow intellectuals, and the lack of any relatives in America. Each time I rehearsed the story, it got weaker. I feared that by the time I got to face him, no story could be told. I wanted to beg someone who would listen, anyone. But each day went by without him appearing. I wondered if I was staking out the wrong house. But the address was confirmed by his old mother's presence, an old lady with bound feet who watered the flowers every day.

Every night I stayed there till nine, thinking that any day he would be back from those lavish banquets, but there was no trace of him at all. I dragged my feet and climbed back to my room. When Lee was out teaching, I knelt before the window and prayed. Sometimes the prayers turned into a chat, as if I were talking to a physical being. Someone was listening to me, patiently and sympathetically. I would talk and cry a little and then chuckle at my own silliness of crying to nobody. The next day I would return to the all-important task of sitting by the president's doorstep. By noon the heat would engulf me, and sweat would drench me and I would nap until a mosquito bite woke me up. The president, whom I had only seen once or twice, became this supreme being who got bigger and bigger with every passing day. I would bring newspapers to read while sitting in sadness. I would teach my classes and quickly return to this hopeless and endless wait.

Often I saw myself as the main character in the famous play we had studied, *Waiting for Godot*. Soon the president became my Godot. I hoped that this was one Godot that would eventually materialize. The waiting became more and more meaningful and significant as it went on day and night. His nonappearance became a thing that I began to accept without complaint. I reasoned that if he didn't know I was waiting for him, how could I blame him? Slowly, in my mind, he was transformed from a bad politician into an okay guy and I sank from desperation into languor. I read and reread the *People's Daily* with its exaggerated headlines and hollow contents. All the headlines seemed to be talking about one thing and one thing only. The Taiwan government, China's old foe, had for the first time in history agreed to hold talks with mainland China. It was a big deal because the island of Taiwan had been separated from the mainland for over thirty years, since Chiang Kai-shek had fled there in 1949. There had been daily shellings from mainland China and numerous defections. Mao had dreamed of retaking the island but couldn't. Anyone who could accomplish this would be regarded as a greater leader than the old Mao. It was a hot and sexy issue that got everyone's patriotic blood boiling. People shouted the national anthem and rushed out into the streets to celebrate. Deng would score big if he got the rich little island to unleash its mighty wallet to invest in the poor mainland. The party would win because people would get richer. They had yet to figure out how such a tiny little island had made such a giant leap into becoming the international financial and manufacturing powerhouse it was today. I could only chuckle at the absurdity. Only a few years ago, anyone who had contact with an ordinary Taiwanese citizen would have been labeled an enemy agent. That was partially the reason why my family had suffered so much, because my uncle lived there. Now the heads of state were courting them like maddened lovers. How times had changed.

One night after a long stakeout, I found an envelope from home lying on my bed. I eagerly opened the letter after crashing into bed and lighting a cigarette, the only way to appreciate each and every golden word from my loved ones. How I wished the letter could talk back.

Dad wrote that the whole family was thrilled at the great news. The reason why he had not responded to the letter sooner was that he had been awaiting my uncle's reply. And he had replied, saying how wonderful it was that I was going to America. To show his ultimate happiness, he had taken it upon himself to book a plane ticket to Lincoln, Nebraska, on August 25 with Northwest Airlines, for which I had to take a bus to Hong Kong.

My heart leaped. My crazy uncle! He had presumed that I was going for certain, that there was nothing to stop me from going. How little he knew about China, but his blind belief brought silent tears to my eyes. How I wished everything could just be that simple. I held the letter to my chest and thanked him with my heart. In the face of all my failures so far, his ticket, my precious ticket, became solid evidence of my dream. It made me believe again.

"I haven't seen you this happy for ages," Lee said, leaning on his bed. "What is the good news?"

"Nothing. My uncle bought the plane ticket for me, that's all."

"Rich uncle from Fujian?"

"Taiwan."

Lee paused and came over to gaze into my eyes searchingly. "Tell me again. You have an uncle in Taiwan?"

"Yes."

"And you can't get your ass out of here?"

"I don't see your point."

"You don't see my point? Haven't you been reading the news?"

"Yes."

"And you still don't see the point?"

"Oh, my."

"Oh, my is right. They are sucking up to the Taiwanese government in a big way. Go run to the dean's home now and tell him about your uncle."

"Wait a second. You want me to tell him about my uncle just like that?"

"Not just like that. Dramatically."

Dramatically it was. I prayed first, then put on a nice shirt. It was 10 P.M., but I could not wait. It was already midsummer. I ran to the dean's home and knocked confidently.

"What do you want at this hour?" He was genuinely upset this time, but I did not care. I had been staked out in the heat for too long.

"I have to show you something."

"What is it that could not wait until tomorrow?"

"Please, just give me a second and read this. It is important that you read it because it concerns the thorny political issue of Taiwan."

"Taiwan? Are you going to Taiwan?"

"Please read it."

As he read painfully in the dim light of his hall, I could see his face twitch uncomfortably. No one in China wanted to offend Taiwan at this point. Anyone who had family in Taiwan was protected dearly like a tenuous bridge that might span the gap between the two courting governments. And the dean, a smart political weasel, understood it well. Hurting Da was hurting the Taiwanese uncle. And who knew how powerful his uncle was? (Uncle not powerful at all.) Who knew what his powerful uncle might do? (Probably nothing.) Report to his government, which would report to the Chinese government, which in turn might cause negotiations to break down? Then he, the dean, would get blamed and all hell might break loose. (Baseless paranoia!) A little man thought a little man's thoughts. Fear got bigger. It was time to be good. It was time to suck up.

The dean said, "I'll see what I can do next week."

My heart sang. "Not next week, tomorrow, please. My uncle is anxiously waiting to hear from me."

There was anger in his face. "How come you never told me about your uncle? We could have gotten you out of here faster."

"I did not think it necessary."

"Good night."

No fake suicide, no hunger strike, just one timely uncle who possessed a blind faith in all things askew, and this world somehow found its rhythm. The next day a pink slip was delivered to me by the party Youth League secretary, Mr. Monsieur. (He had since regained his position.) In his accented Mandarin, he congratulated me and asked me not to fault the party for having blocked me in the first instance; it was just something they had to do. Sure. Last time they did something they had to do, millions died in the Cultural Revolution. I was the lucky one, thank God. I shook his hand, and he hugged me, a very un-Communistic act.

"Bon voyage." He still remembered his French.

"A very, very *bon bon voyage.*"

Getting a passport was like stealing something from those icy-eyed government public security officers.

"Where are you going?" barked the man behind the desk in the shack-like bungalow.

"America."

"Commit any crimes before?"

"No."

"Wife?"

"None."

"Relatives in America?"

"No." If I had any, I would not tell him.

"Duration?"

"One to two years at most."

"Why not longer?"

"I see no reason."

"Are you kidding me?"

"No."

"Everyone goes there and stays. I would," the officer said.

I smiled, not knowing what to say to such an honest man in disguise.

The next trip was to the U.S. consulate to get the all-important visa. Rumor mills had it that each day the Americans gave out only one student visa. And only to a full scholarship student, which I was. You had to be at the door by four in the dark morning to stand in the shadowy line waiting for the door to open at nine; otherwise you would never get in. Only seeing was believing. By nine o'clock the line was hundreds of people long, curving along the street like a snake. Everyone was trying to jump the line, and there were fights everywhere. The scene was like that every day, which explained the existence of the food stands and soybean soup kiosks. There were older folks waiting for immigration papers, but most of the people were red-faced, hot-blooded youngsters speaking various degrees of bad English. All bragged about the schools they had gotten accepted into, and all were anticipating the high probability of rejection and the low possibility of approval. One veteran, a fellow with an admission letter to an obscure master's degree program at Baylor, was describing his many trials of rejection. "You go there, they don't even look at you. One chop and you are rejected," he said.

"How many times have you been rejected?"

"Twice."

"For what?"

"No reason given, pure silent bureaucracy. What is your school?" he asked me.

"A small undergraduate school with a full scholarship."

"And you are an English professor?'"

"Yes."

"You won't get it."

"Why?"

"It doesn't make any sense," he concluded.

"No, it makes sense," another veteran argued. "He speaks English well. If the clerk hears you talk funny, it's bye-bye, study-some-more-see-you-next-year time."

"No, he is overqualified. They are looking for any reason to reject you."

Nine o'clock sharp, Chinese guards in full uniform and fully armed marched out. The thin line distorted itself into a thick mass, choking the entrance. The guards shouted and used the rifle butts to disperse the mobs, but the eager crowd swarmed like mosquitoes. It was not until the appearance of American soldiers that the line got straightened into an orderly shape. And all those American soldiers needed to do was smile and say, "Hello. Hey, get in line."

Hearts were beating fast as the first few applicants came out crying.

"It's going to be a really bad day," the veteran shouted.

"Why do you say so?" I asked.

"The first two girls were going to Stanford for a double E [electrical engineering] major with a full scholarship. If they didn't get it, you are not going to."

Quietly I knelt down, pretending to tie my shoelaces, and prayed silently. In my head I was begging Buddha, Jesus, and, last but more important, my grandfather, a rarely used spiritual weapon that I had only once before deployed. He had helped me through the national college entrance examination. I could see his smiling eyes looking at me lovingly through the thick clouds. He had always loved the fact that I was a little intellectual even when I was just a kid. He had taught me complicated calligraphy at three, and marveled at how I handled the subtlety of each refined stroke. It was he who had instilled in me that we were an intellectual family and should do anything to enhance that reputation for the many generations to come. Uphold it, Da, I could hear him say. Even though he had died long ago, critical moments like this brought his spirit roaring back. *You lovable spiritual warlord. I miss you, Grandpa.*

When I was finally allowed in, I stood gingerly before a young blond male clerk, who perused the documents without looking at the applicant. I might be just another of the thousand worthless applicants to him, but I felt as if I had taken a giant step toward my fate, my destiny. Then he looked up and for one long, agonizing moment stared right into my eyes, searching. My heart grew, expanded, and ballooned, almost choking me. He took his gaze away silently, and slowly he pulled out a pen and wrote something down. A seal was pressed. When he looked up again, his eyes were full of smiles. "Congratulations," was all he said. The word vibrated violently like throbbing waves in my head. *I'm in! I'm in! I'm out! I'm out of here! I'm singing, I'm crying, I'm dancing!* I ran through the hushed hall filled with anguished eyes and the stony stares of uniformed guards. My breath was freed and my steps light. I wanted to fly. Heck, I could fly! But when I was finally out into the streets crowded with even more sweaty and blurry faces, my steps slowed. There were tears in my eyes. I didn't say I got it. Instead I murmured, *Grandpa, Grandpa.* All the way through the crowd, they were trying to stop

me, but I just kept going. I was floating on cotton clouds. The whole world
was beautiful. The streets had never looked so picturesque before. The people, my Chinese people, were all deliciously kissable and hugely huggable.

"He is the lucky one," someone shouted.

"Shit, he got our daily quota. Let's beat him up."

"That fucking bastard."

Whatever their curses, they all sounded like a birdsong of compliments.

In a dizzying, maddening pedaling of my bike, I rushed to the biggest
telegraph building and spent five big yuan to let my anxious family know
the good news. All this flood of beautiful feelings was condensed into five
little words. *Got visa. Home 8/1.*

I spent the next week paying good-bye visits to all my worthy friends. The
Nahs were happy for me but even happier because good old Bob had gotten their daughter a visa through another creative arrangement. To a lesser
man, she was a hopeless case who would never be granted a visa. But nothing would stop Bob. He got the daughter of a high-ranking diplomat a gig
to perform with the People's Philharmonic. She was a so-so cellist who
could never have gotten such a break at home. On the night of her performance, a string snapped, but she continued calmly, and that won her a standing ovation for bravery if not artistry. The next day, when Nah's daughter
came for the visa, it was all signed and waiting for her.

"Everything seemed to work out well for everyone. What an amazing
ending," Nah emoted. "I am so happy to see you young people going places."
The sentimental artist had tears in his eyes. I hugged him and felt his finger
tapping on my shoulder, half a beat fast, always a conductor even in embrace.

"But the best is yet to come," I said.

"What do you mean?"

"Bob is working on your trip to America for a performance."

"Is he?"

"He would not have mentioned it until it materialized."

"What a great man he is."

"I can't agree with you more. He is the greatest."

No good-bye was complete without visits to my two old friends Hui
Ton and Abdullah, who had made my life in Beijing so much more colorful and adventurous. I first went to see Hui Ton, whose government had

assigned him to study the field of telecommunications engineering at a university nearby. As in the old days, he embraced me with his skinny limbs and that unique aroma that seemed to cling to the colorful skirts that all Cambodian men wore. We spent the afternoon chatting about our past but even more about our future. I said I would always remember him, and with tears he replied that he would go home someday and help rebuild his country. And when that day came, he would welcome me to his beautiful home.

Abdullah was now a second-year medical student at Beijing Medical College. He was all needles and herbs. His room still smelled of lamb meat, garlic, and an assortment of spices, except this time there was an additional antiseptic odor. He was probably the only doctor wearing a white coat over a Yemeni striped robe. He gave out a shriek when I gave him the news and said, "You go and make millions!"

"You can come too," I said.

He smiled. "Isn't it interesting? I am staying here and you are going." Then his face turned serious. "You know, I am engaged."

"To whom?"

"Here." He passed me a photo of a tall, busty Chinese girl with a beautiful smile. "She is a kindergarten teacher here. She helps me with my medical studies at night, the Chinese language part, and I love her."

"Congratulations," I said. "No more sneaking around, hey, Abdullah?"

"No more of that for sure, and you know why? Because she was fired from her job after we got engaged."

"Are you bringing her home to Yemen?"

"I don't think so, Da. I'll be staying here as long as we're together."

"Good. I'll know where to visit you when I return, and you'd better be married to her the next time I see you."

The campus was empty in the summertime. And even emptier now that Professor Tu had gone on to better things, on loan as a supervising translator to the UN's Geneva headquarters. I would have loved to have gotten some advice from my dear mentor, the man who I knew would always be kind to students like me. I thanked Buddha for him.

Professor Lulu had traveled to England to study her beloved applied linguistics. But she was said to have gone crazy right after her arrival there. Difficulty adjusting and loneliness must have caused it all. She was escorted back within a month of her departure and was rarely seen on campus afterward. My heart went out to her. Why would someone who had admired the language so much and so long and cherished her gift of learning like precious pearls go crazy upon fulfilling her dream? Someday, I hoped, she would go again.

As for Black Rose, her happy, bouncy shadow hovered all over the blue water of the campus swimming pool where she frolicked with her newly returned husband, her black existence ripening into a maddening love that she felt all over again in this endless summer heat.

And in the hollow echoes of this empty campus, Bo's midnight footfalls were heard, heading for the woods where he had sought peace and calm and pacing back and forth along the wet poolside where his puppy love had once prowled. In the silence of the heat, I whispered my goodbye to him, my friend who had died too young and suffered too much.

Chapter Twenty-nine

A thousand-li journey should start from the earth beneath your feet. The proverb teaches a traveler not to lose himself in the vastness of his grand journey but to be mindful of every bit of preparation. A long journey was, after all, the sum of many brief sojourns, stretching from the one at your feet to the end of the rainbow. Before flight, I felt the desperate need to touch the soil and reconnect with the land that had nurtured me. So I started my trip with a delicate gesture from my heart. In the twilight of a summery day, I strolled alone into our garden and squatted down to carefully pinch up the sticky mud from the roots of our *liu ju tao* and drop it into the small silk bag that I would carry to that faraway America. This was my kiss from the land of my father and his father. A handshake farewell. Now I would forever live attached in a distant land.

Dad called a big reunion of the whole family. The newly grown family—two brothers-in-law—shared rooms crowdedly and contentedly under our slanting, curled roof, days before my departure. Mom lingered around me like a shadow, murmuring something, forgetting it, then repeating the murmur. A son was going afar to a land of foreigners to settle, grow, prosper, and bear fruit. Mother was worried. Her face should have been smiling, but many times she was found crying under her quilt because she would have to kiss her baby son one more good-bye, a long good-bye. Seven years of separation only intensified a mother's love. I could feel it every step I took at home with her following me and constantly asking me what I would like to eat. And whatever I liked to eat, she would quickly cook for me. I kept telling her I wasn't hungry, but she said I should eat as much as she could cook because who knew what they ate there in America. So to satisfy her love and my budding longing, I asked her to cook some of my favorite childhood food, the fried rice noodles that she would make with the freshest seafood bought from the fisherman's wife in the misty morning street. She told me that when I was a young kid, we were so poor that at times she thought the whole family would not survive another day, but then something would happen, little miracles, thank Buddha, and we would live on. Life was miserable then. But her old tears were soon washed off by the new happy tears, and she would say how incredibly fortunate it was that I had graduated with honors from Beijing. And now, even more unbelievable, her young son was flying off to America!

The whole of Yellow Stone was aflame with great anticipation. Dad held court in the sunbathed living room. His guests were the commune cadres who came here every day now to mingle with his acupuncture patients and catch the newest gossip of his traveling son: the sleazy cadre Long, who had issued the order to hang my dad by his thumbs; the neighbor who used to report from his window about all the religious activities in our house; Ar Duang, the merchant, with the same old basket carrying different juicy fruits for Dad every day; and the fisherman's wife who carried the catch of the day to Dad in return for treating her man's bad knees and rotten back.

Dad was at his bragging best when it came to the subject of my American college. No one knew how big or little Lincoln in Nebraska was. Dad told his crowd that it was named after the most famous American president, and all his friends concurred that it must be a fun-filled big city to deserve such a name. And Union College, when translated, seemed like an important name. In a Communist country, the word *union* was a word of power, authority, and legitimacy, with a heavily tainted governmental connotation. In conclusion, it sounded alarmingly good. And of course, college and university had the same good translation, literally meaning "big school." So all of a sudden, Da was going to a big school named Union in a big city named after a bigger-than-life, slave-freeing president. On top of everything else was the eight-thousand-dollar-a-year scholarship mentioned on my I-20. One calculating sugarcane merchant plucked his abacus and told everyone present that it would roughly make Da a millionaire in Chinese currency with the most generous estimate of currency exchange in the seediest small-lane black market. Of course, Dad liked the loose calculation. If Da, his son, was a millionaire, then he automatically became the father of a millionaire.

"Hey, why don't you just take the money?" The sly merchant asked the inevitable question that everyone was itching to ask.

Dad stepped in to explain. "Though the money is there, you can't take it. You have to spend it on the school. And with further schooling, only Buddha knows how far my young son will go."

"Congratulations, another round of drinks," someone suggested.

Dad was all too happy to open another jar of local cheap liquor.

At night the whole family gathered under the moon in the backyard and talked about the past. Uncle had asked Dad to relay to me in detail the complete recent history of the Chen family. I was instructed to put it all down in words when I reached the free world and send it to my uncle in Taiwan. He did not know anything that had happened since he had left for Taiwan forty years ago. Dad had taken care of their parents, and Uncle felt a desperate need to know what had happened to them in the last days of their lives, and their final parting words.

In tears we relived the misery of the Cultural Revolution, but this time it was more. Things I had never heard about I got to hear now. I was, after all, the youngest son. I had not been told many things that had happened before I was born. Dad told me about his youthful but broken dreams, and Mom recalled the day when she was a pretty bride blessed with the most abundant dowry. For the first time I got to see and hear them talk like the young people they once were, romantic, daring, and bursting with hope.

Dad had wanted to move the whole family to Amoy. He had already bought a house in the beautiful island city, and also some cameras so that he could make a living taking photos, which was the newest rage then. He had hoped so much for us children to go to school there and live a good life. But all this was not meant to be. The Red Army came and took everything. He was lucky even to be a teacher, but soon even that teaching job was taken away, and his imprisonment followed. That was when he realized his youth was over, he said. There was no bitterness in his tone. Only defiance, pride, and courage punctuated each teary and bloody episode of his memories. In the end, his smile shone through the tears, and the brilliance of his love gleamed in the darkness as he put his arm over Mom's shoulders, hugging her.

How far they had traveled and how much they had suffered to bring us to this day. Without their suffering, their undying love, and their beautiful spirit, I would not be there today, sitting under this round moon with the river whispering beside us, my heart singing a song of hope for a better tomorrow. With the blinking stars above, I became brave. Fear of leaving vanished, and in my heart, a pledge was born. Their hopes became mine, their lives I would continue to live, and their dreams, through me, would become even bigger.

On the eve of my departure, Dad threw a big banquet in my honor. Ten tables of happy close friends and relatives crowded our house, everyone drinking happy toasts. Dad, at the head, fielded all the inquiries tossed his way, while Mom, a happy hostess, hovered over every table, urging the older guests to eat more and the younger to drink less. I had never seen her that happy before. The glow of happiness came from her heart. Nothing could cover it, not even the soot from our busy chimney.

In the corner were my four best friends, who felt ill fitting among the well-wishers. Half the people there hated their guts; the other half they still had to take revenge on.

"You big-nosed rascal, I can't believe you're going to America. Take me, please," Mo Gong said.

"They'll put you in jail the moment you arrive there," Sen said.

"Are you going to marry one of those blue-eyed blonds?" asked Siang.

"Yeah, like our favorite, Page Eighty-seven?" said Yi, referring to the infamous magazines I had brought them long ago.

"I might. Which one would you choose for me?" I asked.

"Page Ninety-nine."

"No, Page Sixty-seven."

They could never agree on anything.

Professor Wei came by briefly, bringing a sack of precious goose eggs as a parting gift. I asked her to sit down with my parents, but she shook her head, smiling, and I understood her. It would be hard for her to mix with the smokers, the drinkers, and especially my four rascal friends. In the darkness we hugged good-bye, and I knew that she was crying again. She gave me a photo of her fellow Methodist friends and told me to seek them out in New Jersey when in need.

When the last course was served, Mom told everyone that the food was blessed because she had used all the materials in the worship ceremony to thank Buddha, and that all would go well for everyone and her Da.

It was midnight before the last guest left.

Early morning on the twenty-fourth of August, I knelt with Mom and Dad in our attic. Mom had tears in her eyes, praying to the smiling statue of Buddha, and so did Dad, a man who rarely cried. The only other time I saw him cry was on the eve of Grandpa's death when he had begged Buddha to take a few years off his own life to add to Grandpa's. He taught me then what it meant to be a son, and I would forever cherish that. Today he cried again, a happy cry. He asked for Buddha to protect me in that faraway land. His tears moved mine.

On the doorstep, he held me in his arms. "Son, you are going for a long journey all alone. . . ."

"I'll be fine," I assured him.

"Your old father can't help you anymore. . . . I'm sorry. . . . I feel so useless."

"Dad, please. . . ." I hugged him.

"Remember, wherever you go, I'll be watching you. Go far, son."

"I will . . . for you." I nodded and looked beyond. Tears blurred my vision.

Mom wiped her hands on her apron, her tears gleaming in the morning sun. Standing before her, I felt like a little boy again, going away for the first time. I hugged her tight one last time. Words failed me. I took the first step, a heavy step, a thoughtful step, away from the embrace of my mom and looked one last time at the faces that I so adored.

Good-bye, colors of the mountain.

Good-bye, sounds of the river.